I1044585

Africa in the Time of Cholera

Written in a style attractive to nonspecialists, this book combines evidence from natural and social sciences to examine the impact on Africa of seven cholera pandemics since 1817, particularly the current impact of cholera on such major countries as Senegal, Angola, Mozambique, Congo, Zimbabwe, and South Africa. Cholera's explosion in Africa involves such variables as migration, armed conflict, climate change, and changing disease ecology. Myron Echenberg highlights the irony that this once-terrible scourge, having receded from most of the globe, now kills thousands of Africans annually – Africa now accounts for more than 90 percent of the world's cases and deaths – and leaves many more with severe developmental impairment. Responsibility for the suffering of thousands of infants and children who survive the disease but are left with acute developmental impairment is shared by Western lending and health institutions, and by often venal and incompetent African leadership. Cholera is no longer a biomedical riddle. Inexpensive and effective oral rehydration therapy can now control the impact of cholera, and modest investment in potable water and sewage infrastructure would help prevent major outbreaks. If the threat of this old scourge is addressed with more urgency, great progress in the public health of Africans can be achieved.

Myron Echenberg is former Chair of the History Department at McGill University, where he is now Professor Emeritus. He is a former editor of the *Canadian Journal of African Studies* and previously served as President of the Canadian Association of African Studies. Professor Echenberg is the author of *Plague Ports: The Global Urban Impact of Bubonic Plague, 1894–1901*; *Black Death, White Medicine: Bubonic Plague and the Politics of Public Health in Colonial Senegal, 1914–1945*; and *Colonial Conscripts: The Tirailleurs Sénégalais in French West Africa, 1857–1960*, which won the Herskovits Award of the African Studies Association for the outstanding original scholarly work published during 1991.

AFRICAN STUDIES

The African Studies Series, founded in 1968, is a prestigious series of monographs, general surveys, and textbooks on Africa covering history, political science, anthropology, economics, and ecological and environmental issues. The series seeks to publish work by senior scholars as well as the best new research.

EDITORIAL BOARD

David Anderson, *University of Oxford*

Catherine Boone, *University of Texas at Austin*

Carolyn Brown, *Rutgers University*

Christopher Clapham, *University of Cambridge*

Michael Gomez, *New York University*

Nancy J. Jacobs, *Brown University*

Richard Roberts, *Stanford University*

David Robinson, *Michigan State University*

Leonardo A. Villalón, *University of Florida*

A list of books in this series will be found at the end of this volume.

Africa in the Time of Cholera

A History of Pandemics from 1817 to the Present

MYRON ECHENBERG
McGill University

CAMBRIDGE
UNIVERSITY PRESS

CAMBRIDGE UNIVERSITY PRESS
Cambridge, New York, Melbourne, Madrid, Cape Town,
Singapore, São Paulo, Delhi, Tokyo, Mexico City

Cambridge University Press
32 Avenue of the Americas, New York, NY 10013-2473, USA

www.cambridge.org
Information on this title: www.cambridge.org/9780521188203

© Myron Echenberg 2011

This publication is in copyright. Subject to statutory exception
and to the provisions of relevant collective licensing agreements,
no reproduction of any part may take place without the written
permission of Cambridge University Press.

First published 2011

Printed in the United States of America

A catalog record for this publication is available from the British Library.

Library of Congress Cataloging in Publication data
Echenberg, Myron J.
   Africa in the time of cholera : a history of pandemics from 1817 to
the present / Myron Echenberg.
      p. ; cm. – (African studies ; 114)
   Includes bibliographical references and index.
   ISBN 978-1-107-00149-7 (hardback) – ISBN 978-0-521-18820-3 (pbk.)
   1. Cholera–Africa–History–19th century.   2. Cholera–Africa–History–20th
century.   3. Cholera–Africa–History–21st century.   4. Epidemics–History–
Africa.   I. Title.   II. Series: African studies series ; 114.
   [DNLM: 1. Cholera–history–Africa.   2. Disease Outbreaks–history–
Africa.   3. History, 19th Century–Africa.   4. History, 20th Century–
Africa.   5. History, 21st Century–Africa. WC 264]
   RA644.C3E24   2011
   614.5'14096–dc22   2010037101

ISBN 978-1-107-00149-7 Hardback
ISBN 978-0-521-18820-3 Paperback

Cambridge University Press has no responsibility for the persistence or accuracy of URLs
for external or third-party Internet Web sites referred to in this publication and does not
guarantee that any content on such Web sites is, or will remain, accurate or appropriate.

In memory of my mentors at McGill University and at the University of Wisconsin, Robert Vogel and Philip D. Curtin

Contents

Figures, Maps, and Tables

Acknowledgments

Many people have offered advice and support on this project. Two friends who carefully read versions of the manuscript, Dean Echenberg and Judy Rasminsky, used their training in epidemiology and journalism respectively to spot egregious errors and infelicities. My gratitude extends also to many colleagues who listened patiently to my discourses on cholera and offered sage advice and inspiration. They include Charles Becker, Gwyn Campbell, Tamara Giles-Varnick, Catherine Legrand, Margaret Lock, John Saul, and Jim Webb. Adama Aly Pam and Edna Robertson kindly permitted me to read their unpublished texts, and Chris Hamlin and Guy Thompson graciously supplied me with last-minute references. Barbara Schreiner and Belinda Dodson helped me secure permission from the South African Department of Water Affairs to use some of their artwork. Facil Tesfaye helped me as a research assistant with his computer skills and his intimate knowledge of Ethiopian history, and Linda Janeiro worked with Facil to prepare the maps. At Cambridge University Press, two anonymous readers provided constructive criticism; Eric Crahan was a skillful and diligent general editor; and Jason Przybylski kept the manuscript moving steadily forward to publication. John McWilliams of PETT Fox, Inc. was a talented and patient copy editor. Pam Miller, Chris Lyons, Diane Philip, and Lily Szczygiel at the Osler Library of McGill University kept me in mind when cholera publications caught their attention and helped me navigate the Internet in search of material. Finally, my wife Eva, encouraging me at every turn, has been my best critic.

Abbreviations

ANC	African National Congress
ARV	antiretroviral drugs
AWD	acute watery diarrhea
CAR	Central African Republic
CCF	The Concerned Citizens' Forum (South Africa)
CFRs	case fatality rates
COSATU	Congress of South African Trade Unions
DRC	Democratic Republic of Congo
DWAF	Department of Water Affairs and Forestry (South Africa)
ENSO	El Niño Southern Oscillation
FAR	Forces Armées Rwandaises (Rwandan Army)
FRELIMO	Liberation Front of Mozambique
GEAR	Growth, Employment, and Redistribution Strategy (South Africa)
GNUC	The Greater Nelspruit Utility Company (South Africa)
IMF	International Monetary Fund
IMS	Indian Medical Service
IOPH	International Office of Public Hygiene
ISCs	International Sanitary Conferences
JOWAM	Johannesburg Water Management
LCBC	Lake Chad Basin Commission
MDC	Movement for Democratic Change (Zimbabwe)
MERLIN	Medical Emergency Relief International (Britain)
MNR	Mozambique National Resistance
MSF	Médecins Sans Frontières
NGOs	nongovernmental organizations

NIH	National Institutes of Health, Bethesda, Maryland
OCVs	oral cholera vaccines
ORT	oral rehydration therapy
PAC	Pan-Africanist Congress
ProMED	Program for Monitoring Emerging Diseases
RPF	Rwandan Patriotic Front
SADC	Southern African Development Community
SADF	South African Defence Force
SAMWU	The South African Municipal Workers' Union
SAPs	Structural Adjustment Policies
SDE	La Sénégalaise des Eaux
SICAP	Société Immobilière du Cap-Vert (Senegal)
SONEES	Société Nationale d'Exploitation des Eaux de Sénégal
UNDP	United Nations Development Programme
UNHCR	United Nations High Commission for Refugees
UNICEF	United Nations International Children's Fund
VIPs	ventilated improved privies
WER	*Weekly Epidemiological Record*, published by the WHO
WHO	World Health Organization
ZADHR	Zimbabwe Association of Doctors for Human Rights
ZANU	Zimbabwe African National Union
ZAPU	Zimbabwe African Peoples' Union

Introduction

This book has two purposes. It offers an overview of Africa's historical encounters with the seven cholera pandemics from 1817 to the present. Second, it explores the epidemiology of the contemporary African experience during the seventh cholera pandemic, for which evidence is more robust and for which the analysis has immediate policy relevance.

Scientific interest in cholera continues to be significant. Not only did the disease help launch the new field of epidemiology in the late nineteenth century, it also represents a fascinating and complex challenge in the newest research specialties of disease ecology, membrane biology, and trans-membrane signaling. In public health circles, cholera raises questions for global health workers concerned with new and reemerging infectious diseases.

Part One describes the first six cholera pandemics through to 1947, emphasizing how the disease affected Africans. Of course, Africa's experience with cholera cannot be isolated from that of other parts of the globe, especially the Middle East and the Indian Ocean region, long active as favorite routes for cholera's diffusion into the African continent. Nor can the experience of Europe and the Americas be overlooked, especially efforts in the industrializing countries to diagnose and treat this dreaded disease. Chapters 1 and 2 explore cholera's global trajectory and the medical responses the disease provoked. Much of the record of Africa's early experience with cholera has not survived, which may explain why this is the first attempt to produce a study of cholera in Africa. The one major primary source, however, is a remarkable contemporary epidemiological and geographical study by Dr. James Christie, *Cholera Epidemics in*

;t *Africa*, published in 1876.[1] I drew heavily on Christie in Chapter 3,
h case studies from Senegambia, Ethiopia, and Zanzibar. Fortunately,
cholera features prominently in Nancy Gallagher's path-breaking studies of public health in Tunisia in the nineteenth century and Egypt in the
twentieth.[2] Cholera in the Nile Valley and North Africa is the subject of
Chapter 4.

Part Two draws more heavily on primary evidence, especially first-
hand medical and statistical material. It provides a novel historical and
epidemiological portrait of Africans' attempts to deal with cholera outbreaks. No historian is yet to investigate modern cholera in Africa, but
two geographers, Robert Stock and Andrew Collins, have provided valuable insights.[3]

After a long period of quiescence, modern cholera science has rapidly
evolved since the 1970s. The classic medical work, Robert Pollitzer's mon-
umental *Cholera*, published by the World Health Organization (WHO)
in Geneva in 1959, runs over one thousand pages and was meant to be
definitive. Two years later, the seventh cholera pandemic emerged out of
Indonesia and forced researchers to take a fresh look at this enigmatic
and complex disease. The best way to follow research developments after
Pollitzer has been to read the research journals as well as a series of edited
works compiled by leading cholera researchers.[4] Although historical studies of cholera abound, many of them reflecting outstanding scholarship
in English, French, and German, they focus on cholera before 1900, with
one important exception.[5] Just before this study was completed, I was

---

[1] Dr. James Christie, *Cholera Epidemics in East Africa* (London: Macmillan, 1876, reprinted, USA: Kessinger Publishing, 2008). Edna Robertson has recently written an excellent biography, as yet unpublished. See her "Christie of Zanzibar, Medical Pathfinder."

[2] Nancy Gallagher, *Medicine and Power in Tunisia, 1780–1900* (Cambridge: Cambridge University Press, 1983), and *Egypt's Other Wars: Epidemics and the Politics of Public Health* (Syracuse: Syracuse University Press, 1990).

[3] Robert F. Stock, *Cholera in Africa* (London: International African Institute, 1976); and Andrew Collins, *Environment, Health and Population Displacement: Development and Change in Mozambique's Diarroeal Disease Ecology* (Aldershot: Ashgate, 1998).

[4] There have been four compilations. In chronological order, they are: Dhiman Barua and William Burrows, eds., *Cholera* (Philadelphia: W.B. Saunders, 1974); a revised edition by Dhiman Barua and William B. Greenough III, eds., *Cholera* (New York: Plenum, 1992); I. Kaye Wachsmuth, Paul A. Blake, and Orjan Olsvik, eds., *Vibrio Cholerae and Cholera: Molecular to Global Perspectives* (Washington: American society for Microbiology, 1994); and B.S. Drasar and B.D. Forrest, eds., *Cholera and the Ecology of Vibrio Cholerae* (London: Chapman & Hall, 1996). The latest published overview that is of value to researchers and lay readers alike is Paul Shears, "Recent Developments in Cholera," *Current Opinion in Infectious Diseases*, 14 (2001), 553–8.

[5] At the risk of slighting many fine studies, I note the following exemplary contributions by American, British, French, and German scholars: Olaf Briese, *Angst in den Zeiten*

able to enjoy reading and learning from Christopher Hamlin's excellent overview of cholera, published by Oxford University Press in 2009 as part of the *Biographies of Disease* series, edited by William and Helen Bynum.[6] Besides offering an original and insightful view of classic cholera and its players and problems, Hamlin is the first historian to tackle cholera science through to the present, and to argue convincingly that the revolution in cholera therapeutics and toxicology has rendered many historical assumptions about so-called classic cholera obsolete.[7] One belief, repeated in texts so often it became "fact," is that cholera was "Asian" – different from and more virulent than European forms of acute diarrhea. A second position widely held in scientific circles was that cholera in India was subject to "recrudescence"; that is, cholera's agent lingered in a region, persisting in sporadic and asymptomatic cases among a large host population before bursting out in a new pandemic wave. What triggered these revivals was unclear, as is the prospect, now widely accepted, that cholera's ecological niche was not the human body, but a variety of warm seas that harbored genetically unstable organisms.

Statistics for cholera cases and deaths in the nineteenth century are impressionistic and serve only to provide a qualitative picture. For Part Two, the main source since the Seventh Pandemic that began in 1961 are the data published regularly on cholera outbreaks globally and compiled annually in August or September for the previous year's totals by the WHO in their weekly publication, the *Weekly Epidemiological Record* (*WER*).[8] These aggregate data have been supplied officially by member-states of the WHO since 1968, in keeping with their mandatory obligation under the WHO's International Health Regulations, as revised in 2005. Superior data, which are less constrained by political considerations, have been provided since the mid-1990s by the Program for Monitoring

---

der Cholera, 4 vols. (Berlin: Akademie Verlag, 2003); François Delaporte, *Disease and Civilization: The Cholera in Paris, 1832*, translated by Arthur Goldhammer (Cambridge: MIT Press, 1986); Richard J. Evans, *Death in Hamburg: Society and Politics in the Cholera Years* (New York and London: Penguin, Second Edition, 2005); Christoph Gradmann, *Laboratory Disease: Robert Koch's Medical Bacteriology*, translated by Elborg Forster (Baltimore: Johns Hopkins University Press, 2009); Charles E. Rosenberg, *The Cholera Years: The United States in 1832, 1849, and 1866* (Chicago: University of Chicago Press, 1962; reprint, with an an afterword, 1987); and Frank M. Snowden, *Naples in the Time of Cholera, 1884–1911* (Cambridge: Cambridge University Press, 1995).

[6] Christopher Hamlin, *Cholera: The Biography* (Oxford: Oxford University Press, 2009).

[7] Hamlin, *Cholera: The Biography*, 269–70.

[8] World Health Organization, "Cholera," *Weekly Epidemiological Record*, yearly since 1970.

Emerging Diseases (ProMED). This program offers a free online forum for microbiologists, infectious disease specialists, public health officials, and the general public, and has been administered since 1999 through the International Society for Infectious Diseases.[9] A full discussion of the strengths and limitations of the data occurs in Chapter 6.

The two sections of this book tell very different stories. By the late nineteenth century, especially in industrializing countries of western Europe and North America, but also in Africa, cholera became more sporadic and less destructive of human life. Significant improvements in public health coupled with the burgeoning of scientific medicine created a sense that cholera had been "defeated." The French medical historian Patrice Bourdelais sounded this congratulatory note in the title of his recent book largely devoted to a history of cholera, *Epidemics Laid Low: A History of What Happened in Rich Countries*.[10]

For people who do not live in rich countries, cholera has not been "laid low." It remains a debilitating disease, especially life-threatening to infants and children in parts of Asia, Latin America, and Africa. Indeed, with more than 95 percent of the world's cases since 1995, cholera is now an African disease. Chapter 5 examines the significant medical changes in the etiological understanding and therapy developed to treat modern cholera. Chapter 6 provides an overview of how cholera has reemerged as a global threat to Africa from 1971 to the present. Chapters 7 through 9 deal with case studies of risk factors ranging from the changing global environment to armed conflicts and to public health choices exercised by various African governments. The book concludes with an assessment of cholera today in Chapter 10.

Cholera is not a new disease. Its exact origins are ancient and obscure, but the presence of an acute diarrheal disease in the Ganges Basin of the Indian subcontinent has been endemic from at least the fifth century, when Sanskrit texts described an illness with cholera-like symptoms. Modern cholera dates from 1817, when a vicious intestinal infection caused by the *Vibrio cholerae* bacteria left its long-established Indian reservoir and launched what was later recognized as the world's first cholera pandemic (Figure I.1). As four waves of new pandemics followed in the nineteenth century, cholera's horrendous destruction of human lives earned it a deserved reputation as a global scourge.

---

[9] Program for Monitoring Emerging Diseases (ProMed), posted by the International Society for Infectious Diseases as *Pro-Medline*, www.promedmail.org
[10] Translated by Bart K. Holland (Baltimore: The Johns Hopkins University Press, 2006).

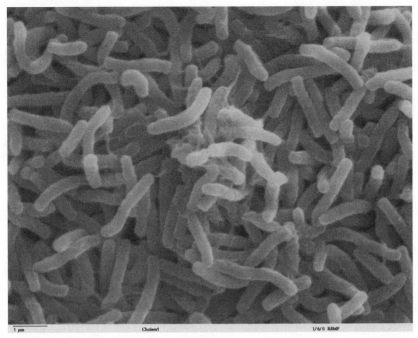

FIGURE I.I. Scanning electron microscope image of *Vibrio cholerae* bacteria (Dartmouth College Electron Microscope Facility).

Two cholera pathogens, the first emerging in the Ganges Delta in 1817 and its descendent launching the Seventh Pandemic from Sulawesi, Indonesia in 1961, have been responsible for at least three of the seven pandemics.[11] Only during the Fifth Pandemic did Robert Koch and his team identify the pathogen as *Vibrio cholerae o1*, which was also responsible for the Sixth Pandemic; the strains that caused the first four pandemics, as well as a cholera-like disease before 1817, have never been determined. The second strain, called *Vibrio cholerae o1* El Tor after the medical inspection and quarantine station port at Sinai on the Red Sea, was first identified there in 1897 by the English bacteriologist Armand Ruffer. How it materialized is not known, but El Tor later appeared in Indonesia in 1937 and caused four major outbreaks through to 1958 while remaining endemic between these episodes.

---

[11] D. Barua and W.B. Greenough III, eds., *Cholera* (New York: Plenum, 1992); and Reinhard S. Speck, "Cholera," in Kenneth Kiple, ed., *The Cambridge World History of Human Disease* (New York: Cambridge University Press, 1993), 642–9.

Vibrio cholerae 01 El Tor exists in either of two serotypes, Ogawa and Inaba. Less virulent than the original or "classic" *Vibrio cholerae 01*, this new strain led many health authorities to hope that it would not be able to create a pandemic. To the surprise of experts, however, after being confined for twenty-four years, the El Tor strain began a global journey from its starting point on Sulawesi Island, Indonesia in 1961. Once it began dispersing, the El Tor biotype proved to be more widespread than its classic cousin. Its capacity to colonize multiple local ecosystems has produced endemic cholera in Africa and North America, a new phenomenon characteristic of the seventh pandemic.

Indian researchers in Madras discovered the third and newest cholera strain, called *Vibrio cholerae 0139* Bengal, in October 1992. Its emergence is discussed more fully in Chapter 5. By 1996, the WHO observed confidently that because *0139* Bengal had not left the region, it was unlikely to cause a new pandemic.[12]

In theory, cholera should not be a great threat to humans. Not only is susceptibility variable, the bacteria can only be acquired in one way: through the consumption of water or food that has been contaminated either by fecal matter from a person with active cholera, or from free-standing bacteria present in plankton or seafood living in infected brackish water. One authority maintains that cholera causes "only a reversible and easily treated biochemical defect," and claims that cholera requires "a very gross level of contamination, greater than for any other known epidemic disease," to produce illness in normal individuals.[13] This explains why cholera rarely infects medical workers involved in its treatment.

That said, cholera clearly was a grave threat to those who were susceptible. Relatively high gastric acidity in the small intestine can kill the cholera bacteria before they can secrete their toxin. Conversely, low natural acidity coupled with gastrointestinal disturbance arising from purging, alcoholism, or infection with other enteric bacteria can place the human target at high risk of alarming illness. Also, pregnant women are more susceptible to cholera. Unlike the case with smallpox or measles, which confer lifelong protection to survivors, residual immunity to cholera persists only briefly, rarely more than a year or two. Finally, researchers hypothesize that humans with blood type O, for reasons not fully

---

[12] *WER*, 72 (1997), 235.
[13] Charles C.J. Carpenter, "Treatment of cholera-tradition and authority versus science, reason and humanity," *The Johns Hopkins Medical Journal*, 139 (1976), 157.

understood, are more vulnerable to bacterial infections like cholera, whereas those with other blood types are more susceptible to viral infections such as influenza.[14]

Apart from the many who acquire asymptomatic or mild cases of cholera, cholera's progress is frightening for those who are more susceptible. Incubation precedes symptoms within a range of from fourteen hours to as long as five days. The variation depends on how long it takes for the cholera vibrios to colonize and multiply in the small intestine after they enter the body via the mouth from contaminated water or food. There, the bacteria secrete a powerful toxin that interferes with the absorption of water, salts, and other electrolytes into the large intestine. In the first stage of symptoms, a sudden and explosive watery diarrhea, classically called the "rice water stool," gushes out of the patient, emptying the lower bowel of fecal matter quickly. Dehydration produces acute and agonizing cramps in the muscles of the legs and feet, and sometimes the arms, abdomen, and back. The sense of prostration is extreme, and lasts from two to twelve hours, depending on the severity of the symptoms.

The second stage, often reached in a day or two, is marked by extreme collapse and continued purging and vomiting. Rapid dehydration and ruptured capillaries produce a grizzly effect in the patient's appearance. The skin becomes black and blue, wrinkled, cold, and clammy to the touch; the eyes become sunken, the cheeks hollow, the voice husky, and the expression apathetic. Blood pressure falls, a pulse cannot be felt at the wrist, and urine is suppressed. Violent convulsions of the leg and stomach muscles can cause terrible pain. Loss of liquid is often so great that blood can run as thickly as tar, and the opening of a vein produces no results. Meanwhile, the patient suffers from the horror of full awareness of her or his plight. By this time the patient may have lost most body fluids. Without fluid replacement, death can occur from circulatory or kidney failure. In the worst cases, a healthy person can be dead in hours.

Feces from acutely infected patients are the main source for spreading the cholera outbreak. In a single day, an individual patient can produce up to twenty liters of stool containing as many as ten million vibrios per milliliter. This frequent and painless diarrhea is accompanied by vomitus of the same whitish appearance, which may contain cholera bacteria; and there is extensive retching and hiccups. The massive loss of water

---

[14] D.L. Swerdlow et al., "Severe life-threatening cholera associated with blood group O in Peru: Implications for the Latin American epidemic," *Journal of Infectious Disease*, 170 (1994), 468–72.

and electrolytes can amount to 8 percent loss of normal body weight. A third stage, for those who survive this critical attack, brings a cessation of vomiting and diarrhea. If the second stage lasts only a few hours, then circulation and blood pressure are restored and the flow of urine resumes. Though recovery seems assured, death can still occur within four or five days should impaired kidney function develop.

Given the truly horrible suffering it has inflicted on patients, it is no wonder that cholera has remained a frightening disease. Deeply embedded in the collective memory of many cultures globally, its association with violent purging of both vomit and feces evokes natural revulsion and shame in both patients and caregivers. The inability to control the bladder and bowels in the process of bodily elimination of waste is a mark of infancy, but its manifestation in adults suffering from cholera is a humiliating sign of dependency, and, among the elderly, a sign of senility.

Attitudes toward feces and their elimination have varied greatly over time, within and across cultures. European aristocracy developed "chamber pots," and monarchs such as Elizabeth I or Louis XIV thought it acceptable to relieve themselves while holding court. By the nineteenth century, however, elimination of body waste became a private act, one that distinguished the proper manners of genteel society from the barbarous public practice of the lower classes and the "other" – often foreigners. The sanitarian movement reinforced this loathing of feces, and germ theory later in the century was able to demonstrate the threat to health that fecal matter could represent. The literature on "dirt and disgust" has been linked to specific theologies such as Unitarianism and belief in a universally benevolent God. A recent study in literary criticism has argued that cholera was a vehicle for the creation of Victorian notions of the social body operating in the nation-state.[15]

On the Continent, a similar horror of feces and filth was also developing. Alfred Le Petit's grotesque caricature purporting that cholera was not contagious and entitled "Un docteur épatant" (an amazed doctor) appeared in *Le Grelot*, a popular Paris magazine, on November 23, 1884. Difficult for readers today to tolerate, the drawing portrays a man placing fecal matter in his mouth while releasing a bouquet of violets from

[15] For the theological dimension, Michael Brown, "From foetid air to filth: The cultural transformation of British epidemiological thought, ca. 1780–1848," *Bulletin of the History of Medicine*, 82 (2008), 515–44; for literary criticism and cholera, Pamela K. Gilbert, *Cholera and Nation: Doctoring the Social Body in Victorian England* (Albany: State University of New York Press, 2008).

his anus. A blue hue of violets symbolized the common association of cholera victims with blue skin color. The caption reads, "[T]o prove cholera is not contagious, Dr. N. consumes a cholera-ridden feces orally; five minutes later, he produces a bouquet of violets ... 'at the other end.'"[16]

Cholera became the quintessential disease of filth, and this association, more than its potential and real lethality, helps explain why it triggers such powerful popular reactions. The symptoms of a cholera attack invoked bodily functions that were hidden from public view in respectable Western society by as early as the late eighteenth century. Those who flaunted such practices as bodily elimination were degraded marginals, vagrants, drunkards, or the mentally ill. Their very behavior was an indicator of their disqualification from civilized society.

Some cultures have used metaphor to express loathing for cholera and its association with filth. In Brazil, it is a matter of deep shame to be considered *imunda*, "filthy," or deficient in personal hygiene. The colloquial expression for cholera was *doença de cachorro*, "a dog's disease," similar to the English phrase "sick as a dog," and was used euphemistically to describe bouts of vomiting and diarrhea.[17]

Modern day sensibility has continued, and with it, deeply ingrained psychological attitudes. Euphemistic language is one indication, and examples include such terms as "night soil" for human feces used as fertilizer, a common practice in parts of Asia but avoided elsewhere. Similarly, having a "bowel movement" is the polite discourse used even between doctors and patients, as opposed to a wide variety of countercultural expressions used by the young, the rebellious, or the uncouth. Another euphemism is the practice of "toilet training," so fundamental to early childhood.

Yet waste elimination is a natural function, and not every culture has considered it abhorrent. Many Africans and Indians use empty areas of public or even private space as makeshift latrines. One of the most difficult adaptations for cultural outsiders is to engage in greetings and conversations with individuals who are in the act of defecating. While fecal elimination as a casual and natural act may be culturally acceptable in some societies, makeshift latrines do represent a public health hazard, and persuading people of the cholera risks involved can pose a challenge to public health authorities.

---

[16] In Patrice Bourdelais and André Dodin, *Visages du choléra* (Paris: Belin, 1987), 75.

[17] Marilyn K. Nations and Cristina M.G. Monte, "'I'm not dog, no!': Cries of resistance against cholera control campaigns," *Social Science and Medicine*, 43 (1996), 1007–24.

For most of the nineteenth century, medical remedies for cholera remained as varied – and often as downright harmful – as they were ineffective. Misunderstanding of cholera's mode of attack on the human body often produced "benevolent homicide," to use Norman Howard-Jones's appropriate phrase.[18] Instead of replenishing fluids and electrolytes, misguided treatments could often involve accelerated loss through purging, the administration of alcohol or morphine, and other undesirable practices. Two such painful attempts at therapy in the nineteenth century were the application by Parisian physicians of a red-hot iron to the spine or the heel. Second, hot and cold water orally or via the rectum was sometimes attempted, as were baths. Although they diverged as the nineteenth century progressed, Western and Indian medical therapies shared a series of assumptions and practices regarding cholera. Western humoral tradition classified cholera initially as a disease of bile because of the patient's thirst and the yellowish tinge to the eyes. In 1817, British physicians sitting on the Bengal Medical Board recommended treatment in four stages, borrowing partly from Ayurvedic Indian practice. First came the Western prescription of liquor to revive strength; second, laudanum (tincture of opium) to calm the stomach and bowels; third, purgatives like calomel, epsom salts, and senna to expel any remaining "morbid secretions"; finally, tonics and a plain diet to restore health to the stomach.[19]

The use of strong spirits aside, this was much like the treatments used by Indian healers. They recommended medicines made up of black pepper, borax, asafetida, aniseed, ginger, and cloves; sometimes opium or hemp was offered to dull pain and relax the body.

Both British and Indian pharmaceutical schools were convinced their treatments were preferable, but neither side showed great enthusiasm for the available medicines, possibly because none really had significant therapeutic value. In the 1840s, Dr. William Scot of the Madras Medical Board spoke for many when he lamented the failures of treatments: "In no disease has the sovereign efficacy of numberless specifics been more vaunted, and in none have the utmost efforts of the medical art been more frequently insufficient, than in cholera."[20] A century and a half

---

[18] Norman Howard-Jones, "Cholera therapy in the nineteenth century," *Journal of the History of Medicine and Allied Sciences*, 27 (1972), 373.

[19] Ira Klein, "Cholera: theory and treatment in nineteenth century India," *Journal of Indian History*, 58 (1980), 35–51.

[20] In David Arnold, *Colonizing the Body: State Medicine and Epidemic Disease in Nineteenth-Century India* (Berkeley: University of California Press, 1993), 183.

later, scientific understanding and therapy, together with the emergence of the less virulent *Vibrio cholerae* 01 El Tor strain, have combined to mitigate cholera's threat to life. Expensive mass antibiotic treatments (with tetracycline or doxycycline) have sometimes been applied with mixed results. The WHO does not recommend these procedures, as we shall see. Clinical trials for an effective cholera vaccine have been under way since the 1990s, but by far the most important change has been the ability to rehydrate patients quickly and effectively by means of an inexpensive and effective treatment, known now as oral rehydration therapy (ORT). As early as 1830, a few westerners recognized this need to restore liquids, but were simply unable to find a way for the cholera sufferer in distress to retain liquids. It would take more than a century before medical therapists successfully administered oral rehydration. Though there is a conventional protocol, the restoration of a cholera patient's fluids and electrolytes can be achieved in a number of ways, some of them remarkably ingenious when necessity must prevail. One such example is the method employed by an Australian military physician accompanying some 7,000 Australian and British prisoners of war during their forced march under Japanese occupation in Southeast Asia in 1943. Cholera was a great killer, but this adept medical officer designed a contraption from a small bamboo tube, an old tin can, and a piece of rubber tubing from his stethoscope, and administered nearly one hundred infusions of salt and water into the veins of his dehydrated patients, saving scores of lives.[21] More conventionally, rehydration by ORT over the past twenty years has become one of the greatest success stories in the annals of modern medicine. This therapy involves the oral administration of gentle concoctions containing sugar, salts, and other products combining to restore life-giving fluids. An added attraction of ORT is that it is as simple and inexpensive to administer as it is effective.

With this simple therapeutic tool readily and cheaply available throughout the world, no one should die from cholera today. Unfortunately, cholera can still be a killer. Horrific deaths from cholera still occur today among the world's most disadvantaged, whether they are civilian refugees in war-torn Darfur, slum-dwellers in seasonally flooded lowlands in Africa and Asia, or those indigenous peoples inhabiting remote corners of the Amazon Basin in South America. Worse, as will be discussed

[21] Don Wall, *The Heroes of 'F' Force* (Mona Vale: NSW: by the author, 1993).

in Chapter 10, cholera may soon become the quintessential twenty-first century disease: a beneficiary of globalization, and sensitive to the complexities of biodiversity and climate change in ways that are only beginning to be understood.[22]

---

[22] See especially Kelley Lee, "The global dimensions of cholera," *Global Change & Human Health*, 2 (2001), 6–17; and Kelley Lee et al., "Global change and health: the good, the bad and the evidence," *Global Change & Human Health*, 3 (2002), 16–19.

PART ONE

THE FIRST SIX PANDEMICS, 1817–1947[1]

<hr>

[1] Delineations for the various cholera pandemics vary among authorities. Pollitzer opts to extend the Second Pandemic to 1851, ignoring a definite lull internationally from the mid 1830s to the mid 1840s. I prefer to follow Speck and close off the Second Pandemic in 1838. These are, after all, artificial conventions. What is clear is that the first three Pandemics ran to the middle of the nineteenth century, and the Fourth and Fifth took place in the second half of the century. The Sixth and Seventh Pandemics were products of the twentieth century. Robert Pollitzer, *Cholera* (Geneva: WHO, 1959); Speck, "Cholera", 642–49.

Cholera Circles the Globe

THE FIRST PANDEMIC, 1817–1826

The first modern cholera pandemic coincided with the beginning of a new era in world history: the economic transformation of the world system. After Britain led a European alliance to defeat France in 1815, peoples' lives everywhere were changed by the economic reordering of their societies. Paramount among these changes was the rise of British hegemony, which was based on a new guiding commercial policy that held that domestic wealth depended on the import of basic goods and the export of new manufactured commodities. What became known as British free trade created new magnitudes of capital and labor in society and generated responses everywhere.

In South Asia, the leading edge of this transformation was the British East India Company, which was on the verge of reordering political power by defeating and replacing the Mogul Empire. In the Middle East, the Ottoman Empire, although not yet destroyed, was rapidly declining into dependency on Europe as it uncomfortably adjusted to the new rules of commerce and diplomacy. In Africa, alternate visions held by charismatic leaders were emerging in response to the changes in long-distance trade, and especially the slave trade. In the Americas, the United States and the former colonies of the Spanish Empire looked on the new British rules of international trade with energy and enthusiasm, as they recognized the economic opportunity offered by these new principles. Finally, in Europe itself, imperial systems were faced with civil unrest between conservatives and liberals – those who wished to maintain the old order and those who

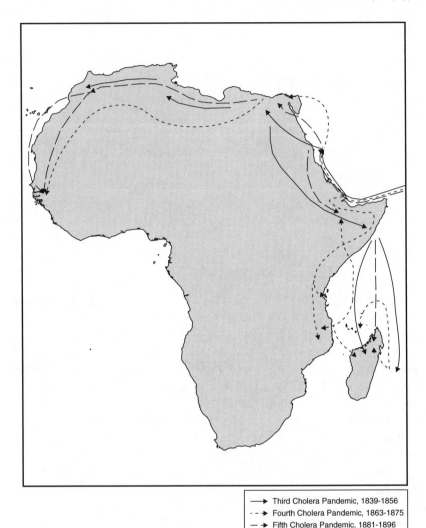

MAP 1.1. Third, Fourth, and Fifth Pandemics in Africa.

demanded that political reforms match the large economic transformations engulfing their societies.

Only in East Asia were conservative forces able to avoid the changes that would play such a significant role in the globalization of cholera. The Qing dynasty in China was either oblivious to the new realities or preferred not to alter Confucian fundamentals of society under such unfavorable terms. Until later in the nineteenth century, a similar attitude prevailed in Japan as well.

It only became clear after the fact that the diffusion of cholera from the Ganges Delta after 1817 was of pandemic proportions. Well before this date, it appears likely that a cholera-like infection did make occasional forays somewhat beyond the Ganges Delta. Indian texts from as early as the sixth century BCE described an acute form of diarrhea that might have been cholera. Arriving in India in the late fifteenth century, the Portuguese encountered an acute diarrhea that was locally called *moryxy*, and that was modified to *mordexim*, from which came the French *mort de chien*. A century later, the Dutch described a similar outbreak in the East Indies, and the Chinese reported an imported outbreak of a cholera-like disease from India in 1669. The first well-documented epidemic began near Ganjam, southern India, in 1781. From there, Bengali troops spread the infection to Madras and back to Calcutta; soon after, British sailors carried the disease to Sri Lanka.[1] In none of these cases – occurring before the days of biomedicine – could the causative agent be identified. Modern usage reserves "cholera" as a term to describe the illness caused by *Vibrio cholerae*, the comma-shaped bacteria first recognized by the Italian scientist Filippo Pacini in 1854, and discovered to be cholera's causative agent by Robert Koch in 1883. Contemporary Europeans after 1817 chose to label this new disease "Asiatic cholera." Following modern convention, it will be assumed throughout this study that cholera began as an international scourge in 1817.

How modern cholera emerged remains a mystery. Extreme climate change may have been a factor. The eruption of Mount Tambora in Indonesia in 1815 is said to have triggered erratic weather, resulting in extreme rainfall followed by disastrous floods and harvest failures. This association between food shortages and cholera was repeated on several occasions after 1815. Dust deflected sunlight, and weather anomalies arose throughout South and Southeast Asia. The unusually hot and dry conditions that resulted may not have been ideal for the cholera bacilli, but they drove desperate villagers to drink from suspect sources, to eat surrogate foods that taxed their digestive systems, and to migrate in a desperate search for sustenance.

Significant details regarding the scale of the First Pandemic are sorely lacking, because only fragmentary accounts, often written years later, have survived. In March 1817, Calcutta and the rest of Bengal experienced a violent outburst of cholera that left hardly a village or town untouched over the entire province. During 1818, cholera reached Delhi,

[1] Speck, "Cholera," 642–3.

Bombay, and most other cities and regions of India, with estimated infection rates running as high as 8 percent of the population.

During its relatively brief decade, the First Pandemic left the Indian subcontinent and struck primarily in Asia, the Indian Ocean islands, and the African coast. Europe and the Americas were spared, and the impact on the Middle East and Africa was probably milder than in subsequent visitations. The patterns of cholera's spread would prove to be typical of later pandemics. Diffusion took place by both land and sea and was closely linked to trade and to warfare, which were often working in tandem. Throughout the nineteenth century, cholera was to be a beneficiary of Western military and colonial expansion coupled with dramatic technological innovation that accelerated the frequency, speed, and volume of global commerce. In 1821, a British military force carried cholera from India to Oman, a Persian Gulf entrepôt focusing on Indian Ocean trade. Growing commercial traffic quickly spread cholera from Oman to Zanzibar. That same year, a British naval force engaged in the suppression of the slave trade brought cholera to Muscat in southern Arabia. Warfare between the Ottomans and Persia in 1822 saw cholera attack both armies near Yerevan, the capital of present-day Armenia.

THE SECOND AND THIRD PANDEMICS (1828–1836 AND 1839–1861)

The Second Pandemic, beginning in 1828, only two years after the retreat of the First, was of longer duration and wider scope. Once again, cholera left the Ganges Delta, traveling by both land and sea, and this time circling most of the globe. Military activities again aided cholera when a British invasion of the Punjab in 1827 helped the Second Pandemic gain impetus. In 1835, Algeria endured a cholera visitation brought by French troops who were continuing the conquest they had begun in 1830. Neighboring Libya to the east and Morocco to the west were also infected. Russia's wars with Persia from 1826 to 1828 and with the Ottoman Empire from 1828 to 1829 helped cholera gain a stranglehold on these regions of the Middle East. The Polish revolt against Russia in 1830 and 1831 brought cholera to the Baltic for the first time.

Expanding trade and improving technology also contributed to cholera's spread. The more rapid mobility of carriers and patients aboard new and improved ships helped make the Second Pandemic a global event. For example, once warfare brought cholera to the Baltic shores in 1831, cholera moved rapidly over water by steamship and over land by rail for the next three years, reaching Britain, Ireland, France, Spain, and Portugal. Faster trans-Atlantic crossings permitted cholera to invade the Americas. In Canada, the United States, Cuba, and Mexico, the disease spread along rivers, roads, and newly built canals. There was even a report that the South American nations of Chile and Peru experienced a light brush with cholera in 1832, but that was never confirmed.

In addition to war and trade, a third element assisted the diffusion of cholera: large gatherings of pilgrims housed in makeshift accommodations. The Hindu pilgrimage at Hardwar in the lower Ganges Valley in 1826 would provide fodder for this cholera outbreak and for the Fourth Pandemic in 1867. Cholera surfaced at the large annual gathering of Muslim pilgrims at Mecca and other holy sites on the Arabian Peninsula for the first time in 1833. Before cholera finally disappeared from the Muslim holy sites after 1912, the disease would make no less than forty appearances there, some of them truly horrific. During the Second Pandemic in 1833, Muslim pilgrims returning from Mecca carried the bacilli west as far as Morocco and east all the way to Mindanao in the Philippines. A second Meccan outbreak in 1836 allowed cholera to travel with returning pilgrims aboard dhows (Arab sailing vessels) bound for the Somali coast of East Africa. Cholera penetrated as far south as the island of Zanzibar and possibly even to Mozambique, as well as into the East African interior aboard caravans.

The Second Pandemic's impact was uneven. Although it probably killed fewer people in Asia than its predecessor, in Europe and America its symbolic effect was dramatic. According to the medical historian J.N. Hays, news of the First Pandemic may have frightened westerners, but the actual arrival of the Second Pandemic invoked emotions and fears not experienced since the bubonic plague of the fourteenth century.[2] Part of this response was the growing assumption that "Asiatic" cholera was a reflection of Asia's barbarity, despite the inability of European medical opinion to comprehend the cause and mode of transmission of the disease.

The world that the third cholera pandemic toured from 1839 to 1861 had changed dramatically since the pathogen had begun its international wanderings in 1817. Steadily growing in trade and empire, Great Britain repealed the Corn Laws in 1846 and proclaimed its commitment to the new doctrine of free trade. Political tensions in Europe culminated in

---

[2] J.N. Hays, *Epidemics and Pandemics: Their Impacts on Human History* (Santa Barbara, CA: ABC-CLIO, 2005), 212–13.

1848, a year of largely failed liberal revolutions, although the new ideology of nationalism took solid hold. From mid-century forward, efforts at nation building and revitalizing imperialism changed the political face of the world.

These new realities were everywhere. In Europe, two new states emerged – Germany and Italy – and nationalist aspirations were strongly contested in two sprawling multinational empires, Austria and Russia. While the Qing continued their decline in China, Japan under Meiji rule chose a dramatic path that would marry nationalism to imperial ambitions in the East Asian region. Through all of these changes, cholera's twin dependence on transport and warfare was well served. Faster movement by river, road, rail, and canal gave the disease superior technical assistance in its spread. Wars for imperial gain or to resist its encroachments, especially the Crimean War, continued to be breeding grounds for the cholera pathogen. In July 1854, part of the French expeditionary force of 55,000 landed at Varna, Bulgaria, where, together with the British, they sought to prevent the Russians from entering the Dardanelles. The French forces brought cholera with them, and they and the British suffered 8,230 cases and 5,030 deaths. Among the victims was the British commander in chief Lord Raglan. The allies forced the Russians to retreat from Bulgaria and chased them into the Crimea, hoping to destroy the Russian naval base at Sevastopol. Cholera spread to the Russian enemy and to the Bulgarians, and thousands died.

Meanwhile, great advances in industry, technology, and science took place in what is sometimes called the second industrial revolution of the nineteenth century. Germany and the United States, although not yet ready to challenge British hegemony, were increasing their share of world industrial output, and confidence in the assertion of their power was growing. In medical science, theories and therapies devoted to infectious diseases improved dramatically, leading to the emergence of germ theory and the new science of bacteriology. Its implications for cholera, however, would take some time to be felt.

As the world economy grew more integrated, huge movements of peoples continued in this period. This economy required greater quantities of raw materials to produce finished products and needed more workers as production dispersed throughout the world. These changes spurred investment by capitalists and migration by the laboring populations seeking new opportunities to escape from poverty. Some of this migration remained less than voluntary; it no longer involved the coerced transport of slaves from Africa to the New World, but instead now relied on contract labor from India, China, parts of Africa, the Indian Ocean, and the Americas. Also moving in great numbers were thousands of Irish, Poles, Jews, Italians, and Greeks, who settled mainly in the rapidly growing cities of North and South America. Nor was global migration essentially a movement across the Atlantic. A second great migration saw Indians and Chinese drawn to the rubber plantations and rice fields of Southeast Asia. The third and most neglected migration involved millions of Northeast Asians and Russians moving into Manchuria and Siberia.[3]

In the Middle East, the holy pilgrimage sites of Islam proved useful to the pathogen once more. More than 15,000 pilgrims died at Mecca in 1846. Another cholera outbreak at the holy city struck two years later, and this time surviving pilgrims carried the disease to Egypt. The same pattern would occur again during a third cholera outbreak in 1855.

Although lightly infected during the Second Pandemic, Africa was not so lucky during the third. Not only did Mecca prove a launching pad for cholera into Egypt in 1848, 1850, and 1855, but Algeria and Tunisia also experienced importations from southern France and Italy during 1849. Morocco was infected in 1851 and again in 1855, the same year that cholera headed south from Egypt into the Sudan, Ethiopia, and the East African coast, and then from Somalia, past Zanzibar, all the way south to Mozambique. Major Indian Ocean islands – Mauritius, Réunion, Madagascar, and the Comoros – also suffered cholera visitations in the 1850s.

Warfare and maritime expansion also operated in East Asia during the Third Pandemic. British troops assembling in Calcutta and Madras for imperial purposes were the likely carriers of cholera into Malaysia and then on to China, where it first touched down near Shanghai in July 1840. It claimed thousands of lives on the Chinese mainland over the next two years. Japan had remained cholera-free since the 1820s, but the opening up by the U.S. Navy of Nagasaki and other ports to westerners in the 1850s brought back the dreaded cholera, which the Japanese labeled "the disease of the Western barbarians." The moribund Tokugawa Shogunate had good reason to blame the "unequal treaties" forced on them for the medical disaster that followed.[4] In 1857, the American battleship *Mississippi* brought infected patients to Nagasaki and triggered a

[3] Adam McKeown, "Global migration, 1846–1940," *Journal of World History*, 15 (2004), 155–89.

[4] Anne Bowman Jannetta, *Epidemics and Mortality in Early Modern Japan* (Princeton: Princeton University Press, 1987), 16; Mahito H. Fukuda, "Public Health in Modern Japan: From Regimen to Hygiene," in Porter, Dorothy, ed., *The History of Public Health and the Modern State* (Atlanta: Rodopi, 1994), 390.

cholera epidemic throughout Japan that, over the next three years, killed in excess of 100,000 people in the capital region of Edo alone.

To the west, greater travel and trade also meant more cholera. Once again, cholera entered Europe through its Russian portal in 1847. Although Moscow was infected in September 1847, a lull set in during the winter of 1847–1848, with cholera halted on the approach to Riga at the Baltic Sea and at the Austrian border. But cholera virtually exploded in 1848, reaching as far north as Norway and Scotland and as far south as Spain; it included England, France, Ireland, and the Balkans in its travels. Paris suffered a death toll of 24,000, and one in twenty-eight of its residents were infected. By the 1850s, cholera had ravaged most of Europe.

The year 1848 also saw terrible cholera outbreaks in the Americas. New Orleans gave cholera purchase into the heart of the continent via the Mississippi River. A year later, cholera crossed the Gulf into Mexico. A ship heading from New Orleans to Panama brought cholera to Central and South America, where infections flared in Colombia as far inland as Bogotá, and on to Quito in Ecuador. Jamaica and Cuba suffered violent attacks in 1850 and 1851. Jamaica lost an estimated 7 percent of its population in the 1850 outbreak. From Cuba, cholera was transported back across the southern Atlantic to the Canary Islands, causing 9,000 deaths, most in the space of a few days. Finally, the large empire of Brazil tasted the bitter pill of cholera for the first time in 1855.

The Third Pandemic finally began to wane in 1860. For some regions, it proved to be the worst pandemic of the century. The list would include Brazil, the Caribbean, the United States, and most of Europe. In the West, cholera solidified its reputation as a gruesome killer, though this reputation was based more on the horrors of patients' suffering than on the only occasionally high mortality rates during specific epidemics. In reality, cholera's morbidity trends were much lower, well below those of nineteenth-century tuberculosis, a much more dangerous disease that ironically was less feared than cholera. In the West, this pandemic coincided with the rise of sanitarianism, initially a British public health initiative linked to new engineering systems that separated sewage lines from those drawing potable drinking water.

THE FOURTH AND FIFTH PANDEMICS (1863–1879 AND 1881–1896)

The world was virtually free of cholera in 1861 and 1862, but in 1863, the Fourth Pandemic began its travels from India to Indonesia.

This pandemic continued to benefit from transformations. Newly industrial and urban societies were sending their young men overseas on missions of conquest and colonization, and the growth of nationalism accelerated in the new states of Germany and Italy. Similar sentiments prevailed among the many nationalities making up the Austrian, Russian, and Ottoman empires.

In a more timid manner, public health and medicine were also changing. One phenomenon that grew was the international concern for better cooperation in defending against the pathogen, which resulted in the establishment of the International Sanitary Conference (ISC). The first two of these conferences were held in Paris during the Fourth Pandemic. The third ISC was held at Constantinople in 1866, and the fourth at Vienna in 1874. Like their predecessors, the two meetings failed to achieve the consensus necessary to produce binding regulations. They did, however, lead the Ottomans to draft comprehensive legislation that later proved important regionally for the pilgrim trade.

Despite these small steps forward, the fourth cholera pandemic may have killed more people than any other. The decade of the 1860s was especially destructive. The following numbers give some indication of the havoc wrought: in 1865, 15,000 deaths among 90,000 pilgrims at Mecca and 50,000 deaths in Egypt; in 1866, 50,000 deaths in the United States and 12,000 deaths on the small island of Guadeloupe; in 1867, 125,000 deaths – a 50 percent mortality rate – among pilgrims at Hardwar.

During these same middle years of the decade, turmoil resulting from empire building helped cholera ravage Germany, Austria, and Italy. To the north and west, the terrible death toll in 1866 saw tens of thousands succumb in Sweden, Britain, Holland, and Belgium. In South America during 1866, tiny Paraguay lost a major war, and a large portion of its army died from cholera, not combat. War victors Argentina and Brazil also paid a price in lives lost to cholera rather than to bullets. The epidemic also spread to Peru and Uruguay. The United States was fortunate not to be visited by cholera during its brutal Civil War, but cholera in 1866 did take advantage of thousands of people suffering in the aftermath from food shortages, inadequate shelter, and unsanitary prisoner-of-war camps, such as the one at Newport, Kentucky. East Asia suffered successive blows between 1865 and 1867, and again from 1877 to 1879. In the latter year, China and Japan had an estimated 89,207 and 105,800 deaths, respectively, each with case fatality rates (CFRs) in excess of 50 percent.

The Fourth Pandemic was Africa's worst. Cholera not only revisited its haunts in Egypt and all of North Africa but also made its maiden voyage south of the Sahara to West Africa, launching terrible epidemics in the Senegal and Gambia river valleys. Cholera's African invasions came from a variety of sources. Ships carried the infection from Bombay via Aden to Eritrea and Somalia on the East African coast, and then caravans transported cholera into the Ethiopian highlands from the port of Massawa on the Red Sea coast.

Most devastating of all was cholera's ability to work its way down the East African coast from 1865 to 1871. Over land, it reached the Great Lakes of Africa through Masai lands in Kenya and then moved south to Tanzania and the bustling entrepôt of Zanzibar. The city lost an estimated 70,000 people in 1869 and 1870. Indian Ocean sailing vessels engaged in the coastal trade also carried cholera down through the Swahili ports to their southern limits just short of Delegoa Bay at Quelimane. During this same period, cholera also called at the Indian Ocean islands of Mauritius, the Seychelles, the Comoros, Nossi-bé, and Madagascar.

Advances in shipping technology assisted cholera's diffusion from the Middle East and elsewhere during the Fourth Pandemic. In the Mediterranean by 1850, although sailing vessels remained dominant in the shipping of merchandise, passengers found the time savings well worth the purchase of more expensive tickets on steam ships. Travel time from Alexandria to Marseilles dropped from between fifteen and thirty days to six. Typically, returning pilgrims bound for a Mediterranean destination traveled by land only to the Red Sea port of Jeddah. Once the Suez Canal opened in 1869, pilgrims could board a passenger vessel taking them through the canal and to the southeastern corner of the Mediterranean at Alexandria in a week. From there, steam travel as far as Gibraltar took less than one week. Rapid passenger travel from Europe to North America also increased the dangers of cholera. Two such cases were the *Leibnitz*, traveling from Hamburg to New York in 1867, which had 165 cholera cases and 105 deaths aboard, and the *England*, bound from Liverpool for New York via Halifax in 1866, with 150 cases and 46 deaths. Some 200 additional cases were recorded in quarantine at Halifax.[5]

The cut-off date for the Fourth Pandemic is disputed. Several historians, and most health scientists who follow them, end the Fourth Pandemic in 1872.[6] Yet this cut-off date excludes the serious epidemic in Hungary that

[5] Pollitzer, *Cholera*, 880.
[6] See, for example, Pollitzer, *Cholera*; Speck, "Cholera," 642–9; and Barua and Greenough III, *Cholera*, 1–36.

continued until 1873, when Russia, Germany, Thailand, Malaysia, and Indonesia were infected. Although it is the case that the Fourth Pandemic waned thereafter, it did not die out. As noted, Japan and China suffered terribly between 1877 and 1879. Clearly, the early cut-off date is biased toward cholera events in Europe and the Americas and neglects international outbreaks within Asia that are well outside the endemic home of cholera in the Ganges Delta.

On the other hand, virtual unanimity exists that the Fifth Pandemic began in 1881 and lasted until 1896. This was the least widespread and devastating pandemic since cholera had begun its global reach in 1817. Countries in the North Atlantic world, applying hard-won sanitarian lessons of prevention through improved water systems, had seen the last of cholera pandemics by the 1870s. Where cholera did strike after 1881, it continued to do so with great intensity and with elevated mortality rates.

In East Asia, the Fifth Pandemic was the worst on record. In Japan, where registrations of cholera infections were now being more accurately tallied, seven separate outbreaks between 1881 and 1895 produced 340,000 cases. The worst year was 1886, when 155,000 cases were registered.[7] CFRs were rarely recorded, but if they ranged close to 20 percent, then somewhere in the vicinity of 68,000 deaths would have resulted. Numbers are not available for Japan's neighbors, but most endured multiple outbreaks between 1881 and 1895. China had six; Indonesia and Korea, five each; the Philippines, two; Sri Lanka, Thailand, and Malaysia might have considered themselves fortunate to have suffered one visitation each.

Cholera was still capable of causing havoc in the Mediterranean, Central Europe, and Russia, where one of its victims may have been the illustrious composer Peter Tchaikovsky. Between 1892 and 1894, Russia experienced two million cases and 800,000 deaths. This high CFR of 40 percent brought with it a familiar trail of riot, murder, and angry attacks on government and medical officials. Tsarists were still rigidly enforcing quarantine, isolation, and disinfection on the shoulders of an impoverished peasantry, and the medical profession had little success in educating peasants on the value of preventive measures.[8] Southern France and Italy each had 10,000 cases and 5,000 deaths in 1884, with port

[7] Fukuda, "Public Health," 391.
[8] Nancy M. Frieden, "The Russian Cholera Epidemic of 1892–1893 and medical professionalization," *Journal of Social History*, 10 (1977), 538–59.

towns of Toulon, Marseilles, Palermo, Naples, and Genoa hardest hit. The next year, Spain lost 60,000 people among its 160,000 cases, mostly in the southeast provinces of Valencia and Murcia. Finally, in 1892, the German port city of Hamburg lost more than 7,500 people, a CFR of 38 percent.

Mild and sporadic outbreaks were the norm in the Americas during the Fifth Pandemic. The closest North America came to disaster was when eight badly infected ships arrived in the port of New York in 1892. Careful inspection and control resulted in only ten cases in the city. In the far south of the Americas, mild outbreaks occurred in Brazil, Uruguay, and Argentina between 1893 and 1895.

In the Middle East and Africa, experience with cholera during the Fifth Pandemic was extensive, though not so terrible as during the Fourth Pandemic. During 1881, 200,000 of the Muslim faithful contracted cholera at the Arabian pilgrimage sites, and more than 30,000 died. From there, the infection quickly spread to Egypt, which experienced two waves. More than 16,000 Egyptians died during the second wave in 1895 and 1896, which was the last visitation of the disease until after the Second World War. Cholera at Mecca once again found its way among returning pilgrims to other African locales, reaching all the way west to Morocco in the early 1890s. Next, cholera took caravan routes south across the Sahara to the Senegalese Valley in 1893 and 1894. The Fifth Pandemic also revisited highland Ethiopia and coastal Eritrea in the same period. By 1896, the pandemic's fire was reduced to smoldering embers.

THE SIXTH PANDEMIC, 1899–1947

After a hiatus of three years, in 1899, cholera began its familiar march once more. In the West, filtration and chlorination of urban water supplies proved a major barrier to cholera, save where political and social tensions spilled over into revolts and warfare. As the twentieth century dawned, violence was close to the surface. Russia teetered on the edge of revolution, and the Balkans were bristling with political tensions. In slightly more than a decade, war on an unprecedented scale would produce a great slaughter, this time on a global canvas, with cholera tagging along as an opportunistic parasite.

Most Europeans never experienced cholera after the 1890s. In Russia, however, turmoil, revolution, and civil war abetted cholera enormously during the years from 1902 to 1925. The worst year recorded was 1910, with 230,000 cases and 110,000 deaths. The cities of St. Petersburg,

Jekaterinoslav, Kiev, and Orenburg all suffered terribly during the civil wars. Nevertheless, as the Red Army consolidated control and conflict began to diminish, so too did cholera. The last bad year was 1922, after which the disease began to wane.

War was also cholera's hand maiden in Central Europe. The Austro-Hungarian Empire experienced only sporadic cholera in 1909, and again in 1913, in its Balkan territories and lands bordering on Russia. Russian and later Serbian prisoners of war created a bad cholera situation from 1914 to 1916. For example, in November of 1914, Austrian soldiers coming from the Volhynia-Podolsk front in the Ukraine brought cholera with them to Silesia. Cholera also ravaged southeastern Europe. Beginning with the Balkan Wars of 1912–1913 and continuing through the First World War and its aftermath, Romania, Serbia, Bulgaria, and Turkey all endured the unwelcome presence of *Vibrio cholerae*.

Cholera could easily have been a factor on the Western Front during the Great War as well. Trench warfare would seem to have provided a golden opportunity for cholera, and it is a mystery as to why it did not strike. A sporadic outbreak did hit the Dutch port of Rotterdam well before the war, in 1909, with twenty-six cases and six deaths, but that was all.

With the glaring exception of Republican China, where cholera remained one of that country's many health challenges, the Sixth Pandemic did not have great purchase in East Asia. China faced cholera outbreaks frequently; its struggles were depicted in the 2006 film *The Painted Veil*, based on Somerset Maugham's 1925 novel. The worst year was 1932, when roughly 34,000 deaths among 100,000 cases were recorded. Cholera in China benefitted from the instability of war and from extreme climatic conditions, and it appeared every year from 1937 through to 1948 as the country was racked by Japanese invasion and internal revolution. Displaced persons and troop movements helped spread cholera from Canton in the south to Manchuria in the north. Disastrous floods in central China and in Manchuria helped produce large numbers of deaths from cholera in 1932 and again in 1939.

Also contributing to China's suffering from cholera was Japanese biological warfare. Cholera seemed an attractive biological weapon because it survived in untreated water and where infrastructure had been damaged by war. In 1936, after its seizure of Manchuria, Japan created the notorious Unit 731 near Harbin to experiment with biological weapons for cholera, botulism, anthrax, bubonic plague, and typhoid. An estimated 200,000 Chinese died from biological warfare. Japanese forces introduced cholera by contaminating water supplies along the Nu River in Yunnan province in early 1942, and by dropping ceramic bombs containing *Vibrio cholerae* over several Yunnan cities. Cholera, however, proved too difficult to control, and when too many Japanese soldiers became infected, the effort was halted.[9]

In Southeast Asia, the region's proximity to the "home of cholera" in the Ganges Delta continued to make it vulnerable. Neighboring Burma, especially in the low-lying and more densely populated delta of the Irrawaddy River in the south, suffered at least five cholera epidemics between 1926 and 1946. In each decade of the twentieth century until 1950, Thailand dealt with bouts of cholera imported from both Burma and China. At various times during the Sixth Pandemic through to 1948, the Philippines, Indochina, and Indonesia faced explosive outbreaks as well.

Compared with earlier global visitations, the Sixth Pandemic trod lightly on the Middle East. Its entry into the Arab heartlands occurred once again through the pilgrim routes to Mecca. The first visitation of the Sixth Pandemic, in 1902, caused 4,000 deaths among pilgrims. The killer returned in 1907 and 1908, and it left over 25,000 dead. Major outbreaks continued in Mecca from 1910 to 1912, when, in retrospect, something of a miracle occurred. For reasons that are not clear, but which may have been attributable to better sanitation, the Saudi Arabian peninsula became cholera-free and remained so thereafter. The same held true for pilgrimages to revered Shia locales in Karbala and Najaf in southern Iraq. Iraq suffered only a light outbreak in Basra in 1923 and on two more occasions later; in all instances, the disease was allegedly imported by travelers from Bombay. Sporadic and light outbreaks in Iran in the 1920s and 1930s were linked to cholera in Afghanistan and to the Punjab. Syria's light cholera epidemic in 1947 was its first since the beginning of the twentieth century, and may have been linked to the Egyptian outbreak of that same year. Apart from the possible link to Syria, Egypt's cholera did not spread to neighbors in North Africa, the Indian Ocean, or sub-Saharan Africa. These regions remained free of cholera during the entire Sixth Pandemic, as did most of Europe and the Americas.

---

[9] See Sheldon H. Harris, *Factories of Death* (New York: Routledge, 1994); Gavin Daws *Prisoners of the Japanese: POWS of World War II in the Pacific* (New York: Morrow, 1994); and "Unit 731 and War Crimes," last updated January 21, 2001, www.ww2pacific. com/unit731.html.

2

Medical Responses

The British took stock of cholera as the First Pandemic abated in India after 1821. They gradually reached conclusions they were to hold through most of the nineteenth century. First, they adopted what became known as anti-contagionism. It held that cholera was caused by peculiar aspects of the Indian environment such as the abrupt drops in temperature and the heavy rains of the monsoon, or by "miasmas" emanating from rotting vegetation or overcrowded dwellings. The death from cholera in 1827 of Sir Thomas Munro, governor of Madras, demonstrated that the disease could be alarmingly random, and that even the most powerful were susceptible. Still, Munro's misfortune excepted, cholera was a much greater danger to the Indian rural poor. The European and Indian elite enjoyed generally healthier living conditions, better diet, sanitation, and hygiene, and they were spared in large numbers for these reasons.

It also soon became fashionable – not only for the British, but in the West in general – to blame Indian squalor and superstition for cholera's persistence and spread. Foreigners came to identify the Hindu and Muslim pilgrimages, and British refusal to regulate these, as the prime culprits. As early as 1831, the French observer Moreau de Jonnès labeled troop movements and pilgrimages as the two major causes of cholera's spread in India, specifically alluding to the Puri pilgrimage in 1821.[1]

In the twenty-first century, it seems difficult to understand that some medical experts could argue that cholera was not contagious, but that was the most popular medical opinion around 1830. Though in a minority, however, contagionists like the German physician Jeremias Lichtenstaedt

---

[1] Arnold, *Colonizing*, 185.

firmly believed that the "non-infectivity of cholera ... belongs in the category of the most dangerous errors of our time."[2]

Frequently, as in France, the official position on cholera was adopted for political and economic reasons, not medical ones. For example, one concern about endorsing contagionism was the fear the state would be unable to retain nurses and other hospital personnel if contagion were officially admitted.[3] As time passed, a majority of the French population came to recognize that cholera was contagious. Nor were therapies any different in France than elsewhere in Europe. They consisted of that harmful stand-by, blood letting, and the less threatening but still unhelpful steam bath, which dehydrated the patient further. Medications were either stimulants or purgatives, often administered simultaneously. They included opium, calomel, belladonna, and absinthe.

Another line of inquiry was being developed by the early sanitarian movement, which had its strongest roots in British soil. Fear of cholera had a significant influence on the first stages of sanitary reform, because it was no longer acceptable to do nothing. The 1832 cholera pandemic stimulated the development of the first British local boards of health. Initially unpaid and locally elected, these bodies lacked expertise and legal power to change living conditions, but they were the foundations on which later progress would be built.

The third cholera pandemic stimulated increased research in mid-nineteenth-century European science as governments and the public anxiously looked for improved treatments and cures. There were two prongs to the inquiries. One was empirical and centered on the continuing concern of the sanitarian movement for improved public health. The second was more theoretical and involved the quest to identify cholera's causative agent.

Nineteenth-century cities certainly posed a challenge to early public health figures bent on sanitary reform. Exponential growth accompanied by inadequate and poorly built housing left migrants to the cities living in dire conditions.[4] Disposal of human and animal wastes posed a terrible problem. Dumping of wastes as well as industrial pollutants into rivers and bays presented a toxic cocktail ideal for water-borne diseases.

---

[2] In Roderick E. McGrew, *Russia and the Cholera, 1823–1832* (Madison: University of Wisconsin Press, 1965), 10.

[3] Bourdelais, *Epidemics*, 55.

[4] J.N. Hays, *The Burdens of Disease: Epidemics and Human Response in Western History* (New Brunswick: Rutgers University Press, 1998), table 142, shows exponential growth of cities.

Factory discharges of airborne pollutants spread asthma, tuberculosis, and other lung infections. Industrial toxins from arsenic or lead too often affected unprotected workers. The food and beverages they purchased from uninspected and usually filthy markets and stalls also exposed them to a variety of ailments.

The driving force for sanitary change in Britain was Edwin Chadwick (1800–1890), a disciple of the philosopher Jeremy Bentham. In 1842, Chadwick issued his famous *Report on the Sanitary Condition of the Labouring Population*, "the single greatest classic of the sanitation movement and one that outsold well-known novels."[5] A bureaucrat, Chadwick was concerned about controlling public health costs, and thought that investments in sanitation would be economical even if the initial outlay was steep. Chadwick envisioned a completely integrated water and sewer service: a steady supply of piped fresh water to each home, and home and street drainage to main sewers from where waste would be carried out of town and perhaps turned into fertilizer. He did not get his way on fertilizers, and it took fear of cholera for the rest of this initially expensive package to be adopted. As cholera threatened again in 1848, the British Parliament passed the Public Health Act and reconstituted the Central Board of Health, a body that had become moribund once the cholera fear of 1832 receded. Some municipalities were very slow to act, but by the later part of the century most cities in western Europe had followed the British lead and had built new water and sanitation systems.

Cholera was also the stimulus to very similar trends in the United States.[6] New York created a Board of Health as early as 1805, but it did little and the city developed no health infrastructure. The rest of the country was no better off. At mid-century, terror of cholera was enormous and fear spurred reforms, even if ignorance of cause persisted. Lemuel Shattuck (1793–1859) was a figure with an influence in the United States similar to Chadwick's in Britain. A Boston publisher and genealogical scholar working on vital statistics for the city, he saw disease as a "penalty for deviation from moral behavior," and could be avoided by a regimen of "Godliness and cleanliness."[7] The return of cholera in the late 1840s convinced him that the state needed to intervene to protect public health. Shattuck chaired the Massachusetts Legislative Commission of

---

[5] Hays, *Burdens*, 144.
[6] Laurie Garrett, *Betrayal of Trust: The Collapse of Global Public Health* (New York: Hyperion, 2000), 283, 290, 292–4.
[7] Hays, *Burdens*, 143.

1849–1850, which found that the environment was poisoning citizens, and called for the state to regulate or eliminate wastes and develop central water and sewage systems. Two further decades would elapse before the state acted.

The quest for the causative agent of cholera began during the Third Pandemic at roughly mid-century. Among the many theories, one that was on the right track was Jacob Henle's argument in 1840 that cholera and other infectious diseases were caused by living and probably vegetal organisms.[8] A theory popular in British India was that of "locality," the notion that cholera lingered in certain districts because of certain unspecified "local" circumstances.[9] This theory was popular with miasmatists, who claimed that cholera rose up in these locales and penetrated the affected person through the respiratory and gastrointestinal systems. The association of cholera with polluted water began to be significant by mid-century. In a letter to the *Times* on September 5, 1849, William Budd (1811–1880), a Bristol physician and pioneer in germ theory, argued that cholera was caused by an organism, "which, being swallowed, becomes infinitely multiplied in the intestinal canal." He also suggested that "water is the principal means of the dissemination of the disease," and that "too much care could not be exercised in procuring pure drinking water."[10] That same year, Budd and two associates published a paper describing microscopic bodies in cholera excreta. In 1849, the British physician Alfred Barring Garrod analyzed the blood of cholera victims and discovered a fifth of the body's volume had been lost. Also in 1849, Félix Pouchet reported finding vibrios in stools of cholera patients.

Independently of these developments in Britain and France, a Tuscan professor of anatomy at the University of Florence named Filippo Pacini (1812–1883) was using his skills in microscopy to conduct pioneering research on cholera.[11] When cholera struck Florence in 1854, Pacini

---

[8] Margaret Pelling, *Cholera, Fever and English Medicine, 1825–1865* (Oxford: Oxford University Press, 1978), 194.

[9] Mark Harrison, "A Question of Locality: The Identity of Cholera in British India, 1860–1890," in David Arnold, ed., *Warm Climates and Western Medicine: The Emergence of Tropical Medicine, 1500–1900* (Atlanta: Rodopi, 1996), 133–59.

[10] In Pollitzer, *Cholera*, 778–9. For a richly detailed examination of water analysis and public health in Britain, see Christopher Hamlin, *A Science of Impurity: Water Analysis in Nineteenth Century Britain* (Berkeley: University of California Press, 1990).

[11] M. Bentivoglio and P. Pacini, "Filippo Pacini: A determined observer," *Brain Research Bulletin*, 38 (1995), 161–5; and Norman Howard-Jones, "Choleranomalies: The unhistory of medicine as illustrated by cholera," in *Perspectives on Biology and Medicine*, 15 (1972), 422–33.

spotted the comma-shaped bacillus with his microscope – the first scientist to do so – and named it *Vibrio cholerae*. He also published a paper describing the organism and showing his slides. For the next two decades, Pacini continued his cholera research in academic obscurity in Tuscany, always insisting that the organism was the cause of the disease. Unfortunately, Pacini lacked a global theory of cholera causation, and his work was ignored. It was a great irony that he died in obscurity in 1883, only months before Robert Koch's independent discovery of the cholera bacillus under his microscope in Alexandria and Calcutta. Posthumously, the international committee on nomenclature gave satisfaction to an Italian request, and in 1965 renamed the bacillus *Vibrio cholerae Pacini 1854* in honor of the Tuscan scientist.

Although, like Pacini, he also lacked an encompassing theory of cholera's causation, a distinguished physician named John Snow (1813–1858) made the most important breakthrough in the history of cholera epidemiology during the Third Pandemic. A London anaesthetist, he was also Queen Victoria's obstetrician.[12]

The 1848–1849 cholera outbreak in London had stimulated Snow's theory that cholera was disseminated by contaminated water supplies. He observed that water drawn from the Upper Thames was of far superior quality to that from the Lower Thames, which contained sewage from upstream. Snow inferred that cholera's spread was linked in some fashion to the mixing of drinking water and sewage. He first published his theory in 1849, and then again in 1855 in an expanded edition that included his observations during the 1855 cholera outbreak in London.[13]

There were two dimensions to his experiments. First, he studied a severe but localized cholera outbreak at a site he made famous, the Broad Street

[12] Snow was the son of a poor coalworker in York, was apprenticed to a surgeon in Newcastle-upon-Tyne, and eventually studied medicine in London. Before turning his attention to cholera, Snow was one of the first physicians to study and calculate dosages for the use of ether, and of chloroform as surgical anesthesia. He personally administered chloroform to Queen Victoria when she gave birth to the last two of her nine children in 1853 and 1857. Together with his publications on ether and on chloroform, this royal endorsement of the procedure greatly advanced public acceptance of obstetric anesthesia. See P.E. Brown, "John Snow – the autumn loiterer," *Bulletin of the History of Medicine*, 35 (1961), 519–28; and Steven Johnson, *The Ghost Map: The Story of London's Most Terrifying Epidemic, and How it Changed Cities and the Modern World* (London: Allen Lane, 2006).

[13] John Snow, *On the Mode of Communication of Cholera* (London: J. Churchill, 1849); and *On the Mode of Communication of Cholera, 2nd edition, Much Enlarged* (London: J. Churchill, 1855). Also, John Snow, "Cholera and the water supply in the south districts of London," *British Medical Journal*, (1857), 864–5.

water pump in the St. James, Westminister district of Soho. Second was his more ambitious attempt to determine the cause of the larger epidemic in South London. Both studies linked cholera to contaminated water supplies: the first, a single local water source, the Broad Street pump; and the second, polluted water drawn from the Thames River.

Snow applied his theory by means of a map he drew of the St. James outbreak showing the density of cases clustered around the pump on Broad Street. Although Snow's map, as well as his dramatic removal of the Broad Street pump handle, have become iconic symbols of the advancement of medical science, professional public health workers and epidemiologists stand in even greater admiration of Snow's larger, if inconclusive, study of how municipal water supplies were linked causally to the larger 1854 London epidemic. Snow's account of the death toll in St. James Parish was harrowing:

The most terrible outbreak of cholera which ever occurred in this kingdom, is probably that which took place in Broad Street, Golden Square, and the adjoining streets, a few weeks ago. Within two hundred and fifty yards of the spot where Cambridge Street joins Broad Street, there were upwards of five hundred fatal attacks of cholera in ten days. The mortality in this limited area probably equals any that was ever caused in this country by the plague.[14]

Snow had great difficulty in persuading the local council to disable the Broad Street pump by removing its handle. For one thing, this pump gave invariably cool and clear water, and was considered by many the most palatable water then available in London. Part of the erroneous argument used against Snow was that sweet-tasting water could not be unsafe. Once the cholera crisis was over, the local officials rejected Snow's theory and restored the pump handle, not wishing to accept that oral-fecal transmission of cholera had taken place.

Snow persisted in his research, aided significantly by an unheralded but invaluable ally, the Reverend Henry Whitehead (1825–1896), a twenty-nine-year-old curate of the local St. Luke's Church. Whitehead conducted personal interviews with 497 of the 896 original inhabitants of Broad Street, and his findings convinced him of the validity of Snow's theory.[15] Of the 137 people in Broad Street who drank from the pump, 80 developed cholera, but only 20 of the 299 who did not use this source became

---

[14] Snow, *On the Mode* (1855), 38.
[15] Henry Whitehead, "The Broad Street Pump: an episode in the cholera epidemic of 1854," *MacMillan's Magazine* (1865), 113–22; and Henry Whitehead, *Experience of a London Curate* (Clapham: n.d., 1871).

infected. The Poland Street Workhouse escaped the outbreak because it had its own pump in addition to a mains supply. Nor was anyone at the Broad Street brewery infected. It had its own deep well and mains supply. An isolated case in Hampstead, Susannah Eley, so preferred water from the Broad Street pump that her sons sent her a large bottle daily by carrier's cart.

Whitehead went further. By April 1855, he had found that the index case at 40 Broad Street, the infant girl, lived in a house whose "privy" and cesspool were only three feet from the pump. The drain leaked and the cesspool had been poorly built.

The Cholera Inquiry Committee now accepted that impure water at the well in Broad Street had been responsible, but only by the narrowest of margins in a vote. Although it recommended abolition of all surface wells and the removal of all cisterns, it was not until 1866 that the Broad Street pump and others were closed down.

Snow's classic mapping of the geographical distribution of cholera constituted one of the earliest exercises in epidemiology ever attempted. Yet his proofs were not accepted, the French Academy did not publish his papers, and he was only acclaimed long after the fact. For most of his career he was "commonly regarded as a voice crying in the wilderness."[16] His colleague and admirer Whitehead remarked that a physician friend of his in 1855 had warned that "Dr. Snow's views on cholera are generally regarded in the profession as very unsound."[17] Perhaps what accounted for this rejection was that Snow's work was epidemiological but not bacterial. He did not discredit the anti-contagionists, who continued to argue that different vapors in various parts of London explained Snow's data.[18] Not until Robert Koch identified the comma-shaped cholera bacillus under his microscope in Alexandria in 1883, and linked it to germ theory and to contaminated water would an acceptable causative theory emerge.

A noteworthy French initiative occurred during the Third Pandemic in 1851. In an attempt to coordinate an international public health response, initially to bubonic plague, but increasingly to global cholera, Paris hosted the first of what would be fourteen International Sanitary Conferences (ISCs), which were held until 1938.[19] With the exception of

[16] Pelling, *Cholera*, 203.
[17] Whitehead, *Experience*, 37.
[18] William H. McNeill, *Plagues and Peoples* (New York: Anchor Books, 1976), 236.
[19] The most recent and thorough account of these conferences is Valeska Huber, "The unification of the globe by disease? The International Sanitary Conferences on Cholera, 1851–1894," *The Historical Journal*, 49 (2006), 453–76.

the fifth ISC held at Washington in 1881, which touched only on yellow fever, and the tenth, at Venice in 1897, where bubonic plague was the main subject, cholera dominated the deliberations of the ISCs. The meetings were essentially gatherings of European powers, each usually represented by one diplomat and one medical expert. The only non-European sovereign power to participate at every meeting was the Ottoman Empire. Beginning with the second ISC at Paris in 1859, the United States usually sent delegates, as did the Persian Empire, starting with the third ISC in 1866 at Constantinople.

The inclusion of the Ottomans was no accident. A dominant theme of most meetings was how to keep cholera out of Europe. The hope was to confine cholera to its British Indian homeland, or contain it in the Muslim lands of the Middle East, which were all under the formal or informal control of the Ottomans.[20] Though many, no doubt, regarded the six months of debate as wasteful and hopeless, at the very least the 1851 conference indicated that health protection was worthy of international political and medical discourse.

The second Paris ISC in 1859 accomplished still less. France hoped that if the diplomats could take another look at the rejected "draft convention" of 1851, a stronger quarantinist outcome might occur. After much debate, the convention was so watered down that even the British agreed to sign, although its delegates argued that steam ships and rail travel made quarantine more illusory than ever. None of the sovereign states ever signed the convention, and it died on the Parisian drawing board.

Changes in public health and in attitudes were pronounced during the Fourth Pandemic. Sanitarianism continued its advance in Europe, the United States, and Asia. In the western enclave of Shanghai, cholera was much reduced through simple precautions such as the boiling of water. In 1870, the wealthy expatriate community there found the money to invest in a ten-year campaign for a pure water supply.[21] In Japan under the Meiji Restoration, the government by 1879 had set up a Central Sanitary Committee in the Interior Ministry to deal with cholera epidemics, and this led to the establishment of Local Sanitary Committees in each town.[22]

---

[20] For India, Mark Harrison, "Quarantine, pilgrimage, and colonial trade: India 1866–1900," *The Indian Economic and Social History Review*, 29 (1992), 117–44; for the Ottomans, Daniel Panzac, *Quarantine et Lazarets: L'Europe et la Peste d'Orient (XVII-XXè siècles* Aix-en-Provence: Edisud, 1986).

[21] Kerrie L. MacPherson, *A Wilderness of Marshes: The Origins of Public Health in Shanghai, 1843–1893* (New York: Oxford University Press, 1987), 81.

[22] Fukuda, "Public Health," 390.

The British in India achieved striking reductions in mortality as a result of introducing better water and sewer systems in Bombay and Calcutta, and more dramatic sanitary reforms in their military installations. Though it is difficult to speak of any consensus among specialists about cholera's causation, a growing number accepted the idea that polluted water was in some way linked to the infection, as was the strategy of preventing cholera from traveling from one place to another. The identification of a precise causative agent remained elusive throughout the entire period.

Cholera diffusion from the Hindu pilgrimage at Hardwar, and especially the annual Muslim visits to Mecca, hardened European attitudes toward the "other." Led by France, this anger was directed toward the states under whose jurisdiction the holy sites lay, the Ottoman Empire for Mecca, and the British Raj in India for Hardwar. At the Constantinople meeting of the ISC in 1866, the French delegates recommended sealing off the Middle East entirely, and forcing pilgrims returning from their holy sites to travel by caravans overland through harsh desert; it was "the best quarantine applicable for large numbers of people," stated one French delegate.[23] In a polemical work entitled *La civilisation et le choléra*, Girette wrote of the need "to preserve Europe from all compromises with the rude and injurious habits of the Oriental populations."[24] France also insisted on the building of quarantine stations and lazarettos at the southern and northern entrances to the Red Sea.[25] The Ottoman delegation refuted the French assumption that overland routes were still viable for thousands of pilgrims. Steam navigation made lengthy desert crossings obsolete, and wells had fallen into disrepair. Despite this, a majority at Constantinople voted in favor of the French proposal. Yet the point was moot because none of the countries was bound by the resolution.

Sanitarianism continued its advance during the Fourth Pandemic. Nowhere were the gains greater than in the United States, and it was not a coincidence that cholera there would soon become a horrible memory rather than a continuing reality. Leading the effort was Dr. Elisha Harris, a member of the new Metropolitan Board of Health of New York in 1866. Harris developed the sanitarian practices Lemuel Shattuck had championed fifteen years earlier in Massachusetts. A contagionist, Harris

[23] Peter Baldwin, *Contagion and the State in Europe, 1830–1930* (Cambridge: Cambridge University Press, 1999), 229.
[24] In Baldwin, *Contagion*, 229.
[25] Harrison, "Quarantine," 117–44.

asserted that water contaminated with fecal matter from other cholera victims was responsible for the disease. His analysis helped give public health an empirical grounding in demonstrable facts.

Major medical breakthroughs in Germany, France, and Britain also occurred in this period. Rudolf Virchow used laboratory studies to show that human illness occurred at what he called the cellular level. In 1862, Pasteur made public his theory of the existence of "germs," the key to the natural process of fermentation. Two decades later, Pasteur wrote in his *Germ Theory of Disease* that infectious diseases were caused by microscopic organisms that attacked Virchow's cells. In the early 1880s, Paul Ehrlich showed that substances in the blood among animal survivors helped fight the disease in other animals. He called these toxins and antitoxins and dubbed them "magic bullets." Meanwhile, in Britain, Dr. Joseph Lister found that putting carbolic acid on a wound or suture site prevented infection at the spot.

The era of the Fifth Pandemic marked a major breakthrough in cholera research. After Robert Koch succeeded in identifying the *Vibrio cholerae* bacillus as the disease's causative agent in India in January 1884, the debate among medical scientists reached a climax, culminating in the triumph of Kochian views by the 1890s on how to intervene against the killer disease. Not content to publish his findings, Koch was also a determined advocate of new public health procedures, which he articulated at numerous scientific conferences. Koch's breakthroughs added strength to the contagionist camp. His identification of cholera's causative agent made possible the use of the laboratory to test for the disease. He was also a strong advocate of state intervention in public health and a believer in quarantine, isolation, disinfection, and the policing of the water supply. Koch's ideas fit Germany's centralizing tendencies in the 1880s, a decade of rising tariffs, antisocialist campaigns, and the beginnings of the German Empire's paternalist welfare-state legislation.[26] Koch's research helped mark a return in centralized states to massive preventive campaigns, this time based on knowledge of the causative agent. Koch's discovery did not sweep away all opposition. His team's research in India in January 1884 had produced a pure culture of the cholera bacteria, but they had been unable to transfer the disease to animals, the third of Koch's own postulates for determining cholera's etiology.[27] Some argued

---

[26] Evans, *Death in Hamburg*
[27] Christoph Gradmann, *Laboratory Disease: Robert Koch's Medical Bacteriology*, translated by Elborg Forster (Baltimore: Johns Hopkins University Press, 2009), 189–91.

that a simple microscopic organism was not a sufficient explanation and that local and general environmental causes might still be factors. Others were unhappy with what they held to be a moral argument, that individual and collective behaviors still played a role in creating an infection.

Yet there could be no denying that Koch's work on cholera from 1883 forward marked a major watershed. As Hamlin points out, Koch brought cholera into the laboratory and medical classroom as part of a new scientific methodology, with new "assumptions, techniques, agendas, [and] habits of inference."[28]

Koch's advances now gave increased support to what had long been the French position regarding prevention. At the Paris ISC in 1894, a large majority of delegates called for the complete reorganization of quarantine stations in the Suez Canal zone at Kamaran and El-Tor, medical inspection of all pilgrims and pilgrim ships prior to departure, tougher rules for the provision of physicians and infirmaries aboard, and increased space and water allowances. What was now novel was British compliance, even though the number of pilgrims from India fell dramatically in the last years of the century. The Ottomans also became more rigorous, passing new pilgrim-traffic regulations in 1888 that called for more control of shipboard conditions. At the opening of the Paris conference in 1894, the Ottomans announced their reorganization of the lazaretto at Jeddah and sanitary improvements at Mecca that consisted of a new hospital and shelters, a pharmacy, provision for more physicians, and a corps of sanitary police. They also modernized inspection sites at El-Tor and at Kamaran Island at the southern entrance to the Red Sea, long a French concern.[29]

Though great progress in prevention was achieved by the end of the Fifth Pandemic in 1896, treatment lagged far behind. Although fading, counterproductive measures such as the use of purgatives continued to have their advocates. A few pioneering physicians still experimented with rehydration of patients, but this therapy had to await twentieth-century developments. Vaccine therapy, a favorite of Pasteur and his followers, made some progress during the Fifth Pandemic, especially when one of the great French scientist's disciples, Waldemar Haffkine, began large-scale cholera vaccinations in India between 1893 and 1896.[30] Nevertheless, the

---

[28] Hamlin, *Cholera: The Biography*, 211.
[29] Harrison, "Quarantine," 117–44.
[30] Ilana Lowy, "From guinea pigs to man: The development of Haffkine's anticholera vaccine," *Journal of the History of Medicine*, 37 (1992), 270–309.

Indian government was not convinced of the vaccine's effectiveness and limited its use largely for those "without a choice in the matter, such as soldiers and prison inmates,"[31]

The problem that haunted vaccine therapy then and now was that it could not eradicate cholera by producing the "herd immunity" effect. This occurs when a vaccine such as that for smallpox or measles surpasses a vaccinated threshold of 80 percent of the population. Yet another obstacle in these early days of immunology was the failure to produce genuine scientific trials that showed the vaccine to be a true indicator of protection. For example, one practice was to give vaccinations after an epidemic had begun, at a point when the outbreak was already on a natural downswing. Finally, antivaccination sentiments at the turn of the century were strong, insisting on the fundamental Anglo-American principle of the inherent human right to medical liberty and choice, and to the sanctity of the body. So strong was this movement that in 1907, the antivaccination lobby won repeal of the Vaccination Acts in Britain.[32]

As the Fifth Pandemic wound down by the end of the nineteenth century, progress in cholera prevention rather than treatment characterized international scientific approaches. Most jurisdictions in the West made great strides in the production of potable water and the removal of sewage. The scientific breakthroughs of germ theory in general and in understanding of cholera causation in particular added to confidence, and to a willingness to spend money on public health. Similarly, effective smallpox-vaccination programs were well in place by the 1890s. All who wished to see could recognize that the low purchase of the Fifth Pandemic itself spoke to these gains.

The international sanitary gatherings between Rome in 1885 and Paris in 1911 and 1912 also emphasized prevention, but were dominated by a French insistence that Europe be defended from "others." Smarting over the British takeover of Egypt in 1883, France now viewed the Suez Canal, to which French engineers had given birth, as "the outer gate of a European sea, at which the nations of Europe have a right to arrest the approach of Asiatic diseases."[33] French demands that the British in India and Egypt and the Ottomans in the Middle East tighten surveillance and

---

[31] Hays, *Epidemics and Pandemics*, 311.
[32] See, for example, Allan Chase, *Magic Shots: A Human and Scientific Account of the Long and Continuous Struggle to Eradicate Infectious Disease by Vaccination* (New York: William Morrow and Company, 1982).
[33] Anonymous French remark in Baldwin, *Contagion*, 230.

quarantine dominated international discussion of cholera control at the ISC meetings from Rome onward.

Nevertheless, from a global perspective, triumphalism was not warranted. Treatment of cholera patients remained focused on older approaches, as illustrated by the failure to save the life of the young Pasteurian Louis Thuillier in Egypt in 1883 (see Chapter 4). Even in such modern countries as France, Italy, and Germany, when cholera did strike during the Fifth Pandemic, it did so every bit as ruthlessly as in the past. France in 1884 suffered a terrible 50 percent CFR on 10,000 cholera cases. In the same year, almost identical figures applied to Italy. Hamburg's 7,582 deaths in 1892 represented a CFR of just more than 38 percent. Such figures made it clear that chances of survival from a case of acute cholera remained poor, even in the most advanced countries of the world.

The picture in other parts of the globe was worse. In the backward Russian Empire, morbidity and CFRs remained unacceptably high. In modernizing Japan, where great strides generally were being made in medicine, 155,000 recorded cases occurred in 1886, one of seven epidemic years during the Fifth Pandemic. Nor did cholera spare one of its favorite hunting grounds, the pilgrimage sites of Arabia, where 200,000 of the Muslim faithful contracted the dread disease in 1881.

Last but not least was India, the "home of cholera." As David Arnold has shown, cholera deaths peaked in India in the year 1900 with a total of 805,698.[34] Cholera morbidity and mortality would not begin to diminish until after the First World War.

By the 1920s, cholera was no longer perceived as a threat to public health in the West. Its retreat not only from Europe and the Americas, but also from Africa, added to this perception. True, cholera remained as an endemic disease in colonial India, but it seemed only to spread internationally in parts of Asia torn by strife and instability. For reasons difficult to explain, international scientific inquiry into cholera stagnated in the interwar period, perhaps because it no longer seemed an urgent threat in the West.

International surveillance and cooperation did slowly improve during the Sixth Pandemic. The old International Sanitary Conferences (ISCs) evolved into the International Office of Public Hygiene (IOPH)

[34] David Arnold, "Cholera Mortality in British India, 1817–1947," in Tim Dyson, ed., *India's Historical Demography: Studies in Famine, Disease and Society* (London: Curzon Press, 1989), 263–5.

under the League of Nations. Both were subsumed by the World Health Organization (WHO) under the UN after its creation in 1948. These bodies were the chief agencies responsible for this improved approach.

During the Sixth Pandemic, the approach to cholera consisted of three elements. First was the filtering and chlorinating of drinking water to provide a safe supply, in view of cholera's close association with contaminated water. Second was the pursuit and application of an anticholera vaccine that would at least diminish the risks of a fatal infection, and at best prevent outbreaks by imparting immunity. Third was the continuing pursuit and development of better rehydration techniques to treat seriously ill patients.

Beginning in the early twentieth century, chlorination of the water supply became a standard procedure where more permanent guarantees of safe water could not be met. Sometimes public health authorities used too much of a good thing. To discourage drinking from contaminated wells, they occasionally used chlorination with bleach to make the water entirely unpalatable. Pollitzer has noted that only in extreme circumstances should this have been done, because it strengthened the prejudice of people against chlorination, which was a very sound method of well-water treatment.[35]

For too long, international methods of assuring clean drinking water foundered because of the excuse of costs. In British India, the failure of the government to address the problem of clean drinking water either in the villages or at the annual fairs was scandalous. Fearing disobedience campaigns, for example, British public health authorities avoided compulsory cholera inoculation unless Indian politicians were strongly in its favor. This same inertia was visible in the absence of rigorous public health measures dealing with annual Hindu pilgrimages.[36] British inertia continued to cost India thousands of lives during the Sixth Pandemic.[37] Although decennial cholera mortality declined from 250,000 in the 1920s to 188,000 in the 1930s, it rose again to 202,000 in the 1940s.[38]

Protection of communities through cholera vaccination was yet another new procedure that held great promise, at least in theory. Haffine's vaccine did not produce persuasive results in India, and experimentation was sporadic. In Europe, studies of the effectiveness of cholera inoculations

[35] Pollitzer, *Cholera*, 931.
[36] Pollitzer, *Cholera*, 79.
[37] Sheldon Watts, "From rapid change to stasis: Official responses to cholera in British-ruled India and Egypt, 1860–c.1921," *Journal of World History*, 12 (2001), 373.
[38] Pollitzer, *Cholera*, 48.

during conflict in the Balkans and among First World War armies found that vaccination was not statistically significant either in preventing cholera or in shortening the carrier state among recuperating patients. By the late 1920s, however, new statistical studies conducted in Calcutta came out more strongly in favor of cholera vaccination. Two further statistical studies in the late 1940s from South Asia recommended vaccination, especially in times of pilgrimage, war, or social breakdown, when regular sanitary measures could not be used.[39]

Inoculation did have its problems. Mass vaccination became a popular, easily grasped, and visible indication that health authorities were doing something. Yet this very popularity became a danger insofar as it instilled a false sense of security. Vaccination could neither eradicate cholera nor provide "herd immunity," and it was, in Pollitzer's view, "a palliative measure" less effective than the provision of safe water in controlling the disease.[40] Several factors made for varying opinions and results of vaccine prevention. The recommended dose was two injections during an interval of seven to ten days, the first with half a milliliter, the second with one milliliter. The larger dose was especially hard on children, and when people did not return for a second dose, their protection was diminished.

Without doubt, the most important breakthrough in the treatment of cholera patients was the advance in rehydration therapy during the Sixth Pandemic.[41] At the beginning of the twentieth century, Sir Leonard Rogers of the Indian Medical Service (IMS) pioneered in the administration of a hypertonic saline supplement, with alkali and potassium combined with purified water. In some instances, this new technique reduced mortality by between a quarter and a third.

Later recognition that glucose added to salts helped patients keep down orally administered solutions was yet another milestone. Initially, however, the British government in India showed its usual hesitation. It allowed water and salt replacement in Indian hospitals, but did little to bring the technique to rural areas, where thousands of lives could have been saved. It was true that early attempts produced mixed results, often because the sterilization of the components was not assured, which contributed to the early unpopularity of the procedure.[42] Although not

---

[39] Pollitzer, *Cholera*, 957.
[40] Pollitzer, *Cholera*, 959.
[41] Joshua N. Ruxin, "Magic bullet: The history of oral rehydration therapy," *Medical History*, 38 (1991), 363–97.
[42] Arnold, "Cholera Mortality," 274.

a justification, perhaps this explains the failure of international health organizations to adopt, endorse, or give research priority to rehydration therapy earlier. Potential cholera victims would have to wait half a century before rehydration became a widespread therapy.

Despite British recalcitrance in India, the international community nevertheless congratulated itself as the Sixth Pandemic faded almost from sight by the middle of the twentieth century. The *Encyclopedia Britannica* in its 1967 edition even went so far as to declare that new knowledge of the etiology of disease and effective controls meant that the sixth cholera pandemic would be the world's last. Similarly, William McNeill, in his classic *Plagues and Peoples* published in 1976, wrote confidently that the end of cholera as a "world scourge" represented a victory of science and world industrialization, which had first spread the disease. McNeill based his assessment on the disappearance of cholera at Mecca and Medina, which, he argued, roughly coincided with compulsory inoculation with Haffkine's 1893 vaccine and the mandatory quarantine of pilgrims.[43]

---

[43] McNeill, *Plagues*, 246.

3

Cholera Ravages Sub-Saharan Africa

Senegambia, Ethiopia, and Zanzibar, 1821–1894

SENEGAMBIA

The only two nineteenth-century cholera visitations of record in Western Africa occurred in the Senegal and Gambia River valleys during the Fourth and Fifth Pandemics, in the years 1868–1869 and 1893–1894 respectively. On both occasions, the likely path of the infestation was by sea from the Mediterranean, though a caravan route from the Maghreb across the Sahara might have been possible.

The region bounded by the Senegal River valley in the north and the Gambia River valley in the south, and extending farther to what is now Guinea-Bissau, had long familiarity with international trade, both in slaves and in products such as gum arabic and ivory. Portuguese traders first arrived in the fifteenth century, and by the eighteenth century, mainly British and French merchants vied for control of the coastal factories and slave pens that were so significant in the involuntary migration of Africans across the South Atlantic. Beginning in the eighteenth century, devout new Muslim leaders led a series of religious wars against the established African polities. Despite failed attempts at tropical agriculture in the early nineteenth century, the European presence grew, often through the efforts of an Afro-European minority who became prosperous in the French and British coastal emporiums. These ambitious men helped European powers develop new trading posts up-river in the region, and they designed ambitious plans for the control and conquest of the interior. As the slave trade dried up after the abolitionist push following the Napoleonic era, so-called legitimate commercial products helped change the regional dynamics. Peanuts became a feature of Senegambian exports after 1830, and the gum trade flourished once industrial demand grew for the product's utility in the textile and confectionery industries.

Sources for the Senegambian cholera outbreaks vary. The most detailed, Adama Aly Pam's doctoral thesis, written in 2005, is based on French colonial archives together with some African oral traditions for Senegal. His is the only study that deals directly with the Fourth Pandemic outbreak of 1868–1869. Ralph Schram provides some statistics from British primary sources for cholera in the Gambia, as does a nineteenth-century writer, Dr. James Christie, who is so valuable for the cholera epidemics in East Africa during the Fourth Pandemic. In 1869, the *Lancet* also published a brief account of the Gambian outbreak. For the Fifth Pandemic in Senegambia, Kalala Ngalamalumbe uses French public and private archives to provide a thorough account.[1]

The French colonial capital of Saint-Louis suffered a severe first wave lasting for two months, beginning in November 1868. For much of this period, this small city of roughly 15,000 people registered more than one hundred deaths a day. By the time the outbreak ended, 1,112 Africans and 92 Europeans perished.[2] A second wave resumed in June 1869 and ran until the beginning of 1870. Although only nine deaths were recorded at the French hospital in Saint-Louis, the list included the colony's governor, Pinet Laprade, who died on August 17. He was followed soon after by a physician, Dr. Maurel.

Cholera quickly spread to French trading posts up the Senegal valley. Dagana lost 10 percent of its population; then Podor and its surrounding villages recorded 180 deaths, estimated at 25 percent of its population. After a pause of several months, the last cholera outbreak occurred at Bakel in May, 1869, when 582 victims were tallied, roughly a quarter of the local population.

Little is known about the cholera measures taken. French authorities established a quarantine against the Moors in what is now Mauritania, which prevented them from crossing from the northern bank of the

---

[1] Adama Aly Pam, "Fièvre jaune et Choléra au Sénégal: Histoire des idées, pratiques médicales et politiques officielles entre 1816 et 1960" (thèse de troisième cycle, Université Cheikh Anta Diop de Dakar, December, 2005); Ralph Schram, *A History of the Nigerian Health Services* (Ibadan: Ibadan University Press, 1971) 102; Christie, *Cholera*, 473–4; "Cholera in Gambia," the *Lancet*, (May 22, 1869), 727, and (June 5, 1869), 727; and Kalala J. Ngalamulume, "City Growth, Health Problems, and Colonial Government Response: Saint-Louis (Senegal) from Mid-Nineteenth Century to the First World War" (Ph.D. dissertation, Michigan State University, East Lansing, 1996). To my knowledge, no research has been done using Portuguese archival sources.

[2] Pam, "Fièvre jaune," 23–30.

Senegal River into Senegal proper. In the Senegal River valley, the arrival of cholera coincided with the rise of an Islamic messianic movement called *madiyanké*, whose leader pointed to the death of Fulbe notables from cholera as punishment for collaborating with the "impious" French. Much farther south, the Malinke population of the Rip area organized armed brigades to close their territory to travelers from contaminated regions. Such efforts to keep cholera out of southern Senegambia failed.[3]

From the Senegal valley, cholera traveled through village after village among the Wolof states, and reached Mandingo country in the Upper Gambia River valley in February 1869. On March 10, it appeared at McCarthy's Island, 180 miles up-river from Bathurst (now Banjul), capital of the tiny British colony of the Gambia. Frightened inhabitants fled east and carried the pestilence as far as 800 miles into the interior of West Africa. Cholera also voyaged down-river to Bathurst, where it was first seen on May 1, 1869. From there, the infection back-tracked north along the coast to Senegal again, appearing by June at Albreda, Dakar, Gorée, and Rufisque. Cholera also turned south from Bathurst, visiting the Portuguese colonial town of Cacheo in September 1869, and then moving the next month to Bissau and to Bulama, the most eastern of the Bissagos islands. Here too, its inland trajectory has left no documentary trace. The only statistics that have survived are for Bathurst, where the outbreak was especially lethal, counting 1,700 dead among a total population of 5,000, a staggering mortality rate of 34 percent.[4]

The fifth cholera pandemic touched down on Senegambia in 1893. This visitation was sea-borne, imported from Bordeaux to Saint-Louis, Senegal, and then spreading up-river and inland during the months of July and August.[5] In the Senegal River valley, the town of Podor sustained 131 victims among 1,396 inhabitants, roughly 10 percent of the population. Dagana lost 73 persons, Matam, 36, and Bakel, 125. These were only the figures officially recorded by the small French medical staff, and they seriously underestimated losses in the outlying villages. The epidemic also extended south and reached the urban centers of Dakar and Rufisque. Saint-Louis recorded 926 deaths in two months among an estimated population of 20,000 in 1893. The local French colonial physician, Gentilhomme, indicated that cholera CFRs in the Saint-Louis hospital were more than 56 percent.[6]

---

3 Pam, "Fièvre jaune," 28–30.
4 Schram, *A History*, 102.
5 Pam, "Fièvre jaune," 33–4.
6 Pam, "Fièvre jaune," 33.

It was assumed, though no medical evidence was provided, that Africans suffered far more severely from cholera than did Europeans. The alleged discrepancy among deaths in Saint-Louis drew a dramatic explanation from Roman Catholic missionaries. The Sisters of the Congregation of Saint-Joseph-de-Cluny erected a statue of St. Roch, patron saint of epidemic victims, and wrote triumphantly:

[T]he Virgin Mary rewarded our confidence, and we escaped the disaster. The *marabouts*, taken by surprise, expressed their amazement for the fact that the Christians did not die, while their own devotees died at the rate of 50 to 60 a day.[7]

No response from the Muslim community of Saint-Louis has been recorded, but the traditional Muslim view held that both the bringing of affliction and the protection of the faithful were manifestations of God's will. Some might also have noted that the better-off Europeans and Creoles of Saint-Louis, most of whom were Christian, largely escaped cholera in 1893, whereas the urban poor were victimized. Class and ethnicity, not religion, were the operative variables in the 1893 cholera outbreak.

ETHIOPIA

Several elements have combined to make Ethiopia's history distinct. Its core area in the fertile highlands was remote from Red Sea and Indian Ocean trade, insulating it from direct commercial contacts for centuries. The development of the plow led to larger agricultural surpluses than could be found elsewhere in Africa, as well as complex patterns of land ownership and deep divisions between poor peasants and rich landlords. A venerable Christian tradition produced a culturally distinct ruling class and literacy among its aristocracy and religious authorities. Political instability ushered in a long period of strife beginning in the seventeenth century, but in the nineteenth century strong princes restored some internal stability.

Atse (Prince) Tewodros sought to revive the emperorship in mid-century, though his authority was limited to the northern highlands of the country. He committed suicide in 1868 when a British expeditionary force invaded to punish him for having mistreated their consul and having held a number of Europeans as prisoners. Expansion and consolidation occurred after *Atse* Menelik of Shoa took the emperorship and ruled

---

[7] In Ngalamulume, "City growth," 235.

until his death in 1913.[8] At the defining battle of Adwa in 1896, Menelik defeated a large Italian army and secured Ethiopian independence, very much the exception to the rule in the era of European conquest.

Economic changes helped fuel the political. After the British treaty with Zanzibar prohibited the export of slaves in 1847, Ethiopia helped meet the demand in the Red Sea and Persian Gulf. Slave exports from the Ethiopian lowlands provided revenue to the princes through tolls, and thus helped the aspiring empire builders buy firearms to supply their powerful armies.

Even if somewhat insulated from outside currents, especially during the early part of the nineteenth century, Ethiopia could not escape the cholera pandemics. Contacts with the Red Sea, Mecca, and the Egyptian Nile helped bring cholera outbreaks during the Second Pandemic in 1834 and 1835, the Third in 1856, the Fourth in 1866 and 1867, the Fifth in 1893, and the Sixth in 1906.[9] The 1835 outbreak was especially devastating for Shoa and other northern provinces, as well as for caravans traveling inland from the Red Sea port of Massawa. The Ethiopian Church organized religious processions in the streets to invoke God's mercy, while the nobility fled the region. Reports of a serious drought followed by famine probably helped cholera proceed from north to south and on into Central Africa.

The next outbreak in the mid-1850s was called *naftanya fangal*, literally "riflemen killer," because it struck down victims so swiftly.[10] It thwarted the military plans of Tewodros, the ambitious ruler of Gojam. He and his army had planned a march on Tigre to suppress a rebellion there, but when cholera struck, Tewodros, his court, and all of his forces fled to the Begemder highlands, where the epidemic petered out.

A decade later, Tewodros reacted in the same manner to yet another cholera invasion, this time with more devastating results. The fourth cholera pandemic came by sea directly from Bombay via Aden to Eritrea and Somalia on the East African coast. Caravans then transported cholera into the Ethiopian highlands from the port of Massawa. Tewodros

---

[8] The primary source for Menelik's reign was written by his chronicler Guebre Sellassie. See Guebre Sellassie, *Chronique du règne de Ménélik II, roi des rois d'Ethiopie*, translated from the Amharic by Tesfa Sellassie and annotated by Maurice de Coppet (Paris: Maisonneuve Frères, 1930).

[9] The only published work for nineteenth-century Ethiopian cholera is Richard Pankhurst, "The history of cholera in Ethiopia," *Medical History*, 12 (1968), 262–9.

[10] Pankhurst, "Cholera," 264. *Naftanya*, or *neftegna*, was the name given to the empire's settler-soldiers who helped extend the empire southward in the late nineteenth and early twentieth centuries.

attempted to cut off all contact with the coast, but cholera made its way first to Tigre, and then to other provinces of the northern highlands. By May 1866, cholera found Tewodros and his entourage on the southern shore of Lake Tana. Once again, the entire royal court and army fled to the higher ground of Begemder. This time, however, many of the estimated 100,000 fugitives fell sick and perished. Tewodros dispersed his troops, which only helped cholera reach the Oromo lowlands.[11] As we will see later in this chapter, this pandemic eventually made its way overland and by sea as far south as Mozambique and Madagascar.

The Fifth Pandemic revisited highland Ethiopia and coastal Eritrea in 1893, as well as the French colonial port of Djibouti. There it killed the colonial administrator and the military physician. Cholera was called *ye nefas beshita* in Amharic, "the disease of the wind," because it was popularly believed to have been brought from the coast by winds from the northeast.[12] The disease added more misery to starving peasants whose draft animals were dying in an ongoing rinderpest epizootic, which had been raging since 1888. One estimate suggests that Ethiopia may have lost one-third of its population to the famine and cattle plague that had so devastated agricultural production.[13] In 1893, a British traveler, Theodore Bent, visited the northern provinces of Ethiopia and offered his impressions of the catastrophe:

Civil war, famine and an epidemic of cholera have, within the last decade, played fearful havoc ... villages are abandoned, the land is going out of cultivation ... It is scarcely possible to realize, without visiting the country, the abject misery and wretchedness which has fallen upon the Ethiopian empire during late years.[14]

Classic cholera made its final appearance in 1906. As was typical of the Sixth Pandemic, the outbreak was much milder and seems to have been confined to the province of Wallo. No official reporting of cholera was to come from Ethiopia again until early in the twenty-first century.

ZANZIBAR

Together with the nearby East African coast, Zanzibar fell victim to each of the first four cholera pandemics in 1821, 1836, 1860, and 1869 and

[11] Pankhurst, "Cholera," 266.
[12] Pankhurst, "Cholera," 268.
[13] John Iliffe, *The African Poor, A History* (Cambridge: Cambridge University Press, 1987), 12–13.
[14] In Pankhurst, "Cholera," 267.

1870 respectively. In the nineteenth century, dramatic commercial and political changes marked the Indian Ocean coast of East Africa and the large off-shore islands of Zanzibar and Pemba.[15] Trade involved the lucrative export of ivory and slaves from the vast interior of the continent, together with slave plantation exports of coconuts, grain, and especially cloves. Early in the century, Indian merchants shipped ivory, the most profitable export, through Bombay, from where it was reexported west and east. The export trade in slaves from the East African coast reached a high of 100,000 per decade during the 1830s and 1840s, then declined to 65,000 per decade in the 1850s and 1860s. Slaves working on the labor-intensive clove plantations of Zanzibar Island in the 1870s numbered 188,000.[16].

The core group in the East African ports were the Swahili, who were the product of centuries of intermarriage and cultural interaction between Africans, Arabs, Persians, and others, but who remained closer to their African forbearers. Zanzibar City and Island rose from little more than a fishing village in 1700 to a highly pluralist trade emporium a century later. Handsome stone houses of prosperous merchants from all over the Indian Ocean marked its rising status as a trade center. Arab immigrants from the Hadhramaut and Oman, as well as Swahili entrepreneurs from the mainland, mingled with Banyan Hindu traders from western India. By the 1830s, Zanzibar had become prosperous enough for the sultan of Oman, Seyyid Said, to move his capital there. Rounding out the population was a labor force of African slaves and a smattering of westerners, such as American whalers and traders, especially from Salem, Massachusetts, together with German, French, and British merchants, seamen, and missionaries.

Political transformation centered on Zanzibar, where an Arab dynasty from Oman grew wealthy on the Indian Ocean commerce, and succeeded in extending its influence on the East African coast and at strong points

---

[15] An extensive literature exists. See especially Edward A. Alpers, *Ivory and Slaves in East Central Africa: Changing Patterns of International Trade to the Late Nineteenth Century* (Berkeley: University of California Press, 1975); R.W. Beachey, *The Slave Trade of Eastern Africa* (London: Rex Collings, 1976); Frederick Cooper, *Plantation Slavery on the East Coast of Africa* (New Haven: Yale University Press, 1977); Johani Koponen, *People and Production in Late Precolonial Tanzania: History and Structures* (Helsinki: Finnish Society for Development Studies, 1988); and Stephen J. Rockel, *Carriers of Culture: Labor on the Road in Nineteenth-Century East Africa* (Portsmouth, NH: Heinemann, 2006).

[16] Paul Lovejoy, *Transformations in Slavery: A History of Slavery in Africa* 2nd ed. (Cambridge University Press, 2000), 61–2; 155–6.

in the interior.[17] The rise of the Omani Zanzibar trading empire depended on a naval alliance with Great Britain, and the price to be paid was the growing pressure of British consular officers and missionaries to secure the abolition of the East African and Indian Ocean slave trade. A major milestone occurred in 1873 when British Consul-General Sir Bartle Frere pressured Sultan Bargash to sign a treaty abolishing all shipments of slaves by sea, and which gave the British navy power to search and escort vessels to Zanzibar for trial if they contained slaves. The treaty also closed the public slave markets on Zanzibar. By 1890, Zanzibar became a British protectorate, two years after the Imperial British East Africa Company had gained a concession from Zanzibar to the coast of what is now Kenya. Under direct British tutelage, the sultan proclaimed all slaves acquired after 1890 to be free, all sale of slaves banned, and all inheritance of slaves limited to the master's children alone.

Before the Fourth Pandemic, accounts of cholera outbreaks in sub-Saharan Africa were thinly documented. All this changed with the cholera epidemics in East Africa beginning in 1865, thanks to a remarkable book published in 1876 by Dr. James Christie, personal physician to the sultan of Zanzibar from 1865 to 1874.[18]

A former clergyman and dedicated abolitionist, Christie provided a richly detailed eyewitness epidemiology of the cholera outbreak of 1869 and 1870 on Zanzibar Island. He also constructed a narrative of earlier East African cholera epidemics based upon his consultation of oral testimony and fragmentary documents of the British consulate in Zanzibar. He further offered a pioneering ethnographic and geographic survey of the African cultures of the interior through which cholera passed, based on a careful reading of Western travel literature. Unusually for that time and long after, Christie conducted extensive interviews with African and Zanzibari travelers who had observed cholera outbreaks in the interior. Determined to understand the Indian Ocean culture, Christie learned Swahili to communicate directly with his informants.[19] Not only did he offer sharp insights into disease and society in Zanzibar, Christie also described the spread of cholera from Mecca in 1865 to the Red Sea and the Indian Ocean as far south as Mozambique and Madagascar, and to North and even West Africa during this period as well.

---

[17] Cooper, *Plantation Slavery*, 269–71.
[18] Unless otherwise indicated, all references to Christie's views on the East African epidemics are from his *Cholera Epidemics in East Africa*.
[19] Robertson, "Christie," 40.

Although his ethnography shared the bias of British travelers against African societies of the interior, his attempts at thoroughness are remarkable for his time. His writing deserves more consultation than the scanty mention he receives in only a handful of modern studies of East Africa. More shocking is the neglect of this rare and indispensable historical source in the medical literature dealing with cholera. Christie's graphic and often horrific account of the epidemic also provided path-breaking insights into cholera causation, though his observations made little impact in the Britain of his age or after.

Why this should have been so remains something of a mystery. When his book appeared in 1876, it received praise from leading medical journals such as the *Lancet* and the *London Medical Record*, and in more popular publications such as the *Geographical Magazine* and the *Glasgow Herald*.[20] Christie was opposed to British colonial expansion in East Africa, and disliked the imperial pretensions of the powerful British consul, John Kirk, who later became virtual ruler of Zanzibar.[21] More directly, Christie made short shrift of air-borne theories of cholera diffusion that were popular with physicians in India, as well as with British policy makers at the India Office, who were apprehensive about cholera theories that could be traced to British commercial and public health policies in India and on the pilgrimage routes to Mecca.[22]

Whatever the reasons, Christie's potentially groundbreaking study of cholera's epidemiology was ignored after the immediate flurry of praise following publication. Until its reprint as a rare book by Kessinger Publishing in 2008, copies of the original were scarce and rarely consulted. Davies, one of the few to read Christie, states that the copy of Christie's book he used in mid-1957 was the same one the author had presented to the British Medical Association library more than eighty years earlier; the pages had not been cut.[23]

Christie was born in Strathaven, Scotland in May 1829 and educated at the University of Glasgow. He took a master's degree in theology, and in 1856 was ordained as a Nonconformist Minister. Health problems with his throat forced him to abandon the ministry, and in 1860 he completed his medical studies. After working for a time in mental hospitals, he left for Zanzibar in 1865 to become personal physician to the sultan.

[20] Robertson, "Christie," 57.
[21] Edna Robertson calls him "an anti-colonial doctor"; "Christie," 68.
[22] Harrison, "A Question," 133–59; and Watts, "From Rapid Change," 321–74.
[23] J.P.N. Davies, "James Christie and the cholera epidemics of East Africa," *East African Medical Journal*, 36 (1959), 1.

He soon became a close friend and associate of Bishop Tozer, the Anglican head of the Universities Mission to East Africa, and of a British businessman on the island, Captain Hugh Fraser, a former officer in the Indian navy. In 1871, the three men published a pamphlet entitled "The East African Slave Trade and Measures for its Abolition."[24]

Christie returned to Glasgow in 1874. He spent the next eighteen months researching and writing his book, while taking up general practice. In 1876, when his book was published, he became surgeon and then physician to the Glasgow Western Infirmary. Leaving behind his interest in cholera, Christie published on dengue fever in 1881 and lectured on public health at Anderson's Medical College in Glasgow, where he became professor of physiology in 1884.[25] Still active in research, he wrote the chapter on tropical skin diseases for a text on dermatology, and was editor for many years of the *Sanitary Journal of Scotland*. He died on January 2, 1892; his obituaries described him as a warmhearted and generous teacher.[26]

In his preface, Christie carefully details the development of his interest in cholera. The initiative seems to have originated with Dr. J. Netten Ratcliffe, president of the Epidemiological Society of London, to whom Christie dedicates his book. Ratcliffe had written in 1870 to Bishop Tozer asking for epidemiological information on cholera in or near Zanzibar beginning in 1865, and he passed the query on to Christie. Christie responded with extremely detailed yet succinct notes in 1870 and 1871, which found their way into the *Lancet* in 1871 and 1872.[27] Christie confides that, before leaving for Zanzibar at end of 1865, news was spreading of a severe cholera outbreak in Arabia and its extension to the European and African shores of the Mediterranean. On the alert for signs of cholera, he found that it had reached the Somali ports but was allegedly arrested by the southwest monsoon; all of East Africa was reported free of cholera by December of 1865. Christie admits that at the time he had no "particular interest" in the study of cholera, and the subject passed "out of his recollection." But in 1869, Christie heard that cholera was advancing on Zanzibar from the northwest along the Masai caravan route ending at

[24] Davies, "James Christie," 1–2.
[25] James Christie, "Epidemics of Dengue Fever: Their diffusion and aetiology," *Glasgow Medical Journal*, 16 (September, 1881), 161–76.
[26] Robertson, "Christie," 69.
[27] Dr. James Christie, "Notes on the cholera epidemics in East Africa," *Lancet*, (1871), 113–15; 186–8; and "Additional notes on the cholera epidemics on the east coast of Africa," *Lancet*, (1872), 573–4.

Pangani on the East African coast. "At that time my mind was unbiased by any theory regarding the propagation of cholera epidemics, for I had none …" Aware cholera would reach Zanzibar, he spent time on treatment and clinical study, and this occupied him throughout the epidemic when it struck in November 1869.

After the epidemic, he was pleasantly surprised to read an editorial in the *Lancet*, stating that his reports constituted a "New Chapter in the History of Epidemic Cholera." No doubt, Radcliffe was also pleased with his protégé, whom he appointed secretary of the Epidemiological Society for the Indian Ocean and Eastern Africa. When Christie received a second inquiry from Radcliffe asking for more information on the diffusion of cholera in East Africa, he launched himself into a prodigious research effort. His method was to interview all sorts of visitors to Zanzibar, whether African, Swahili, Arab, or westerner, about disease and the geography of the East African interior, large parts of which were then unknown to Europeans. Most of this research made its way into his impressive book.

Zanzibar was among the first regions outside South Asia, and clearly the first in sub-Saharan Africa, to experience modern cholera. Its growing commercial links with Oman and its older Indian Ocean trade made it an obvious target. Christie could find no traces in the collective memory regarding the early outbreak of 1821 and no documentation in Zanzibar, but he surmised that Arab traders shipping slaves from Somali ports north to the Arabian Peninsula and the Persian Gulf had transported cholera to East Africa.

The 1836 cholera visitation to the region was linked to Mecca, where an outbreak earlier in that year enabled cholera to travel with returning pilgrims aboard dhows bound for the Somali coastal ports of Mogadishu, Merka, and Brava. Dhows engaged in coastal trade in turn carried cholera as far south as Zanzibar and Mozambique, and caravans brought the disease to the African interior.

Cholera's impact on Zanzibar and the East African region during the Third Pandemic is better documented. One of the best sources is the eyewitness account of the rakish British traveler, Richard Burton. Some mention of cholera in Uganda in 1858 and 1859 also appears in the journal of John Speke. In 1859, Burton's plans to explore the Rufiji River were thwarted by a violent cholera epidemic extending from Muscat to Zanzibar and the interior. Arriving in Kilwa, Burton learned that the population had never encountered cholera before, and that the disease had killed half the town. Burton had seen cholera during his childhood in

Britain and as an adult during visits to India and Italy, but had never observed "such ravages as it committed at Kilwa."[28] He estimated that locals treated the patients "sensibly" with opium and a locally distilled spirit, "and did not, like the Anglo-Indian surgeons, murder patients with mercury, the lancet and the chafing-dish."[29] Burton lost most of his crew to cholera at that time, and found it impossible to hire replacements out of fear of the illness. He also provided one of the most harrowing accounts of a town under siege to cholera ever recorded:

> Soil and air seemed saturated with poison, the blood appeared predisposed to receive the influence, and people died like flies ... The poorer victims were dragged by the leg along the sand, to be thrown into the ebbing waters of the bay; those better off were sewn up in matting, and were carried down like hammocks to the same general depot. The smooth oily water was dotted with remnants and fragments of humanity, black and brown when freshly thrown in, patched, mottled and parti-coloured when in a state of half pickle, and ghastly white, like scalded pig, when the pigmentum nigrium [sic] had become thoroughly macerated.[30]

Captain Speke had much less to say, partly because he was not an eyewitness to cholera. During Speke's visit to the young Kabaka Mutesa of Buganda in April 1862, Mutesa spoke of how his people had endured a severe mortality from a disease that bore all the signs of cholera in the late 1850s, but that it had vanished as mysteriously as it had arrived.[31]

Christie relied on the estimates of Colonel Rigby, the British consul-general, for cholera statistics on Zanzibar before 1869 and 1870. For the cholera outbreak of 1860, Rigby reported 7,000 to 8,000 cholera deaths in Zanzibar City and suburbs, and 20,000 for the entire island. Death tolls were very high among slaves, and very low among Europeans. Only a handful died, all of whom were sailors, as in case of two aboard the American whaler *Zantho* then in harbor.

The Fourth Pandemic was Africa's worst, striking Egypt, all of North Africa, Senegambia, and the Horn. Most devastating of all was cholera's ability to work its way down the East African coast from 1865 to 1871. Overland, it reached the Great Lakes of Africa through Masai lands in Kenya, and then moved south to Tanzania and the bustling entrepôt of

---

[28] Richard Burton, *The Lake Regions of Central Africa, A Picture of Exploration*, Vol.2 (New York: Horizon Press, 1961 reprint of original edition, London: Longman, 1860), 319.

[29] Burton, *The Lake Regions*, 319.

[30] Richard Burton, *Zanzibar, City, Island and Coast*, Vol.2 (London: Tinsley Brothers, 1872), 343–4.

[31] In Christie, *Cholera*, 116.

Zanzibar. Indian Ocean sailing vessels engaged in the coastal trade also carried cholera down through the Swahili ports to their southern limits just short of Delagoa Bay at Quelimane.

A major annual fair in Berbera, Somalia during the northeast monsoon season from mid-November to mid-April was almost as an attractive an opportunity for cholera as Mecca. Berbera was more village than fixed town, and when caravans of up to 3,000 people arrived, traders and their slaves would be sheltered in tents. The same held true for arrivals by sea from all over the Indian Ocean, so that at its peak in March of each year, Berbera's population approached 60,000. Unlike southern Somali ports, Berbera had direct trade not only with the interior and with Arabia, but from India as well. When the site became infected by cholera in March of 1865, thousands died as fleeing traders and their slaves spread cholera inland via caravans and by sea. The intrepid explorer and missionary David Livingstone recorded cholera's arrival near the headwaters of the Congo River beyond Lake Tanganyika. He seems to have been stricken with the disease and to have recovered. Suspecting the water, Livingstone began boiling it, and he and his party recovered, though all had lost weight.[32] Porters working the caravans of the interior were rarely so fortunate. One party traveling to the coast near Zanzibar set out with 150 persons, but only 7 survived the trip.

The cholera epidemic of 1869–1870 in Zanzibar City and Island, which Christie witnessed, left disaster in its wake. Caravans from the East African interior brought the pestilence to Pangani, a Swahili port opposite the southern tip of Pemba, and it soon made its way to Zanzibar Island. By November, cholera was raging with "uncontrollable fury." In his report to the Epidemiological Society, reprinted in the *Lancet*, Christie estimated deaths at 15,000 for Zanzibar City and suburbs, and 25,000 for the Island as a whole. He added that mortality among Arabs and their slaves was not less than 10 percent, for nationals of India, 6.5 percent, and for Africans, 25 percent at the very least.[33] The population fluctuated greatly with the trading seasons; the city and suburbs reached 80,000 at its peak, and the island itself ranged from 300,000 to 400,000 depending upon the size of the slave-labor force on the plantations. Losing what could have been from 10 to 20 percent of its entire population, Zanzibar's death toll from cholera represented one of the worst recorded

---

[32] In Christie, *Cholera*, 244–5.
[33] Christie, the *Lancet*, (1871), 188. In his book, Christie raised his estimate for the entire island to 30,000. Christie, *Cholera*, 418–19.

anywhere. Overall, for the entire East African interior, coast, and Indian
Ocean islands, Christie speculated that cholera caused the death of "several hundreds of thousands." He may not have been wrong, given that
missionary eyewitnesses reported that just inland from the coast of what
is now Kenya and Tanzania, villages were totally depopulated, with rotting corpses everywhere.

By 1870, cholera had reached its southern limits in East Africa, stopping just short of Delagoa Bay in Mozambique. It also penetrated the
Upper Zambezi valley in the interior. On the coast, it visited Quelimane in
February and the city of Mozambique in May. Christie reported that the
British consul in the town of Mozambique, Lyons McLeod, described it as
"the filthiest city in the universe, not even excepting that of Lisbon," and
blamed the high death toll in Mozambique generally on the "filthy habits
of the Portuguese." Christie, on the other hand, attributed the spread
and destruction of cholera in the south to extensive slave trading in the
Mozambique channel between the African mainland and Madagascar.
In the summer, cholera touched down on the Indian Ocean islands of
Mauritius, the Seychelles, the Comoros, Nossi-bé, and the northwestern
Malagasy port of Majunga. At Quelimane, a Portuguese military expedition about to head up the Zambezi was infected, losing about a third
of the force and obliging the expedition to be canceled. An estimated
5,000 deaths were recorded in Quelimane and its environs. Cholera did
not leave the south until at least March of 1871. Mauritius, frightened
by cholera's approach, established a quarantine of fourteen days for all
Indian Ocean vessels in December 1870, to no avail. The deadly disease
arrived a month later. One island in the Comoros group, Johanna, lost
378 out of a total population of 2,000.

Cholera's impact on Zanzibar was made worse by bad timing. The
Muslim fasting month of Ramadan fell in December of 1869, a time
of scorching heat, which unfortunately coincided with the peak of the
epidemic. Christie somewhat naively hoped that the medical emergency
might persuade Muslims patients and their next of kin to break their
daily fasting, but was informed that believers regarded major epidemics
like cholera as God's will, and not a reason to disregard a pillar of the
faith. So many people expired on the street trying to make their way home
that people initially suspected sun stroke or heat apoplexy as the cause
of death. The worst death toll was recorded in Melinde, the poor northern section of Zanzibar City, inhabited by both slave and free Africans.
Conversely, no deaths were recorded in the more comfortable quarters
inhabited by the Europeans or by the Banyan Indian merchants. On the

other hand, American and European sailors aboard ships in Zanzibar harbor counted nineteen dead.

High African mortality was linked both to overcrowded living conditions in Zanzibar, and especially to the extensive East African slave trade. Efforts by Britain to diminish if not abolish the Zanzibar slave trade had some bearing on the subject. A signed treaty stipulated that no slaves could be imported from the mainland to Zanzibar between January 1 and May 1, the period coinciding with the northeast monsoon. During the rest of the year, marked by the onset of the southwest monsoon, an estimated 20,000 slaves arrived, many shipped down in early May from Kilwa Kivinje on the mainland. Each slave imported cost two dollars of duty for the trader. Demand was highest, as were prices, in early May of each year, so slave traders were in the habit of gathering a large number of slaves awaiting shipment to Zanzibar in Kilwa each April. Cholera in 1870 struck at precisely this time, ravaging these poor souls. Calling it "one of the blackest pages in history," Christie recounted how human beings were being discounted for sale at four shillings and two pence without finding purchasers. Some, nevertheless, were still being shipped on to Zanzibar, as Christie grimly reported:

The dhows [from Kilwa] were literally packed with slaves as close as they could possibly stand, some of them suffering from cholera, many of them in a dying state, and all of them in a condition of extreme emaciation. In this condition, and without having had either food or water on the passage, they were landed at the Custom-house of Zanzibar. On the passage, not only the dead but the dying were tossed overboard; and not only the dying but those who were in such a state of emaciation as not to be deemed paying the dollar of duty for, were treated in the same way before entering the harbour. Gangs of living skeletons were landed, with death imprinted on every feature; full grown men and women as naked as the hour of their birth.

Observing that even "cattle were never treated in such a manner," Christie explained that, because slaves were dying at the rate of 200 a day at Kilwa and were virtually worthless, merchants were offering them at fifty shillings a dozen for the few takers who gambled that a handful might survive and leave a margin of profit.

Dhows plying the sea lanes to Zanzibar were often rife with sickness. When cholera broke out aboard ship, the captain would make for the nearest harbor or return to Zanzibar. In one case, an entire company perished, save one man. When entire crews died, abandoned dhows simply drifted.

Christie did treat a few whites for cholera, all of them crew members of ships anchored in Zanzibar harbor. The American barque *Sterling*, arriving from Aden on December 11, 1869, lost at least two sailors among the four who were stricken. The barque *Corsair's Bride*, described as a model of cleanliness, had two of its European crew who had never gone ashore infected, one of whom died. The steamship *Malta* experienced four cases. All were taken ashore and three died, including the ship's engineer.

Yet another vessel, a Portuguese brig with a mixed crew from Mozambique and the Malabar coast, provided Christie with a clue to cholera's causation. The ship arrived from Bombay bound for Mozambique in January 1870 with a clean bill of health. Just before departure, it took on water at Zanzibar and quickly found itself with sixteen cases of cholera and four deaths.

The extraordinary merit of Christie's book on cholera is its epidemiological insight into the Zanzibar outbreak of 1869–1870. It would be unreasonable to expect that a young physician with no experience with outbreaks of infectious disease would be unerring in his account. As a physician treating cholera patients, Christie, like Koch in Egypt in 1883, remained bound to unsound therapies such as the prescribing of carbolic acid at the first sign of symptoms. Also, because he wrote up his notes as the epidemic unfolded, and put together his publication within a year of his return to Scotland, the text could have been more tightly edited, especially concerning causative theories. Early in his book, he comes close to endorsing early sanitarian and miasmatic notions of how the "decomposing blood and offal" of slaughtered animals "undoubtedly poison the atmosphere, lower the state of health and tend to predispose to disease, even although [sic] they are not sufficient to account for the origin of cholera."

By the time he was wrapping up the conclusion to his study, in the aftermath of the ISC meeting of 1874 in Vienna, Christie dismissed the air-borne theory of cholera diffusion so popular with British medical authorities in India, and stated unequivocally that polluted water, ingested through the alimentary canal, is the causative factor. He also provided a carefully researched account of what in later terminology would be called the index cases.

A leading proponent of the aerial theory was Dr. Bryden, statistical officer attached to the sanitary commissioner with the government of India. Bryden, in two reports on East African cholera, written in 1870 and 1874, claimed that atmospheric "waves" were responsible for cholera's diffusion. East African cholera corresponded closely to the monsoon winds and seasons of the Indian Ocean, and could not advance against the monsoon winds. Christie carefully showed how cholera was present in East Africa before the northeast monsoon, and was able to advance against it.

In place of fetid air, Christie argued for contaminated water. He confirmed the ISC findings at Vienna that cholera is a disease of filth, in which the ingestion of contaminated water into the alimentary canal is the main manner in which cholera's "causative agent" is introduced to the body. It is the passage of this agent via fecal contamination that is the vehicle for cholera's spread, usually by polluted water. A decade before Koch would identify the pathogen as *Vibrio cholerae*, this unheralded pioneer epidemiologist, using personal observation, extensive interviewing, and an exhaustive examination of the printed literature in English, built his argument throughout his book.

Christie understood the great East African epidemic of 1864–1871 as a single phenomenon. He begins in chapter two by insisting that each and every epidemic in East Africa arrived by means of diffusion from Mecca. Returning pilgrims were the key carriers. To and from Mecca, they consumed bad water and endured poor transport conditions, whether on overland caravans or aboard flimsy dhows. Cholera, in short, was propagated by infected humans.

For Christie, the key point of the Zanzibar outbreak was that it completely skipped over those Europeans living on shore and over the Banyans. The main issue was how the agent got access to the alimentary canal. Water was the main vehicle, and so a "judicious sanitary arrangement" would prevent ravages of cholera. Some wells in Zanzibar were only a few feet from cesspools, but in the Banyan quarter, their principal well was not in the immediate vicinity of the cesspools.[34] Christie added that cultural factors helped explain the success of the Banyans in avoiding cholera. Strict caste rules dictated how water had to be drawn from their own wells by a member of their own caste, or else they would consider themselves defiled. As for Europeans on shore, they had a secure source of drinking water some distance away from the town, and took the extra precaution of filtering and sometimes boiling the water. Ships, on the other hand, drew water from polluted streams just before sailing, and cholera often broke out as they left port, or when they were a day or two at sea.

---

[34] Although this analysis is very similar to John Snow's findings for London in 1854, there is no indication that Christie had ever read Snow or was otherwise aware of his work. He never cited him.

Although contaminated merchandise could also be a factor in the transmission of cholera in East Africa, Christie saw water as the key:

[W]ater tainted with the discharges of those suffering, or who have suffered from cholera, is, immeasurably, the most important medium of diffusion of the disease in an epidemic outbreak.

Christie's eyewitness observations provided him with many examples of the atrocious sanitary conditions of Zanzibar. Sewers did not exist, and the filth and garbage of the town were swept toward the beach from the narrow flooded streets during the monsoon rains. Members of both sexes and all classes used the sea beach and the stream beside it as a public toilet, and the general area was foul even in years without cholera. Christie noted that all who visited Zanzibar remarked on its squalor, whether it was "the odious state of the sea-beach, even in the best kept part of town," or the dirty African quarters of Zanzibar, which Richard Burton described graphically as a "foul mass of densely crowded dwelling places, where the slaves and the poor 'pig' together."[35] During his visit to Zanzibar in 1866, David Livingstone had voiced similar opinions, and was so offended by the stench that he labeled the town "Stinkibar."[36]

More pertinent to Christie's epidemiological argument about foul water were his descriptions of the source of drinking water aboard European vessels and Indian Ocean dhows. His account left little doubt about the dangers resulting from the methods employed:

While all this traffic is going on – while thousands of negroes are crossing the streams, bathing in them, and using them as a public convenience, a gang of negroes may be at work, not many hundred yards distance, filling water casks for the shipping.

No wonder that there had been nineteen outbreaks among European and American sailors. Christie observed that experienced captains preferred to take on water in Indian Ocean ports at Nossi-bé, Mayotte, or especially the Seychelles, where water supplies were reputed to be plentiful, cheap, and healthful. Unfortunately, some ships watered at Zanzibar. Christie also observed a dozen Indian Ocean dhows taking on water from the same polluted streams. The drinking and cooking water aboard the dhows was stored in wooden tanks or casks that were never cleaned. Men transferred the water from the creek into canoes using goat skins.

---

[35] In Christie, *Cholera*, 305.
[36] David Livingstone, *Last Journals*, Vol. 1 (London: [s.n.], 1874), 17.

Without washing the canoe or cleansing their feet, the men then stepped into the canoe when it was nearly full and, sitting in the water, they paddled alongside the dhow. They then used the goat skins to bail the water from the canoe to the casks. Christie added that the water was usually taken on the day of departure, and in 1869 and 1870, cholera frequently broke out on the second day after sailing, at which point the infected dhow would either head for the nearest coastal port, or return to Zanzibar.

Not content to provide numerous examples of polluted water, Christie focused on what he came to believe were the first Zanzibari cases of late 1869 in the fetid Melinde district, located in the northern part of the town. He admits that his inspection of the Melinde house after the epidemic was over removed the blinkers from his eyes:

I had always a difficulty in accounting for the great and sudden mortality which appeared in the Melinde district at that time, and this led me to the conclusion, while the epidemic was raging, that there must have been, in the district, some local cause of which I was not cognisant. I could not at the time, trace it to the water supply, and I was led to entertain the opinion that the generative agent of cholera was air-borne, in some mysterious, unknown manner ...

But in inspecting the house and preparing his book, Christie found his answer:

Nearly all the inmates of this house died of cholera: the well received the soakage of the cesspool; it was extremely liable to direct contamination; the water was widely used in the district; the deaths in the house preceded the general outbreak, and there was an absence of an otherwise adequate cause to account for the great mortality which prevailed within a short space of time among the population supplied from the well. Viewed in the light of other facts, I have no hesitation in regarding this and similarly situated wells as having been the chief foci of dissemination in Zanzibar.

Christie also had a medical researcher's concern for control and prevention of cholera. He had praise for the decorum shown by the Zanzibari populace, and the stoicism with which they accepted their fate. He observed no flight from the city, found gloom rather than panic to be the prevailing mood, and admired how Africans did their best to cope. Ruling authorities, on the other hand, did nothing to address cholera control. Although quarantine, he noted, was never entirely effective, quarantine laws would have confined the disease to narrower limits and were worth implementing in the future. More to his point about the dangers of polluted water, he pointed to the example of Europe's larger cities, which found it was cheaper in the long run to invest in "ample and pure water," than to do nothing and thus reap the consequences of disease and death.

James Christie was an outstanding pioneer epidemiologist. It is a pity that his directives were ignored both in his time and much later. Like John Snow before him, but without access to the quality of records available in London, Christie researched the nature of a cholera outbreak after it had burned itself out. Eventually, municipal authorities and business-men in Britain and in the West generally came to appreciate the benefits Snow and other sanitarians recommended. In time, and long after the fact, John Snow's pump handle became an icon of historical epidemiol-ogy. Christie was never so revered, even posthumously, although a new study of cholera's history recognizes that Christie's appreciation of the cultural dimensions of the Zanzibar epidemic was both prescient and an exception among Victorian approaches.[37] As we will see in Part Two of this study, too many decision makers in Africa continued this failure to invest in safe water supplies. Nevertheless, as his biographer Edna Robertson observes, Christie's book on cholera in East Africa was "the supreme achievement of his life." She shows how Christie distinguished himself in Glasgow after he left Africa in 1874, as an accomplished expo-nent of public health, and as a champion of medical treatment for the poor.[38]

[37] Hamlin, *Cholera: The Biography*, 61–3.
[38] Robertson, "Christie," 69.

4

Cholera in North Africa and the Nile Valley

Tunisia, 1835–1868, and Egypt, 1823–1947

Tunisia's first and lightest brush with cholera took place in 1835 during the Second Pandemic. The country suffered three major cholera epidemics thereafter, in 1849 and 1850, when 56,000 died; a less severe one in 1856, when the toll in Tunis alone was roughly 6,500; and during the Fourth Pandemic in 1867 and 1868, when as many as 20,000 perished. This chapter relies extensively on Nancy Gallagher's definitive study of medicine in nineteenth-century Tunisia.[1] Thanks to her efforts, Tunisia offers one of the few African case studies of cholera supported by primary sources. Gallagher demonstrates that cholera as a public health issue helped discredit the local Tunisian ruling elite, and played an essential role in encouraging French imperialists to annex the country in 1881.

Nominally a dependent *beylik*, or province within the loosely structured Ottoman Empire, what is now most of modern Tunisia developed virtual independence in the early eighteenth century when Husayn Bey (1705–1725) established a hereditary dynasty. The Husaynis reigned until 1957; their reign survived the French protectorate from 1881 to 1956, but not Tunisian independence.

The Beys, or governors of Tunis, built a strong economy based on agriculture, trade, commerce, and, informally, privateering. Tunis was one of the major ports of the so-called Barbary pirates, who reaped profits from the seizing of European cargoes, and often their nationals, who were then

---

[1] Nancy Gallagher, *Medicine and Power in Tunisia, 1780–1900* (Cambridge: Cambridge University Press, 1983).

held for ransom, sometimes for years. As piracy waned toward the end of the eighteenth century, shrewd and stable Husayni rule helped Tunis transform itself into the most prosperous of the North African ports, known as "the Shanghai of the Mediterranean" by the 1790s.[2]

By then, close to half the ships from North Africa calling at Marseilles came from Tunis. Trans-Saharan caravans brought slaves, gold dust, and gum arabic. Locally produced commodities such as wheat and olive oil were sought after by southern European merchants, and Tunis also manufactured and exported red felt caps throughout the Muslim world. Under the Beys, Tunisian merchants came to control three quarters of the international trade.

The Tunisian boom ended by 1825. The impact of European innovations associated with the Industrial Revolution began to erode Tunisian manufactures and artisanal production. Growing more powerful militarily and especially at sea, Europeans imposed their terms of trade not only on Tunis, but among non-European competitors globally. To make matters worse, North Africa suffered from a prolonged drought in this period, hurting local agriculture.

France was the main beneficiary of this increasing European influence in North Africa. As early as 1824, the French consul in Tunis, backed by the French navy, imposed a new trade treaty upon Husayn Bey's government. In despair, Husayn Bey sought to invoke his nominal links with the Ottomans, but they were preoccupied with the Greek War of Independence. This French commercial treaty marked the start of a steady erosion of Tunisian economic independence, leading first to European control of the economy by the 1860s, followed by the military imposition of a French protectorate in 1881. In nearby Algeria, French imperial expansion came even earlier. French troops occupied Algiers in 1830, and by mid-century had launched a conquest of the vast interior.

In an effort to respond to these commercial and political threats, the beylik government of Tunis grew increasingly indebted to European, and especially French, banks. The first large foreign loan from a prominent French bank in 1863 obliged the beylik government to raise taxes, increasing the resentment of the Tunisian population. This act was the major cause of armed resistance in the countryside during the spring and summer of 1864. The Bey crushed the uprising with some difficulty and imposed large indemnities on the rural tribes. Crises multiplied, as heavy rains flooded some areas while drought persisted in the wheat-growing

---

[2] Gallagher, *Medicine*, 33.

northwest. Extreme weather coupled with brutal government extraction triggered widespread famine in 1865 and 1866, punctuated by a severe cholera outbreak in 1866 and a typhus epidemic two years later.

Among the concessions gained by Europeans were several pertaining to health as well as to commerce. The major European powers acquired the right to establish consulates anywhere in the country, to subject their own nationals to European law, and indirectly, to acquire a voice on health issues. In 1835, Ahmad Bey (r. 1837–1855) created a sanitary council, whose major duty was to exercise surveillance and maintain quarantines to keep out cholera. European physicians played a significant role in the sanitary council, even when Ahmad Bey took credit for his government's vigilance in keeping the 1835 outbreak mild, and for preventing other visitations that struck neighboring Algeria and Libya in the mid-1840s.

In 1847, Ahmad Bey, hearing of the major cholera outbreak in Mecca among pilgrims, ordered his sanitary council to mount a strict forty-day quarantine for ships from infected regions. Maintaining tight naval surveillance for this long a time was wishful thinking. Nor could Ahmad control overland routes from Algeria and Tripoli. Cholera struck the eastern Algerian hinterland in November 1849, and then made its way to Tunis in December. Ahmad ordered three separate and temporary isolation hospitals for Jews, Christians, and Muslims, and on the advice of his personal Jewish physician Abraham Lumbroso, Ahmad and his court moved to nearby Carthage on December 5.

A member of a prominent Jewish family of Livorno, Italy, and a longtime resident himself in Tunis, Lumbroso left valuable records on the impact of the 1849–1850 outbreak. On December 17, he identified the index case, a visiting Jewish merchant who died in the *hara*, or Jewish quarter, two days later. All were puzzled at the time as to why only Jews died during the initial weeks. As Lumbroso put it, "[The disease] spread to nearby houses, all inhabited by Jews, as if that germ had some sort of knowledge and avoided all other sects except the Jews."[3] Contaminated water in the crowded and impoverished Jewish quarter most probably caused the outbreak. The Jewish custom of mourning the deceased by visiting the bereaved would have enabled *Vibrio cholerae* to spread from one household to many.[4]

Slowly, cholera advanced beyond the Jewish quarter to the rest of Tunis during January and February of 1850. By the time the epidemic died

[3] In Gallagher, *Medicine*, 49.
[4] Gallagher, *Medicine*, 49–50.

TABLE 4.1. *Religious groups in Tunis during the 1849 cholera epidemic*

	Deaths	Cases	CFRs (percent)	Population	Mortality per 1000
Jews	3,400	7,700	44	28,500	119
Muslims	3,900	8,500	46	94,500	41
Catholics	300	475	63	27,000	11
total	7,600	16,675	46	150,000	51

Source: Gallagher, *Medicine*, 107–13.

out, all residents of Tunis had experienced terrible mortality rates, even if those for Jews were highest. Table 4.1 provides Gallagher's extrapolations based on Lumbroso's meticulous records.

Fragmentary evidence from contemporary popular culture in Tunisia offers valuable insights into local attitudes toward cholera. One parable using a religious idiom is careful not to scapegoat either Christians or Jews:

The cholera, after having passed from France to Algeria, went from this last country to Tunis. While still on the road, he arrived at Carthage and met the marabout of Sidi bu Said. Sensing the imminent danger to the Muslims of Tunis, who were under his protection, the saint awoke from his long sleep and said,
"Where are you going, Oh bold one?"
"To Tunis."
"What for?"
"For what I do everywhere! I need victims!"
"Well then, take them from the Jews, take them from the Christians too. I hold neither one nor the other dear. As for the Muslims, they are mine. I cannot bear that you touch them."
This was agreed. The cholera pursued his journey. He was soon before the chapel of Saint Louis, the French saint. He was no less jealous of the health of his co-religionists. He also rose from his tomb and asked the cholera, "Oh unhappy one, where are you going?"
"You know where! To Tunis!"
The saint replied, "I am the protector of the Christians of Tunis. You must respect them. You must not touch them."
This was agreed. The cholera again took up his route, which led directly to Tunis leaving La Goulette [the predominantly Jewish suburb] to the left. If he had only encountered another saint who was the protector of the Jewish nation, he might not have entered the city at all.[5]

---

[5] J. Guyon, "Lettre sur l'état de choléra dans la régence de Tunis," *Gazette médicale de Paris*, 5 (1850), 401, cited in Gallagher, *Medicine*, 50–1.

Tunisians, like people all over the world, struggled to understand and contain the scourge which descended upon them. One recourse was to special prayers. The scholar and poet Mahmud Qabadu composed the following invocation, which read in part:

You are the merciful and our mercy.

You are compassionate when angry with your creatures.

Your power has superiority over the feverish.

You who possess all possession.

We have no means or power save through your all powerful will.

You who created medicine; it is shameful for our hearts and bodies to complain about our misery.[6]

Muslim Tunisian physicians had never seen cholera before, and Islamic medicine offered them no historical precedents. They did call on their links to the Ottomans for some redress. One text was written in 1831 by Mustafa Behçet, the *bash hakim* (chief physician) of Istanbul. Trained there, and literate in several European languages, he based his treatise on an Austrian manual on cholera, adapted for use in Ottoman regions. Written in the classical style of Islamic medicine, the text described how this new disease originated in India and displayed symptoms attributed to the burning of the bile. A convinced contagionist, he believed cholera was transmittable from person to person like plague. Unfortunately, like his Austrian colleagues, Behçet's treatments were unsound or ineffective. He recommended bleeding, holding vinegar, garlic, or ammonia to the face as protection, and the burning of tar, incense, gum arabic, pine leaves, and other aromatic plants used in Islamic medical practice to purify the air. Behçet's treatise was translated from Turkish to Arabic in Tunis and was believed to have circulated widely.[7]

Ahmad Bey turned to religious authorities in hopes of divine intervention. He authorized the reading of a daily invocation based on Koranic verses in the Great Mosque in Tunis. Read by a *sharif*, a descendant of the Prophet Muhammad, the words were believed to have been effective, because immediately after the first invocation the cholera outbreak abated and soon disappeared. A minister of Ahmed Bey proclaimed that the *shurfa* (plural of *sharif*) would no longer have to give proof of their holy ancestry.[8]

[6] In Gallagher, *Medicine*, 55.

[7] Gallagher, *Medicine*, 58.

[8] Gallagher, *Medicine*, 55–6.

Not all responses to cholera were benign. Popular anger in the provinces turned against European physicians believed to be agents of Satan. In Bizerte, after seven of the eight patients treated by Dr. Mancel died in March 1850, a riot ensued and the French physician and his family were fortunate to escape with their lives. The flight of Ahmad Bey to Carthage, and his subsequent decision to move farther away to Muhammadiya once his new palace was constructed there in late February 1850, proved unsettling to the Muslim population, though threats of urban disturbances did not materialize. Aware of the potential unrest, when another wave of cholera flared up in March 1850, Ahmad relaxed the tight cordon and allowed his troops to disperse. Many soldiers came from the Sahel, and some carried cholera with them as they returned home. The Kairouan region was badly hit as cholera's second wave continued through the summer before gradually fading away in the fall.

Although Tunisia's experience with cholera in 1849 and 1850 was its worst, recurring epidemics in 1856 and 1867 brought with them political tensions and public anxieties that helped weaken the beylik governments. Ahmad's successor, Muhammad Bey (r. 1855–1859), was more anti-Western and chose not to flee Tunis or accept any of the measures suggested by the sanitary council when cholera broke out in neighboring Tripoli in July 1856, and spread to Tunis a month later. Muhammad's decision to visit the sick in Tunis earned him respect and gave encouragement to the population, especially when the epidemic proved mild and no further visitations took place during his reign.

A decade later, in 1867, cholera's return found the Tunisian political economy in disarray, and the population weakened by famine and angry at the heavy tax burdens imposed by the beylik government. No longer could it be said that Jews were cholera's main victims. In Tunis, impoverished and jobless European immigrants, an estimated 7,000 from Malta and 4,000 from southern Italy (mainly Sicily), suffered unspecified losses to cholera.[9] The noted Tunisian chronicler Ahmad ibn Abi Diyaf, known as Bin Diyaf, has left graphic accounts of despair in the countryside in the 1860s as a result of cholera and drought. In November 1867, he described how thousands of Bedouins had abandoned their possessions and migrated to Tunis in search of public assistance. Many squatted in the street, enduring, hunger, cold, and of course, exposure to cholera:

Every morning, coffins were seen going back and forth from the maristan [hospital/asylum]. The number dying per day rose to about a hundred. The treasury

[9] Gallagher, *Medicine*, 68.

was exhausted from burying them and from paying for the shrouds. The city was reeking from rotten corpses and refuse. People were falling sick in the alleys. The doctors cautioned against this and warned that another sickness would come and it did [his reference to a severe typhus outbreak in 1868].[10]

Although few statistics have survived, and European physicians described the 1867 outbreak as mild, it became deeply embedded in Tunisian collective memory, which calls the year 1867 *bu shalal*, colloquial Tunisian Arabic for severe dysentery.[11]

The cholera outbreaks in Tunisia were political as well as social disasters, and clearly helped destabilize the country. Gallagher does not share McNeill's argument that failure to cope with infectious disease discredited traditional leadership and facilitated the reception of European medicine. She cogently suggests this is unlikely because Europeans lacked understanding or effective treatment for cholera.[12] She argues instead that the political failures of the beylik governments to prevent economic collapse during the 1860s and 1870s discredited them with the public and paved the way for French colonial takeover. In this process, cholera contributed by placing yet another insoluble problem on the government's plate.

Like its North African neighbors, Tunisia faced no serious bouts with cholera after 1867. The region was lightly touched for the last time during the fifth cholera pandemic in 1893. Afterward, Tunisia, like the rest of Africa, escaped entirely from the Sixth Pandemic, and it also avoided the devastation wrought in Africa by the Seventh Pandemic (the subject of Part Two). It is always difficult to account for why a pandemic fails to strike, but an argument can be made that Tunisia's public health system, developed in part under the aegis of its prestigious Pasteur Institute in Tunis during colonial times, continued to function efficiently after independence in 1956.[13]

EGYPT, 1823–1947

It is no surprise that cholera was a frequent visitor to Egypt during the nineteenth century. Major epidemics, usually transmitted by pilgrims returning from Mecca, broke out six times: in 1831, 1848, 1865, 1882, 1895, and 1902. After a hiatus of forty-five years, when even

[10] In Gallagher, *Medicine*, 77.
[11] Gallagher, *Medicine*, 63.
[12] McNeill, *Plagues*, 264; Gallagher, *Medicine*, 60.
[13] Kim Pelis, *Charles Nicolle: Pasteur's Imperial Missionary: Typhus and Tunisia* (Rochester: University of Rochester Press, 2006).

epidemiologists began to believe that modern public health had rendered the disease obsolete, a terrible cholera epidemic erupted in 1947, in the later years of the Sixth Pandemic. Lying at the crossroads of Europe, Asia, and Africa, Egypt was vulnerable to imported epidemics.[14] Its contact through the Red Sea to Arabia, the Persian Gulf, and the Indian Ocean had deep historical roots; and, of course, the thousands of Egyptian and other African pilgrims returning from Mecca annually exposed the country to a series of punishing cholera outbreaks. Egypt also illustrated how technological changes affected the environment and contributed to waterborne diseases, whether cholera in the nineteenth century or bilharzia in the twentieth.[15]

Egypt was also a case where technological changes designed to improve the economy ironically increased the nation's vulnerability to cholera. To illustrate the point it is helpful to examine the changing politics of public health in Egypt under the rule of Khedive Muhammad Ali and his successors.[16] An Albanian-born soldier of the Ottoman Empire, Muhammad Ali seized power in Egypt in 1805. During the next four decades, he built the most powerful military force in the Muslim Mediterranean, and extended Egypt's influence throughout the Middle East and the Upper Nile Valley. He gained complete autonomy from the Ottoman Empire, founded a hereditary dynasty, and carried out significant reforms and innovations. He created a conscript army trained in the Western manner, transformed the agricultural economy by introducing cotton as a cash crop, and concentrated his attention on the sorry state of public health in Egypt. Horrific epidemics of cholera in 1831 and of bubonic plague in 1835 persuaded him of this need.

He also adopted the maritime quarantine system prominent in the Mediterranean, and allowed European consular representatives to organize a quarantine board. Alarmed at the poor health of his soldiers, Muhammad Ali sponsored a European-style medical school to train Egyptian military physicians. This was extended to include other medical personnel, including midwives and smallpox vaccinators. His agent in these medical initiatives was a French physician, Antoine Barthèleme Clot,

---

[14] For scholarship that situates Egyptian epidemics within the Ottoman world, see Daniel Panzac, *Population et santé dans l'Empire Ottoman (XVIIe-XXe siècles)* (Istanbul: Editions Isis, 1996), and his *Quarantine et Lazarets.*

[15] John Farley, *Bilharzia: A History of Imperial Tropical Medicine* (Cambridge: Cambridge University Press, 1991).

[16] Laverne Kuhnke, *Lives at Risk: Public Health in Nineteenth-Century Egypt* (Cairo: The American University in Cairo Press, 1992), 3–5.

known as Clot Bey.[17] What began as a reform designed to modernize the military soon benefited the wider civilian public. Students and graduates of the Egyptian School of Medicine energetically addressed the serious infectious disease epidemics suffered by Egypt with principles and practices of clinical medicine that were evolving in Paris.

Egypt's water supply had always been linked to the Nile, but important changes occurred in the nineteenth century. By the late 1840s, Muhammad Ali's economic reforms, designed to permit Egypt to compete with Western powers, involved the promotion of cotton as a cash crop. When his government constructed new irrigation systems to water the cotton, low levels of water for the towns resulted, which increased the risk of infection as people used and reused water in which human excretions were likely to be found.[18] Along with ground wells, the Nile and its branches supplied most of the country with water. Running streams can be self-cleaning, but the shift to perennial cotton agriculture meant reliance on slow-moving canal water. Nile Delta towns like Damietta held major fairs in June and July each year, before the annual Nile flood, and they received large numbers of visitors when waters were at their lowest and most dangerous levels.[19] In 1865 and 1883, for example, newly introduced irrigation works for industrial crops created standing water in the canals, and those people drinking from the canals suffered terribly, whereas those drawing water directly from the Nile escaped the brunt of the cholera.[20] As for Cairo, it was a city of cesspits that flooded and spread filth at high Nile, or dried up and left human waste to blow in the wind at low Nile.

Though we lack details, cholera's first appearance in Egypt in 1831 may have been the worst.[21] One in twenty Egyptians may have perished, an estimated 150,000 of a total population of about 3 million. Close to 40,000 of Cairo's 250,000 inhabitants fell in only twenty-eight days.

[17] Antoine Clot was born in Grenoble and trained in medicine and surgery at Montpellier. He practiced briefly in Marseilles and then went to Egypt to become Muhammad Ali's chief surgeon. His long career there was distinguished as a physician, teacher, and after 1836, director of medical adminstration in the Egyptian government. He wrote valuable studies of bubonic plague and one collection on the Egyptian cholera epidemic of 1831. See A.B. Clot Bey, *Relation des épidémies de choléra-morbus qui ont regné à l'Heggiaz, à Suez et en Egypte* (Marseilles: Feissat ainé et Demonchy, 1832).

[18] Kuhnke, *Lives at Risk*, 12–13.

[19] Philip D. Curtin, *Disease and Empire: The Health of European Troops in the Conquest of Africa* (Cambridge: Cambridge University Press, 1998), 128–30.

[20] Timothy Mitchell, *Rule of Experts: Egypt, Techno-politics, Modernity* (Berkeley: University of California Press), 2002), 65.

[21] For this epidemic, see Clot Bey, *Relation*; and Kuhnke, *Lives at Risk*, 50–56, who provides the statistical estimates.

Even though these figures were crude estimates, Egypt had one of the highest mortality rates in the world during the nineteenth century. Clot Bey was so overwhelmed by what he observed that he remarked that the entire city of Cairo "seemed headed for destruction in only a few days."[22] This new disease caught everyone unaware. It bore no name in Arabic, but because people died as if blown over by a strong gust, they attributed its arrival to a pestilential "yellow wind" (*al-rih al-asfar*).[23]

Panic and flight were universal soon after August 16, when cholera first appeared simultaneously in several quarters of Cairo, and took 335 victims in two days. A mass of Europeans fled to Fayyum, on the west bank of Nile bordering on the desert. Whereas the Egyptian elite had been stoic in the face of earlier epidemics of bubonic plague, cholera now provoked panic, especially among most Turks, who followed the example of their Pashas and either fled Cairo or locked themselves inside their homes.[24] The streets of Cairo were clogged with continual files of camels carrying the fugitives' belongings, as well as columns of peasant laborers rushing home to the provinces. Funerals filled the streets with trains of mourners. In Alexandria, commerce came to a standstill, and consular officers of the various European powers formed the first quarantine board in the country. The effort to protect Alexandria was in vain. When it became clear that a *cordon sanitaire* was stopping provisions but not cholera from entering the city, the consular authorities recalled physicians manning the cordon and dissolved the board. At the entrance to the Mahmudiyah canal in the Nile Delta, where many pilgrims stopped, the site became heavily infected, and the army regiment garrisoned there was almost wiped out.

Concerned with his military forces, Muhammad Ali ordered many of his 90,000-man army out of the cities and to the desert fringe. The practice of flight seems to have helped somewhat, as Egypt lost an estimated 2,000 sailors and 5,000 soldiers to cholera, a death rate lower than for the civilian population. An angry Muhammad Ali ordered the dismissal of all medical officers who had abandoned their posts during the cholera crisis.

When cholera struck for a second time seventeen years later, the disease confronted a different Egypt. Muhammad Ali's expansionist ambitions had been thwarted by several European powers, led by Britain, which had its own imperial ambitions. Muhammad Ali was required to disband much of his conscript army, and by 1848 the aging ruler had retired from

[22] Clot Bey, *Relation*, 12.
[23] Kuhnke, *Lives at Risk*, 51.
[24] Clot Bey, *Relation*, 12–13.

direct supervision of government affairs. An expanded medical corps now addressed public health issues of the civilian population. Alerted to the threat of cholera when it broke out in Mecca, they sought this time, with partial success, to quarantine and control the returning pilgrims. Perhaps that was why the impact of the 1848 cholera epidemic was significantly reduced. This time, an estimated 6,000 Cairenes lost their lives, and the entire country's losses were pegged at around 30,000.[25]

Nevertheless, disorganization, fear, and flight trumped public health control measures. With Muhammad Ali now retired, his viceroy, Ibrahim Pasha, fled Cairo, first for Alexandria, and then on to Constantinople as cholera advanced. Abbas Pasha, Muhammad Ali's heir, took over the duties of government but he too soon fled, this time to Upper Egypt. The Governor of Cairo was an early cholera victim, thus Egypt's capital had no chief executive during the epidemic. Though cholera was kept out of Upper Egypt, it did severe damage in some delta towns. One devastated site was Tanta, a town of 17,000, where a semiannual trade fair was taking place in July and where thousands of merchants from Egypt and other lands had gathered. Worse, the holy fasting month of Ramadan was about to begin, at the height of the summer heat. The Nile was just beginning to rise, but water levels were still low in delta canals. If all this were not enough, Tanta was overwhelmed by the arrival of more than 150,000 visitors, yet lacked a resident sanitary or medical officer. As cholera preyed on this easy target, the Tanta trade fair dispersed in panic and flight, lasting only four days instead of the usual seven.

When cholera returned to Egypt for the third time in 1865, it could now benefit from the new technologies of steamship and rail to travel farther and faster. The Fourth Pandemic's stop in Egypt was a prelude to its wider invasion of North Africa and southern Europe. This time Egypt's toll was an estimated 60,000, double that of 1848. In Alexandria, the business class fled cholera in panic: Thirty thousand departed by sea within two weeks, risking their lives to obtain passage aboard boats not fit for sea travel, and spreading the pathogen to ports all over the Mediterranean – to Marseilles and Valencia in the West, and Malta, Cyprus, Smyrna, and Beirut in the East.[26] Ironically, when the Khedive Ismail, like his predecessors, fled to Constantinople, he found cholera had preceded him, though it seems that he and his entire retinue were spared.[27]

---

[25] Kuhnke, *Lives at Risk*, 59.
[26] David S. Landes, *Bankers and Pashas: International Finance and Economic Imperialism in Egypt* (London: Heinemann, 1958), 242.
[27] Kuhnke, *Lives at Risk*, 67.

Attempts by Egyptian health authorities to keep the cholera epidemic in Mecca from entering the country failed, in part because of complete disregard for control measures displayed by ships' captains. When the newly invigorated quarantine board alerted control stations at Suez, they received false declarations from ten steamers carrying 900 to 1200 passengers each. The captains' official statements declared their passengers to be in fine health, and suggested the few deaths that had occurred were due to "ordinary" diseases. The pilgrims duly proceeded on land to board the Suez-Alexandria rail line, where cholera broke out at both ends of the line. Further investigation revealed that the ships had cast their cholera fatalities overboard.[28]

Nevertheless, lessons could have been learned if Egyptian authorities had made connections about contaminated water and cholera. In Upper Egypt, for example, villages close to the Nile, which drew their water from the river, escaped infection, whereas those only a kilometer or two away, relying on polluted canal water, did not.[29]

The cholera epidemic of 1882–1883 illustrated how closely tied to the politics of international public health Egypt had become. When cholera broke out in Mecca in 1881, the International Quarantine Board in Alexandria ordered strict measures to protect Egypt. These included twenty-eight days of detention at the three Red Sea quarantine stations. Within days, the camps were swamped with pilgrims and had become a danger to health, yet the board ordered an extension of the quarantine. Rations and water ran out. Some pilgrims were detained for as long as forty days, and a group of enraged detainees burned the lazaretto and fled the camp. Egyptian nationalists used the incident to arouse further anti-foreign feeling. They pressed for the abolition of the quarantine board and demanded that a board of health in Cairo, under Egyptian control, be placed in charge instead. In September 1881, the quarantine board restricted movement through the canal, and by the end of the year, the British Foreign Office as well as the Suez Canal Company were deluged with complaints from shippers, and with bills requesting compensation for the delays.

Meanwhile, cholera easily crossed over the Red Sea, arriving first at Damietta, not far from Port Said, then headed for Cairo, Alexandria, and the rest of the Lower Nile Delta. It exacted a toll of more than 58,000 lives in the country in 1883. Cholera also devastated some of the British

[28] Kuhnke, *Lives at Risk*, 65–6.
[29] Kuhnke, *Lives at Risk*, 66.

military forces occupying the country. Before the British garrison could withdraw from Cairo to Suez, it suffered an appalling 139 deaths among its 183 cases. Only then did the British improve the water situation for its troops in Cairo and Alexandria.[30]

This same outbreak also represented a great opportunity for European scientists to advance their understanding of the killer disease. In an attempt to isolate the cholera pathogen, both the French and the Germans arrived in Alexandria in 1883 with substantial personnel, funding, and equipment.[31] The French team consisted of Drs. Emile Roux and Louis Thuillier of the Pasteur Institute in Paris, together with Dr. Isidore Straus and a veterinarian, Dr. Edmond Nocard; the team arrived on August 15. Robert Koch headed the German team, which arrived nine days later. Koch was supported by bacteriologists Georg Gaffky and Bernhard Fisher and a chemist, Hermann Treskow. Because the European hospital facilities were already conceded to the French, the Germans worked at the Greek hospital. The French team performed twenty-four autopsies and made microscopic examinations of the stools and vomitus of cholera patients, but they did not isolate the one cholera pathogen among the many microorganisms they observed.[32] In mid-September, tragedy struck when the twenty-seven-year-old Thuillier came down with a fatal case of cholera. The intervention of his colleagues, all distinguished medical scientists, consisted of ice champagne, frictions of the extremities, and subcutaneous injections of ether. In what was normally fierce national competition, Robert Koch graciously offered the eulogy at Thuillier's funeral in Alexandria, and served as one of the pall bearers. The disheartened French team returned to Paris.

Meanwhile, based on ten autopsies, Koch's German team reported that an extraordinary number of microorganisms were observed in the stools. Yet in the walls of the small intestine of cholera victims, Koch noted that a specific bacterium was found in each case. Koch was convinced these bacteria "stand in some relation to the cholera process," but could not be sure whether their presence was the cause or the result of the infection.[33] Because cholera was dying out in Egypt in the fall of 1883, Koch requested and received permission from British authorities

---

[30] Curtin, *Disease and Empire*, 130.
[31] Anne-Marie Moulin, "Révolutions Médicales et Révolutions Politiques en Égypte (1865–1917)," *Revue du monde musulman et de la méditerranée*, 52/53 (1989), 115–16.
[32] Norman Howard-Jones, *The Scientific Background of the International Scientific Conferences, 1851–1938* (Geneva: WHO, 1974), 46–7.
[33] Howard-Jones, *Scientific*, 47–48; Gradmann, *Laboratory Disease*, 184–8.

to travel with his team to Calcutta, where an epidemic was then raging. Coincidentally, they arrived in Calcutta on December 11, Koch's fortieth birthday.[34]

Here, the results were much better. Within days, they obtained a pure culture of the cholera organism from a twenty-two-year-old who died only ten hours from the onset of infection. Koch wrote:

> Up to now, 22 cholera victims and 17 cholera patients have been examined in Calcutta, with the help of both the microscope and gelatin cultures. In all cases the comma bacillus and only the comma bacillus has been found. These results, taken together with those obtained in Egypt, prove that we have found the pathogen responsible for cholera.[35]

Koch and his team made a triumphant return to Germany. The Kaiser gave 100,000 marks in gold to Koch personally, and he was awarded a military decoration. The Berlin press heralded Koch and his team as scientific soldiers who had won a great victory over disease, and French competition, in the same manner that Prussia had defeated Napoleon III more than a decade earlier. A complex and unfinished research process, the etiology of cholera was reduced in the popular mind to a simple, metaphorical discovery.[36]

Koch clearly deserves credit for his research on cholera. His conviction that contaminated drinking water was the primary means whereby *Vibrio cholerae* infected humans, and his emphasis on public health measures to prevent outbreaks, saved many lives. These contributions should not ignore his many medical failures. He developed a product called tuberculin, an extract of tuberculosis bacteria suspended in glycerin, but he kept the formula secret to hide weaknesses in the research. No one ever saw the animals he claimed to have cured with the product, and it was removed from the market after it caused harmful side effects and even deaths.[37] Later in his career, he visited Africa on several occasions, where he asserted his medical hypotheses – with often disastrous results – on such disparate diseases as bubonic plague, sleeping sickness, rinderpest, and east coast cattle fever.[38]

[34] Thomas D. Brock, *Robert Koch: A Life in Medicine and Bacteriology* (Madison: Science Tech Publishers, 1988) 159.

[35] In Brock, *Robert Koch*, 140.

[36] Gradmann, *Laboratory Disease*, 194–201.

[37] Gradmann, *Laboratory Disease*, 15–16.

[38] Myron Echenberg, "'Scientific Gold': Robert Koch and Africa, 1883–1906," in Chris Youe and Tim Stapleton, eds., *Agency and Action in Colonial Africa: Essays for John Flint*, (London: Palgrave, 2001), 34–49.

Koch's breakthrough could not immediately benefit Egypt. In 1895 and 1896, a second wave of cholera during the Fifth Pandemic killed more than16,000 Egyptians. Six years later, in 1902, Egypt lost 34,000. It seemed that the new science could not overcome the shocking neglect of urban living conditions by successive governments, including the British after 1883. Egypt's population was so densely concentrated in the Lower Nile that once cholera broke out in the country, it was next to impossible to keep the streams and canals from being polluted and the disease from spreading.

Keeping cholera out proved indeed to be the best solution. The 1902 epidemic was the last one in Egypt for the next forty-five years, just as Mecca was able to avoid cholera after 1912. It would take a new technology – air travel – to break the spell.

In September 1947, Egypt may have been the first country to fall victim to cholera as a result of air travel of infected persons, in this case, from India. To be sure, the airplane was a technological advance that afforded *Vibrio cholerae* rapid access to thousands of new victims. Unlike earlier outbreaks, this one began before the annual return of the Mecca pilgrims. Some of the first victims were laborers working at the British airfields near al-Qurayn, a trading town of 15,000 on the eastern fringe of the Nile Delta, and close to the Suez Canal.

The origins of the 1947 epidemic took on a political and often polemical aspect, as Egyptian nationalists were quick to blame the British occupiers, or even the Zionists in Palestine.[39] The Islamist Muslim Brotherhood even went so far as to see cholera as deliberate germ warfare. The WHO neither confirmed nor denied an Indian origin, and A.M. Kamal, Under-Secretary for Preventive Medicine in the Ministry of Health and Egypt's leading epidemiologist, maintained that although an Indian origin was possible, it could not be proven medically because the index case was never found. The Indian link could have been from at least two sources. The British did import some Indian technicians and workers for their al-Qurayn airfield, and Indian Muslim traders in the Nile Delta did come to the town for business.

Whatever its external origins, cholera could hardly have chosen a better point of diffusion than al-Qurayn. Each year, thousands of merchants from all over Egypt and elsewhere gathered at the town for the

---

[39] Gallagher devotes an entire chapter to the politics of cholera. See *Egypt's Other Wars*, 140–59.

annual date fair. Also billeted there in 1947 were 6,000 workers from the British airfield. Their panicked departure helped spread cholera before any local controls could be enforced. Merchants who scattered from the date fair also contributed to the diffusion. Cholera reached Cairo in late September, then continued on to Ismailia, before reaching all the remaining provinces of Lower Egypt. By October, cholera gained entry into Upper Egypt, though its impact there was mild. After the end of October, the epidemic waned and the last cases appeared in December 1947. Over three months, cholera caused roughly 35,000 cases and about 20,000 deaths, numbers reminiscent of nineteenth-century outbreaks.[40] This terrible CFR of more than 57 percent made it arguably the worst outbreak of the entire Sixth Pandemic. Apart from the possible link to Syria, Egypt's cholera did not spread to neighbors in North Africa, the Indian Ocean, or sub-Saharan Africa. These regions remained free of cholera during the entire Sixth Pandemic, as did most of Europe and the Americas.

The 1947 outbreak was clearly unexpected, yet Egyptian public health authorities reacted swiftly. The ministry of health quickly diagnosed the outbreak as cholera and mounted a cordon in an unsuccessful effort to contain the disease within the Nile Delta. Given that al-Qurayn housed so many temporary visitors to the date fair, people resorted to various means to break the cordon. One involved hiring of smugglers to help people negotiate the fields after dark, swim the Ismailia canal, or hide in car trunks.[41]

The ministry's good intentions to provide treatment for patients and quarantine facilities for contacts were not matched by efficient practices. The rural locations were often makeshift, little more than army tents; badly overcrowded and unsanitary, the locations were guarded by police who often used force in futile efforts to prevent escape from the isolation centers. Villagers were terrified of the medical isolation teams. As panic rose, people turned to concealment of cases to avoid internment. One family even disposed of a dead body down a well. Perhaps the most notorious case was that of a cabbage seller who wheeled his cart into Cairo and was found to have been concealing two men who had died of cholera. The cabbage seller became part of a satirical cartoon directed against prominent government personalities.[42]

[40] Gallagher, *Egypt's Other Wars*, 136.
[41] Gallagher, *Egypt's Other Wars*, 117–18.
[42] Gallagher, *Egypt's Other Wars*, 122.

The 1947 cholera outbreak has become a part of popular collective memory. The novelist Andrée Chedid discusses the cholera outbreak in *The Sixth Day*, which was later adapted into a movie by Yusuf Chahine, an Egyptian film producer.[43] Chedid captures the attitudes of many people in the delta toward the isolation camps. In the following long passage, she uses the voice of the nephew, who is describing to his elderly aunt what had happened in her village, to which she had returned from Cairo on learning of outbreak:

I found out in the end where they had taken my father and brother: under tents, right out in the desert. I've been there. At first they chased us away with sticks, my mother and me, but we returned shouting out the names of our people, so they should know we hadn't deserted them, that we were near them. In the end I crept into one of the tents. It was horrible! The same face everywhere: blue, hollow, the tongue hanging out. The patients lie one beside the other in the sand, vomiting; two of them were already dead and left lying there. I called again, they all looked at me in a dazed way. A nurse came in wearing boots and a mask, he pushed me outside – before I could find my people. No one who hasn't lived through all this knows anything about it. Never shall I forget – Since then we've hidden our sick and even our dead![44]

Memories of the 1947 epidemic are not confined to novels or cinema. The outbreak generated considerable popular resistance as well as social and political mobilization.[45] Inhabitants of the Mediterranean town of al-Rashid (Rosetta) stoned ambulances taking suspected cholera patients to hospital. Near Alexandria, a thousand inmates of an isolation camp tried to break out and stoned police guards. The Muslim Brotherhood volunteered to distribute flyers printed by the ministry of health, to interpret them locally, and to help in cordoning infected areas. Members of Young Egypt, a nationalist political movement formed in the 1930s, organized committees to fight cholera and accused the British of having helped cause the epidemic. The *Wafd*, Egypt's leading opposition party, chastised the ministry of health for its secretive policies and for its failure to contain the epidemic, but its youth wing also helped during the national crisis.

The Egyptian government did accept international offers of assistance. The United States was asked to supply anticholera vaccines and eventually produced enough vaccine for six million people. Under the direction

[43] *The Sixth Day* (London: A. Blond, 1962), in Gallagher, *Egypt's Other Wars*, 122.
[44] In Gallagher, *Egypt's Other Wars*, 122–3.
[45] Gallagher, *Egypt's Other Wars*, 124–8.

of the newly formed WHO, laboratories in Bombay rushed in vaccine, the Soviet Union donated a million units, and Turkey donated half a million. Many countries volunteered to send medical missions and supplies. The ministry of health had to sort out this wide sampling of unproven vaccines. In a later study, Kamal found that the vaccine program had done more harm than good, not only because cholera spread too rapidly to be controlled in this manner, but also because syringes were not always sterilized and cases of hepatitis resulted.[46]

In an article published in 1948, Kamal provided a much more positive picture of Egypt's experience during its cholera emergency in 1947.[47] His argument was that a self-governing Egypt, proud of its expanding public health system, was able to inject cultural sensitivity into its approach to the epidemic. New technology now facilitated surveillance procedures. Mayors of rural villages possessing telephones communicated news of the outbreak, enabling the national health service to bring in medical workers quickly. Control of travel through the dispensing of written permits by health officials kept Upper Egypt from suffering huge losses through cholera's diffusion. Although this isolation measure hurt the national economy, it kept the two parts of Egypt separated completely for six to ten days.[48] Second, bowing in the direction of recovering patients who were still infectious, medical workers showed discretion in isolating large numbers of contacts and keeping them confined for stretches of two weeks or more. Space constraints and the difficulties of feeding large numbers led medical workers to discharge patients between the twelfth and fourteenth days of confinement, based on three successive negative rectal swabs. Although it was sometimes true that some patients still excreted cholera vibrios as late as the fifteenth day, it was difficult or impossible to keep them isolated that long when they objected that they had clinically recovered. As it happened, according to Kamal, this policy did not lead to any recurring cases in their households, though it did earn much goodwill and cooperation among the public. In another example of cultural sensitivity, health officials provided the dead with religiously proper ablution and burial in the presence of some relatives.

[46] Gallagher, *Egypt's Other Wars*, 137.
[47] A.M. Kamal, "Cholera in Egypt," *Journal of the Egyptian Public Health Association*, 3 (1948), 184–90.
[48] Kamal, "Cholera in Egypt," 186.

CONCLUSION TO PART ONE

The Egyptian cholera of 1947 was one of the few medical emergencies during the sixth cholera pandemic. Although new technology had been a permissive factor in expanding the pandemic reach of cholera from 1817 onward, by the end of the century scientific advances had also contributed to the disease's retreat. Despite deprivation and displacement brought on by warfare and overcrowded urban living conditions, international public health officials, after several false starts, had made significant gains in the prevention and control of cholera. Sanitarian concern for cleanliness led to the emphasis on clean drinking water, and to filtration and chlorination of urban water supplies. Recognition of *Vibrio cholerae* as the disease's causal agent spurred on efforts at surveillance, the quest for an effective vaccine, and scientifically based rehydration therapy. In the most industrialized societies, moreover, cholera's retreat became a virtual disappearance as a result of improvements in standards of living that included welfare-state reforms in housing, public health, and nutrition.

Not all peoples shared in this happy change in fortune. In densely populated China and India, the sixth cholera pandemic did exact its customary heavy toll. Civil war and Japan's invasion displaced millions of Chinese civilians and exposed them to death from cholera and other diseases. In India, endemic cholera did decline, but more slowly than it would have if the British Raj had shown less reluctance to intervene actively.

Egypt of 1947 again excepted, the African continent was spared the Sixth Pandemic. Almost entirely under direct European colonial rule, Africans benefited indirectly from advances in global public health. Colonial authorities developed improved infrastructure in their new or newly expanded capital cities. Dedicated sewage disposal lines were kept separate from piped drinking water in the city centers where colonial officials and their families lived. African elites serving in the colonial economy were also beneficiaries, and the poorer African settlements were not yet so crowded and bereft of clean water as to expose them to severe risks of cholera.

One consequence was the death of the popular assumption that Africans were more susceptible to cholera than whites, either racially or culturally. When Africans suffered more heavily from cholera than Europeans in the French colonial capital of Saint-Louis du Sénégal during the 1893 cholera outbreak, Roman Catholic missionaries attempted to explain the discrepancy by invoking the superior protection their faith gave them as opposed to Senegalese Muslims. But better-off Europeans and Creoles of Saint-Louis, most of whom were Christian, lived in superior housing and drank from a recently modernized municipal water system, amenities not available to the poorer Muslim majority.

Similar arguments were made about the greater susceptibility of people of African descent during the terrible cholera epidemic that struck Brazil in 1855 and 1856.[49] In this catastrophe, Brazil lost somewhere between 160,000 and 200,000 victims to cholera in a population of almost 8 million. Some estimates suggested that African deaths outnumbered European deaths by more than two to one. Though the statistics are unreliable because of the ambiguous racial categories, in Brazil as elsewhere, cholera came down hardest on the poor, and this meant people of color, whether of African or Amerindian descent.[50]

Over the course of the six pandemics, it cannot be said that Africa experienced more devastating, and certainly not more frequent, visitations than other parts of the world. Kenneth Kiple challenges the assumptions raised by the Third Pandemic's devastating impact on people of African ancestry in the United States, the Caribbean, and Brazil. Their truly appalling fatality rates led to the facile belief, nurtured by emerging Social Darwinist notions, that nonwhites, and especially Africans, had less physical capacity to withstand cholera than did whites.[51] Kiple carefully lists the elements placing Africans at a tremendous environmental disadvantage in the New World. Living in crowded and filthy conditions with uncertain water supplies, Africans, whether still slave or recently freed, were far more exposed to cholera infection. Kiple adds that they often lived along waterfronts where cholera cases would first appear, and that their poor nutrition could have depleted the stomach acids that can protect against severe infection. Almost a century earlier, Dr. James Christie, to his credit, explained alarming slave and free African cholera deaths in Zanzibar by emphasizing environmental factors, rather than explanations based on race.

When Pollitzer completed his excellent compendium on cholera in 1959, the Sixth Pandemic had petered out. Many optimistically thought the world was finally free from the global scourge of cholera, but Pollitzer was not so sanguine. Although praising the improvements in accessing

---

[49] Donald Cooper, "The new 'Black Death': Cholera in Brazil, 1855–56," *Social Science History*, 10 (1986), 483.

[50] For more on this subject see Kenneth Kiple, "Cholera and Race in the Caribbean," *Journal of Latin American Studies*, 17 (1985), 157–7.

[51] Kiple, "Cholera and Race," 157–7.

potable water, especially in the West, he continued to fear that "the uncontrolled movement of large population groups" from endemic to cholera-free areas could still trigger a new surge.[52] Expert though he was, he could not anticipate the global changes that would make *Vibrio cholerae* a highly adaptive and serious reemerging pathogen, and a grave concern for global public health in general and for Africa in particular. Africa's unhappy experience during the new seventh cholera pandemic forms the theme of Part Two.

---

[52] Pollitzer, *Cholera*, 980.

PART TWO

THE SEVENTH PANDEMIC

Introduction: Cholera Changes Its Face

The Seventh Pandemic was different from the first six in several respects. Its agent was a new biotype of the cholera pathogen, *Vibrio cholerae o1* El Tor. Evolutionary biology suggests why El Tor was able to replace the more virulent classic cholera.[1] Natural selection favored the more benign El Tor; although classic cholera killed its victims more quickly, it lost opportunities to infect more potential hosts. Patients with milder El Tor, less severely ill, were more mobile and could infect others at greater distance and over a longer period of time. Classic cholera in the earlier pandemics traveled from country to country and moved only as quickly as available transport permitted, but the Seventh Pandemic leap-frogged continents by air and benefited from faster ships, trains, and automobiles.[2] It also lasted longer than any of the earlier pandemics. After forty-eight years it shows no sign of abating today.

The diminished impact of the sixth cholera pandemic led many experts to believe that the world was seeing the last of this terrible calamity. Europe's last case dated back to the 1920s, and Mecca's to 1912. Regular reports of cholera did surface from time to time in its traditional home in South Asia, but pandemics seemed to have disappeared.

Researchers first labeled the new biotype (*Vibrio cholerae o1* El Tor) "paracholera" because it was initially confined not to cholera's original home in the Ganges Delta, but, from its first appearance in 1937 through to 1960, to Indonesia. The name indicated that researchers did not regard

---

[1] Randolph M. Nesse and George C. Williams, "Evolution and the origins of disease," *Scientific American* (November, 1998), 86–93.
[2] Lee, "The global dimensions," 9–10.

El Tor as "true" cholera capable of unleashing a global pandemic.[3] Suddenly, in January of 1961, El Tor began to spread from its starting point around Makassar on the major island of Sulawesi, Indonesia to launch what soon became known as the seventh cholera pandemic. What caused the new biotype to become a global threat is not clear. A local military rebellion probably helped in spreading the new cholera variant as increased troop movement drove many civilians into crowded urban areas.[4]

Once cholera left Makassar, it moved first to the central and northern parts of Sulawesi, and then to the neighboring island of Java and the rest of the Indonesian archipelago. By August 1961, cholera crossed international boundaries to southern China, reaching Macao and Hong Kong, and then moving to the Philippines and other Southeast Asian locales. Making its way slowly, El Tor only reached India in 1964; over the rest of the decade, it followed a familiar nineteenth-century route to western Asia. By 1966, it was present on the borders of the Asian republics of the Soviet Union. Exhibiting an erratic rhythm, cholera slowed its expansion in 1967 and 1968 to the point that the WHO recorded the lowest incidence since it began the present system of notification.[5] In 1969, however, cholera became more widespread, striking Laos for the first time. The first global phase really began in earnest in 1970 when cholera El Tor reached throughout the Middle East, struck the Soviet Black Sea ports of Odessa and Kerch, and hit Africa hard beginning with Guinea in West Africa. At this stage, the new wave of cholera spared the Americas and most of Europe, though it did infect such old haunts of southern Europe as Lisbon, Barcelona, and Naples, allegedly carried from North Africa by seasonal workers and tourists. One disappointed cholera expert lamented that cholera was no longer in global decline, but that with the African explosion and the invasion of Europe, cholera now "dominated the world's health problems."[6] He was particularly alarmed at its increased endemicity, although his concern seemed an exaggeration.

---

[3] For the early years of the Seventh Pandemic, see A. M. Kamal, "The Seventh Pandemic of Cholera," in Dhiman Barua and William Burrows, eds., *Cholera* (Philadelphia: W.B. Saunders, 1974), 1–14. In 1974, Dr. Kamal was Professor Emeritus of Epidemiology and former Director of the High Institute of Public Health, Alexandria, as well as a former Under-Secretary of State in the Egyptian Ministry of Health.

[4] Herbert Feith and Daniel S. Lev, "The end of the Indonesian rebellion," *Pacific Affairs*, 36 (1963), 32–46.

[5] *WER* 44 (1969), 461–8. The *WER* of the WHO published world cholera statistics every summer as part of its annual review of the disease. Unless otherwise stated, cholera statistics for the Seventh Pandemic come from these various annual reports.

[6] D. Barua, "The global epidemiology of cholera in recent years," *Proceedings of the Royal Society of Medicine*, 65 (1972), 423.

For most international public health specialists, the first wave of the Seventh Pandemic in Asia aroused concern but not panic. In 1961, statistics compiled by the WHO under International Health Regulations, which made reporting of national cholera cases mandatory, showed that there had been 12,197 cases and 1,969 deaths (an elevated CFR of 16.1 percent); in the following year, Asian countries reported a slight increase in cases to 13,393, but a drop in the CFR to 14.8 percent. What was an orderly reporting of cases became subject to panic by 1966, when countries started to report national cases erratically; they unilaterally turned to discredited nineteenth-century measures, including the disinfection of mail and printed matter and the prohibition of imports of such diverse products as canned fruit, iron beams, carpets, teak, and mineral ore. Some countries took ill-advised but expensive measures to demonstrate their alleged sophistication in public health matters. Iran vaccinated its entire population as a preventive in the 1960s, and the Sudan did likewise beginning in 1970, despite WHO advice that this was both a costly and ineffective procedure.

After the first wave of the Seventh Pandemic of the 1960s, cholera's original heartland of Asia did not suffer greatly, although endemic zones persisted in Bangladesh, India, and Indonesia. Considering the size of their populations, none of these three experienced major outbreaks. A mild appearance of cholera at the Muslim holy site of Mecca in 1974 aroused concern from health authorities with historical memories of how pilgrims involuntarily helped spread the disease in the nineteenth century. Fortunately, only a few cases were diagnosed among the one million Meccan pilgrims, and the disease was not disseminated from there as in the past.

As for Europe, its generally mild experience with the Seventh Pandemic did not apply uniformly. A cholera outbreak in Lisbon in 1974 coincided with the political revolution that toppled a long-lasting and oppressive dictatorship; the disease spread from the Portuguese capital to engulf the entire country. In the early 1990s, Russia, Romania, and a few other former Eastern-bloc countries saw cholera's return as part of a general breakdown in public health surveillance and control. Meanwhile, the Americas remained untouched by the Seventh Pandemic until the disease exploded in 1991, beginning with Peru and creating a public health shock from which Central and South American countries were only recovering at the turn of the twenty-first century.

For Africa, the Seventh Pandemic proved to be especially devastating. Chapter 6 provides an overview of its impact on Africa and indicates the various risk factors at play. Subsequent chapters provide case studies: Chapter 7 shows how environment and geography was one set, and armed conflicts and the dispersal of refugees were another; Chapter 8 treats public health choices among stable and weak states. Chapter 9 highlights the current cholera epidemic in Zimbabwe, a quintessential failed state. The conclusion in Chapter 10 offers perspectives on cholera's future. We now turn to Chapter 5 to examine the major medical changes in cholera research.

5

Medical Changes

The cholera pathogen has changed in the past thirty years and so has scientific research on the subject.[1] Indeed, the standard text on cholera now describes its poison as "one of the best understood of all bacterial toxins."[2] Two Indian scientists working at the Medical College of Calcutta in the late 1950s led the way in this breakthrough in the chemistry of cholera. S.N. De and P.K. Dutta were the first to demonstrate how cholera toxins did their damage. Water and salts pass freely through the intestinal wall into the gut to keep fecal matter in the bowels moist. The cholera toxin destroys this smooth process by causing overproduction of enzymes and, in effect, flooding the large intestine, draining chloride and bicarbonate ions. Cells worst affected are those in the nerves lining the gut. Loss of salts also causes convulsions in the muscles of the abdomen and legs.[3]

A better grasp of how the cholera toxin worked was only one breakthrough. A series of new understandings involved the kinds of strains of the cholera vibrio in the environment, and how cholera survived outside the human body.

---

[1] This is made clear in the most recent medical text written by an impressive international team of experts from Bangladesh, India, the United States, and the WHO in Geneva. See Dhiman Barua, and William B. Greenough III, eds., *Cholera* (New York: Plenum, 1992). The book comes thirty years after Robert Pollitzer's *Cholera*, and seventeen years after the multiauthored volume with the same title edited by Dhiman Barua and William Burrows.

[2] Barua and Greenough III, *Cholera*, xi.

[3] Christopher Wills, *Plagues: Their Origin, History and Future* (New York: Harper Collins, 1996), 118.

Scientists recognize the existence of several strains of *Vibrio cholerae* with a similar effect. As we have seen, the so-called classic *Vibrio cholerae*, possibly responsible for all six of the earlier pandemics, gave way to *Vibrio cholerae 01* El Tor during the Seventh Pandemic. The early 1990s witnessed not only the accelerated spread of El Tor, but also the emergence of a new strain of toxigenic cholera called *Vibrio cholerae 0139*, or "Bengal" serotype.

Some called this new strain the potential beginnings of an eighth cholera pandemic. The first reports on *0139* were from Madras, India in October 1992, but its origins probably were in the *chars*, the temporary islands off the coast of the Sundarbans area in the southwestern coastal districts of Bangladesh.[4] Most of these islands emerge only at the end of the monsoon, and migrant fishers arrive in October to fish in the Bay of Bengal. It is not an accident that the Bay of Bengal has facilitated the emergence of various strains of cholera over time. It receives the waters of five major rivers of the Indian subcontinent, each carrying large amounts of agricultural and industrial waste. Brackish water extends some distance up-river for all these water systems. One of the new hypotheses is that humans created "hot systems" in which mutations of *Vibrio cholerae* were selected and amplified through new environmental pressures. A second hypothesis maintains that a natural climate cycle involving the El Niño Southern Oscillation, or ENSO, triggered the change.

The *chars* are remote, and communication with the mainland is limited, so the new strain went unnoticed until it struck humans in December 1992. The first *0139* Bengal epidemic lasted more than four months, with 46,965 cases and 846 deaths (a CFR of 1.8 percent) in the six southern districts of Bangladesh. In September 1993, three months after its decline in the southern areas, *Vibrio cholerae 0139* moved to the northern part of the country. In January 1993, it completely replaced *Vibrio cholerae 01* across the border in Calcutta, and an epidemic in India followed from March to May 1993. Over the next ten years, however, *0139* spread only within Asia, appearing in China, Pakistan, Nepal, and Malaysia, as well as in Bangladesh and India, where it accounts for roughly 15 percent of the laboratory-confirmed cholera cases.[5] Only in India was this new

---

[4] Rita R. Colwell, "Global climate and infectious disease: the cholera paradigm," *Science*, 274 (1996), 2026.
[5] *WER*, 78 (2003), 273.

strain persistent most years; elsewhere it was sporadic. Its behavior was no different from *Vibrio cholerae o1*. Populations in the affected regions possessed no immunity to the new serogroup, and so the proportion of adults among the cholera cases is abnormally high, although the CFRs are low.

Noting that this was the first non-*o1* serogroup to produce epidemic cholera, the WHO stated that the toxin it produced was identical to that of *Vibrio cholerae o1*, and the clinical disease should be considered the same one. Monitoring it carefully month by month, the WHO stated in 2003 that "[n]o evidence is currently available to show whether or not this strain could become a new threat."[6] Yet an alarmist view can be found in the literature. Paul Epstein, who is otherwise careful in his judgments, exaggerates the danger and erroneously states that by 1996, *o139* Bengal had reasserted its dominance over El Tor, and threatened "to become the agent of the world's Eighth Cholera Pandemic."[7]

For almost a century, it was scientific dogma that the only reservoir of cholera was in the human intestinal tract. Highly host-adapted, the *Vibrio cholerae o1* was believed incapable of surviving longer than a few hours or days outside the human intestine. Yet even if this position dominated the literature since Koch's day, the pioneering bacteriologist was less convinced. His prescience led him to speculate that it was ultimately a question of whether the bacteria could find nutrition elsewhere in nature. His observations were not followed up by researchers for more than seventy years, for he had remarked:

There remains still the important question to be answered, whether the infectious material can reproduce or multiply itself outside the human body. I believe it can ... I would not certainly assume that multiplication ... takes place ... in river water without any assistance, for these fluids do not possess the concentration of nutritious substances which is necessary for the growth of the bacilli. But I can easily imagine that ... some spots may contain sufficient concentrations of nutritive substances [for bacilli to flourish].[8]

The leading scholar investigating the ecological aspects of new cholera studies has been Rita Colwell, who conducted seminal research in the

---

[6] WER, 78 (2003), 273.

[7] Paul R. Epstein, "Climate, Ecology and Human Health," in Andrew T., Price-Smith, ed., *Plagues and Politics: Infectious Disease and International Policy* (New York: Palgrave, 2001), 43.

[8] In Rita R. Colwell and William M. Spira, "The Ecology of Vibrio Cholerae," in Barua and Greenough III, *Cholera*, 107.

Bay of Bengal, and later in Chesapeake Bay.[9] Associated initially with
the Centre for Diarrhoeal Disease Research in Dhaka, Bangladesh, where
she eventually became its chair, and currently attached to the Maryland
Biotechnology Institute at College Park, Maryland, Colwell has made
outstanding contributions to scientific knowledge of cholera.

It was long asserted that *V. cholerae 01* was taxonomically separate
from *V. cholerae non-01*, the so-called non-agglutinable vibrios found in
aquatic environments. Using DNA and DNA hybridization, Colwell and
her associates demonstrated that these two vibrios were a single species,
and that there was only one chromosome missing in the harmless cholera
strains, which prevented them from producing toxins.[10]

Colwell and her associates helped answer questions about the cholera
vibrio's survival in an aquatic milieu. They found that toxigenic *V. cholerae 01* El Tor acquired the ability to shrink to the size of a large virus as
a hibernating organism in water or inside algae. These bacteria adapted
well to the brackish water of estuaries, attaching to shells of shrimps and
in the guts of clams, mussels, and oysters, and were able to survive long
periods of starvation by moving into dormancy.

This new work changed the focus and the locale of cholera research
entirely, because these dormant forms cannot be recovered on bacteriological material routinely used in cholera microbiology laboratories. In
nature, *Vibrio cholerae 01* is subject to ultraviolet rays via sunlight, as
well as to variations in oxygen tension, making study in laboratories
difficult. Colwell and her associates found that in the natural environment, they were forced to use techniques of microscopy, allowing for very
limited recovery from nonaquatic environments. For example, cultural
organisms were rarely found after five to seven days under any conditions
of storage.

Survival on dry surfaces is very short, a matter of hours, and *Vibrio
cholerae 01* is therefore extremely sensitive to desiccation. It was found
that moister soil, by adding uncontaminated sewage, kept cholera alive
up to ten days.[11] This new research has been facilitated by technological
advances over older culture methods. New microscopy equipment permits direct detection of even minute samples of cholera, as few as one or
two cells of *Vibrio cholerae* per liter of water.

[9] See especially Colwell and Spira, "The ecology," 107–27. Spira later moved to the
   Department of International Health, in the School of Hygiene and Public Health, Johns
   Hopkins University.
[10] Wills, *Plagues*, 122.
[11] Colwell and Spira, "The Ecology," 110.

Cholera's ability, enhanced in saline waters, to enter into dormancy as a response to nutrient deprivation, elevated salinity, or reduced temperatures, is in fact a common strategy of bacteria in nutrient-poor environments. The adaption mechanism involves the production of dwarfed cells, which are not an anomaly in aquatic environments. *V.cholerae 01* is able to shrink to 300 times less than its usual size in order to require less nutrition.

The researchers also investigated the microflora that served as cholera's nutrients in its aquatic environment. They determined key variables to be temperature and salinity, adherence to surfaces, and colonization of macrobiota with semitransparent exoskeletons, zooplankton blooms, and copepods. Copepods, which have the diameter of a sewing thread, resemble miniature shrimps. The implications for the spread of cholera are enormous. Cholera vibrios are able to survive in association with such common aquatic vegetation as water hyacinths and the blue-green bacterium *Anabaena*, as well as other zooplankton and shellfish in the aquatic environment. Cholera outbreaks therefore lack a common source and have a broad distribution as a result of tidal ebb and flow and seasonal flooding. As ocean currents sweep coastal areas they are able to transport plankton and their bacterial passengers.[12]

Human agency helps significantly in this proliferation of oceanic algae blooms. The major environmental conditions are the destruction of wetlands, poor erosion control, excessive use of fertilizers, and coastal sewage dumping.[13] The "red" tides from oxygen-rich blooms or the "brown" tides from oxygen-poor ones, can ruin beaches and devastate shoreline birds and their habitats.[14] This process of climate change and its impact on plankton and algae, and on cholera, was clearly operative as a result of ENSO's role in bringing cholera to the Peruvian coast in late 1990, and it was so recognized at the time.[15]

Finally, this new ecologically focused research approach was able to show that climate change represented a greater danger for humans than sanitation issues. A single copepod can carry millions of cells of *Vibrio cholerae*, so there is enough for clinical cholera to occur in humans.

[12] As early as 1992, Paul Epstein sounded this alarm with reference to cholera. See Paul Epstein, "Cholera and the environment," *Lancet*, 339 (1992), 1167–8.
[13] J. Patz, P. Epstein, T. Burke, and J.Balbus-Kornfeld, "Global climate change and emerging infectious diseases," *Journal of the American Medical Association*, 275 (1996), 220.
[14] Epstein, "Climate, Ecology," 32.
[15] N.L. Tamplin and C.C. Parodi, "Environmental spread of *Vibrio cholerae* in Peru," *Lancet*, 338 (1991), 1216–17.

During a plankton bloom, several copepods may be ingested in a glass of untreated water. Chances of consumption increase during periods when copepod concentration in water is high, that is, in times of plankton blooms.

The explosion of cholera in Peru beginning in January 1991 provides an example of how ecology can trump human agency. In Peru during the Seventh Pandemic, it was not the dumping of bilge water by a ship from Bangladesh or China, but a climatic phenomenon that triggered the major cholera outbreak in the Americas.[16] In an example of thoroughness, Peruvian researchers checked the harbor master's logs for Chimbote and found that only two ships had arrived from East Asia, both from Hong Kong, and that no antitoxin antibodies were found in blood samples collected from the crews.[17] The ENSO event of 1990–1991 brought warmer waters to the Peruvian coast and, coupled with plankton blooms driven by El Niño rains, may have helped amplify the population of *Vibrio cholerae* already present by decreasing salinity. ENSO and warm temperatures in 1997 and 1998 saw a cholera upsurge again in Peru. The strong rains associated with this same phenomenon also led to outbreaks of Japanese encephalitis in Vietnam, Malaysia, Nepal, Papua, New Guinea, and in Australia's Cape York region. Similarly, in Bangladesh, ENSO in the period from 1980 to 1998 correlated with a rise in cholera cases.[18] Researchers recognize the longer term global implications of the ENSO phenomenon. Over the past twenty-five years along the East Coast of the United States, an increase in marine-related illnesses has correlated with ENSO events, the most recent of which was the strong El Niño winter of 1997–1998.[19]

The implications of climate change for cholera's diffusion are serious. Cholera remains a summer disease because colder temperatures bring about dormancy of the bacteria. An increase in global temperatures would be welcome news for *Vibrio cholerae*. So too would be rising sea levels, which would change the balance between fresh and salt water in

---

[16] Colwell, "Global climate," 2027.

[17] Rosa R. Mouriño-Pérez, "Oceanography and the seventh cholera pandemic," *Epidemiology*, 9 (1998), 355–7.

[18] Colwell, "Global climate," 2025; Mercedes Pascual et al., "Cholera dynamics and El Niño-Southern Oscillation," *Science*, 289 (2000), 1766–9, who show that ENSO is related to the melting of the snow pack in the Himalayas, which triggers a weather sequence involving the monsoons.

[19] Jonathan A. Patz et al., "The Potential Health Impacts of Climate Variability and Change for the United States: Executive Summary of the Report on the Health Sector of the U.S. National Assessment," *Environmental Health Perspectives*, 108 (2000), 367–76.

estuarine environments of cholera-prone regions of the Bay of Bengal, Indonesia, Thailand, Egypt, Nigeria, and Mozambique. Flooding with salt water would also produce conditions favorable to the longevity of *Vibrio cholerae* in more inland lagoons in these regions.[20]

For a very long time, cholera diffusion was believed to be dependent on humans. As late as 1974, WHO Deputy Director-General Pierre Dorolle observed: "[It was] not through water – or for that matter through food-stuffs – that cholera is transmitted on an international scale. It is spread by those who have it, particularly in the benign form, and by healthy carriers."[21] Cholera and its diffusion are much more complex issues than was once assumed. Dorolle's focus on human carriers, whether asymptomatic or suffering from acute cholera infection, no longer sufficiently accounts for cholera's diverse means of spreading. Nor are *Vibrio cholerae* fragile bacteria capable of living only a few hours without a human host. On the contrary, the bacteria are marine organisms with permanent niches all over the world, whether in warm estuarine and coastal water along the Pacific, Atlantic, and Gulf coasts of the United States, or in Australia, the island nations of the South Pacific, Africa, Southeast Asia, and throughout Europe. The bacteria are even present in the interior lakes of Africa, at first glance believed inhospitable to marine organisms.[22] Cholera endemicity is currently widespread in Bangladesh, in Africa, and in Central and South America.[23]

Efforts to apply the lessons that follow from cholera's epidemiology in order to control its ravages remain frustrating. Public health measures until recently have reflected older nineteenth-century approaches, and have been slow to adapt to the newly emerging understandings of the disease. Largely unsuccessful measures have included quarantine of goods and travelers from infected places and vaccination, although the provision of safe drinking water and the proper disposal of human waste are older but still valuable approaches. Education and attention to personal hygiene are newer steps, but, though useful, cannot stop cholera's spread.

[20] Andrew Collins, "The Geography of cholera", in B.S. Drasar, and B.D. Forrest, eds., *Cholera and the Ecology of Vibrio cholerae* (London: Chapman & Hall, 1996), 267–8.
[21] Pierre Dorolle, "International Surveillance of Cholera," in Dhiman Barua and William Burrows, eds., *Cholera* (Philadelphia: W.B. Saunders, 1974), 428.
[22] Roger Glass and Robert Black, "The Epidemiology of Cholera," in Barua and Greenough III, eds., *Cholera*, 130, 138.
[23] A. Huq et al., "Detection of *Vibrio cholerae* o1 in the aquatic environment by fluorescent-monoclonal antibody and culture methods," *Applied and Environmental Microbiology*, 56 (1990), 2370–3.

Nineteenth-century governments targeted travelers and merchants moving from Asia to Europe. Later, an expanding set of International Health Regulations stressed quarantine services to prevent disembarkation of cargoes and individuals in ports. Quarantine measures may have slowed the disease, but they caused much inconvenience and economic loss, and were especially ineffective against mild cases and those asymptomatically infected. Recent evidence has shown, in fact, that cholera cases among travelers have become rare, on average one case per 500,000. They are less likely to occur because of the low risk of exposure to vibrios locally than through protection from vaccination, antibiotics, or personal hygienic practices.[24]

Modern techniques to prevent or contain cholera have involved water purification, oral rehydration therapy (ORT), prescription of antibiotics, and the employment of oral cholera vaccines (OCVs). Each of these four approaches is discussed in turn.

Cholera is a water-borne disease and efforts to understand and control it have turned on this obvious relationship between the vibrio and water. Several natural events can transform water into a danger. Floods can cause an overflow of waste-water treatment plants, failure of septic systems, or combined sewer overflows that contaminate surface waters or wells. During droughts, contaminants may be concentrated in available water sources, and multiple use for cleaning and bathing and drinking does occur.

Even more fundamental is the role played by water temperature, a major variable in determining the ability of pathogenic cholera bacteria to survive. The organisms require several consecutive weeks in which the water temperature ranges between ten and thirty degrees Celsius. This is, of course, a very broad range and found in many waters globally. The second variable, however, serves to limit cholera's possibilities dramatically. Those species that are pathogenic to humans require salinity between 5 and 30 percent. Oceans are too saline, and most fresh water bodies insufficiently so, but inland coastal areas and estuaries are ideal. A third variable is the presence of organic nutrients such as algae. A high concentration can compensate for the lack of elevated concentrations of salt.

Nutrients and the role of food handlers are additional epidemiological factors, as we have seen. Research has indicated that *Vibrio cholerae o1*

---

[24] Only six American travelers visiting South America in 1991 developed cholera, all contracted from high risks associated with unboiled water. David L. Swerdlow, M.D. Allen, and A. Ries, "Cholera in the Americas: Guidelines for the clinician," *Journal of the American Medical Association*, 267 (1992), 1498.

can survive in a variety of food for up to five days at ambient temperature, and up to ten days within a range of five to ten degrees Celsius. The pathogen can also survive freezing, but low temperatures usually have prevented a level of contamination sufficient to produce an infective dose in humans. In fact, the number of cholera cases produced by infected food is minute when compared with polluted water.

Awareness of the fundamental role of drinking water in cholera transmission has led to greater emphasis on filtration as a control measure in recent years. In the past, prevention concentrated on large filtration projects, combined with chlorination of municipal water supplies. Recently, public health has stressed simpler, low-tech filtering. In Brazil, Mexico, India, and Bangladesh, filtering by means of domestic sari cloth has reduced by as much as 50 percent the number of cholera vibrios in the raw water of ponds and rivers commonly used for drinking.[25] Another simple protection has been the introduction in South Asia of closed-mouth water jugs, or *sorai*, to counteract contaminated household water.

In Africa, lime juice, a common component of food sauces, has long been a traditional remedy or preventative for gastro-intestinal illnesses. The traveler Richard Burton described how Arab and Swahili people in East Africa consumed lime juice and mint, along with lots of coffee, to treat cholera-like diseases.[26] More recently, research in both Guinea and Guinea-Bissau has indicated that lime juice as well as tomato sauce, with their higher acidity, can inhibit transmission of *Vibrio cholerae* in food and water, in contrast to a more neutral peanut-based sauce, also popular in West Africa. A controlled Danish study in Guinea-Bissau during a severe cholera outbreak in 1996 found that lime juice in sauce eaten with rice gave a powerful protective effect, and that lime juice was also helpful when mixed with drinking water. The researchers recommended that the use of lime juice, an inexpensive and common food source, should be further encouraged throughout Africa to prevent or control cholera transmission.[27]

---

[25] A. Huq et al., "Simple water filtration for cholera prevention," *Proceedings of the U.S.-Japan Cholera Meeting. U.S.-Japan Cooperative Medical Science Program*, Tokyo, Japan, 2001, 15.

[26] In Christie, *Cholera*, 84.

[27] For Guinea, see M.E. St.Louis, J.D. Porter, A. Helai, and K. Drame, "Epidemic cholera in West Africa: The role of food handling and high-risk foods," *American Journal of Epidemiology*, 1331 (1990), 719–28. For the studies in Guinea-Bissau sponsored by the Danish Development Research Council, see Amabélla Rodrigues, et al., "Protection from cholera by adding lime juice to food-results from community and laboratory studies in Guinea-Bissau, West Africa," *Tropical Medicine and International Health*, 5 (2000),

Still more dramatic has been the success of oral rehydration therapy. Three leading researchers consider ORT a spectacular boon to the clinical management of cholera:

> [ORT therapy is] one of the most dramatic success stories of modern medical research and its application to a major public health scourge. Using rapid rehydration, a seriously ill patient in profound shock with no detectable pulse or blood pressure is able to sit, talk, and eat within a few hours and can return to work within two or three days.[28]

The history of rehydration therapy has deep roots. From as early as the 1830s, a few prescient physicians saw the desirability of restoring lost liquids to cholera victims even if theirs was a tiny minority opinion. Two German expatriates in Russia in 1830, the chemist Dr. Herman and the physician Jaenichen, were pioneers. Herman observed that the thickening of the blood among cholera patients prevented its circulation and resulted from the evacuation of liquids that cholera produced. Based on this reasoning, Jaenichen infused a saline solution intravenously that was quite similar to the one recommended by the WHO almost 150 years later, and which brought some improvement to his patients. Dr. William O'Shaughnessy in Scotland and Dr. Latta in England developed similar insights during the second cholera pandemic in 1831 and 1832. Latta's success improved when he realized he needed to continue saline treatment throughout the duration of the disease, but the great majority of physicians spurned these practices. In 1849 in the United States, for example, calomel and blood letting remained mainstays of therapy, even though they both clearly increased dehydration, and therefore, mortality.[29]

Not until the twentieth century, and then only slowly, did science develop around the question of how the cholera toxin caused the elimination of such a substantial amount of fluid from its victims. It came to be understood that there occurred a tremendous passage of fluids back and forth through the cells of the gut in a healthy individual. On a daily basis, about seventeen liters of water enter the small intestine, and sixteen liters are absorbed from it, with one liter going to the colon, to pass out in feces or to blood. Normally this absorption and secretion were balanced, but

418–22; and A. Dalsgaard, et al., "Application of lime (*Citrus aurantifolia*) juice to drinking water and food as a cholera-preventive measure," *Journal of Food Protection*, 60 (1997), 1329–33.

[28] Dilip Mahalanabis, A. M. Molla, and David A. Sack, "Clinical Management of Cholera," in Barua and Greenough III, eds, *Cholera*, 253.

[29] Carpenter, "Treatment," 154.

in a cholera patient, secretion in the small bowel increased while absorption diminished because of the action of the cholera toxin. Hydrating the patient merely increased the passage of fluids; a victim could discharge as many as thirty liters of fluid in a day, more than twice the body's weight. But the restoration of salts and glucose through oral therapy halted this process of loss.[30]

A Briton and an American contributed significantly to the development of ORT in the first decade of the twentieth century. Sir Leonard Rogers, using an intravenous hypertonic saline solution and taking aseptic precautions, was able to lower the CFR to 30 percent in Calcutta. In the same period, A.W. Sellards described acidosis in cholera and used alkali replenishment to treat patients in the Philippines.

Not until the 1950s was the physiological principle upon which ORT was ultimately based articulated by scientists. The principle was that glucose enhanced the absorption of sodium in the mammalian gut. But scientists did not immediately consider the implications of this process for patients with acute diarrheal illness. The transfer of this basic insight to the clinical practice of medicine occurred within the next two decades and was a "truly remarkable achievement."[31]

The first steps were taken by U.S. Navy researchers in South Asia. Beginning in 1960, medical teams headed by Commander Robert Allan Phillips, whose career was closely tied to cholera research, worked in Dhaka on rehydration under the Cholera Research Program at the South East Asia Treaty Organization's Laboratory.[32] The period coincided with the new global surge of cholera, the Seventh Pandemic. The Phillips teams in the 1960s measured precise quantities of water and electrolytes lost by cholera patients, and were able to reduce mortality to less than 1 percent through intravenous clinical management of isotonic saline and alkali plus oral water solution. Their key discovery was the importance of glucose. If it were included in the oral solution, it enabled patients to absorb the electrolytes and water effectively. Phillips, however, did not believe that ORT therapy could stand alone without intravenous hydration.

True oral rehydration as the first line of response in cholera emergencies developed incrementally and slowly. In 1953, the Indian physician H.N. Chatterjee experienced some success in Calcutta using an oral

---

[30] W.E. Van Heyningen and John R. Seal, *Cholera: The American scientific experience* (Boulder: Westview Press, 1983), 217.

[31] Barua and Greenough III, *Cholera*, ix.

[32] Van Heyningen and Seal, *Cholera*, 67–8.

glucose-sodium electrolyte solution without intravenous transfusions.[33]
But Chatterjee's procedure was dismissed by the international scientific
community, possibly because he also used exotic Indian plants to halt
vomiting and diarrhea, steps that seemed "too foreign and unscientific."[34]
Thirteen years later, an Iraqi medical resident, Dr. Qais Al-Awqati,
attempted an oral electrolyte solution after having read about ongoing
research in Dhaka and Calcutta. During a six-week cholera emergency
in Baghdad in 1966, Al-Awqati achieved satisfactory results when he
treated the majority of his 500 cholera patients with an imprecisely measured glucose-sodium solution, allowing physicians to reserve intravenous treatment exclusively for patients in shock.

What finally drew ORT to international attention were breakthroughs
by U.S. and South Asian investigators in 1968 and soon after. The two
Americans, Richard Cash and David Nalin, were both twenty-six years
old, residents beginning careers with the U.S Public Health Service, and
assigned to Dhaka by the National Institute for Allergies and Infectious
Disease. At Matlab Bazaar in rural East Pakistan in the fall of 1968,
faced with a limited supply of intravenous liquids during a cholera emergency, Cash and Nalin were forced to improvise with orally administered
salt and glucose rehydration. Their study confirmed that some cholera
patients could be rehydrated with ORT alone, and field staff could be
easily trained to administer ORT.

The most spectacular breakthrough was led by Dilip Mahalanabis
during the Bangladesh War of Independence in 1971. He and his teams
proved that ORT in an emergency could save lives otherwise bound to
be lost.[35] By the end of May, the civil war produced six million refugees
crossing the border to India from East Pakistan. A cholera outbreak in
June with a CFR of 30 percent developed among exhausted, exposed, and
malnourished refugees. With lack of personnel, transport, and supplies of
intravenous liquid, Mahalanabis's only recourse was to administer fluids orally. He organized two teams at Bongaon on the border, where an
estimated 350,000 refugees were camped, joined daily by an influx of at
least 6,000 more. The teams arranged a fifty-mile run from Calcutta by
a shuttle of vehicles transporting prepackaged, inexpensive glucose-salt

---

[33] H.N. Chatterjee, "Control of vomiting in cholera and oral replacement of fluid," Lancet
(1953), 1063.
[34] Ruxin, "Magic bullet," 394.
[35] D. Mahalanabis et al., "Oral fluid therapy of cholera among Bangladesh refugees," The
Johns Hopkins Medical Journal, 132 (1973), 197–205.

packets. The teams treated more than 3,000 in Bongaon hospital during the first three weeks of the outbreak, employing inexperienced personnel who were quickly instructed in procedures. With patients on the floor, and as many as four children or two adults to each bed, the teams were able to lower the CFR to 3.6 percent, gaining local cooperation by calling the oral solution "drinking saline," because saline was already widely known regionally as a curative treatment. The success at Bongaon drew the attention of the WHO and the United Nations Children's Fund, and marked an international watershed for ORT. In the twenty-first century, ORT includes home-administered solutions consisting, for example, of rice-based nourishment in the form of cereal or paste, as well as salt and glucose solutions in water. ORT was, in short, a fine example of how mothers could help their children survive cholera and other acute diarrheal illnesses.

Within less than a decade, ORT, which reduced CFRs from 50 percent or more to 1 percent or less and at very low cost, was hailed as a miraculous achievement. A *Lancet* editorial on August 5, 1978, hailed what it called "the simple cure" as a momentous scientific breakthrough: "The discovery that sodium transport and glucose transport are coupled in the small intestine, so that glucose accelerates absorption of solute and water, was potentially the most important medical advance this century." As techniques and understanding of ORT improved in South Asia, the principles spread elsewhere as well. Peru made excellent use of the technique during its cholera crisis in 1991. Although Peru recorded the stunning total of more than 300,000 cases, public health workers were able to keep the CFR to a remarkably low 0.9 percent. Charles J. Carpenter justifiably labels the Peruvian success "a magnificent example to the rest of the world." He notes, moreover, that the Peruvian medical accomplishment was based on a "simple, inexpensive, but remarkably effective approach to the treatment of this disease."[36]

The WHO has strongly endorsed ORT by means of oral rehydration salts (ORS) packets. One example of these ORS packets is manufactured by Jianas Brothers, a St. Louis, Missouri firm. Each packet contains twenty grams of glucose, three and a half grams of sodium chloride, one and a half grams of potassium chloride, and either two and nine-tenths grams of trisodium citrate, or two and a half grams of sodium bicarbonate. Mixed with one liter of water, these packets are available without

[36] In Barua and Greenough III, *Cholera*, ix.

prescription. Competitors' products have slightly less sodium concentrations, so larger volumes of sodium need to be used.[37]

No treatment is without some risk, of course. Researchers have warned that even ORT can facilitate pathogen transmission when locally prepared rehydration solutions are administered without sufficient attention to disinfection or storage.[38]

Not all clinicians everywhere have been quick to respond to as simple, inexpensive, and effective a protocol as ORT. Charles Carpenter puts it strongly: "... the major obstacle in this disease [cholera] has been the mindless adherence to traditional therapeutic approaches, approaches which were never soundly based on careful or controlled clinical observations."[39] In the United States, especially among pediatricians, it was argued that ORT was a simple and somewhat crude protocol more suited to third-world countries, and because it was less technologically sophisticated than intravenous therapy, it therefore could not be superior. Financial considerations of an expensive curative system were also operative. Intravenous therapy meant keeping a child in hospital overnight and led to maximum insurance reimbursement, as opposed to treating a child with oral rehydration packets and then sending him or her home.[40]

The third approach to cholera treatment, chemoprophylaxis through antibiotics, has not been effective in altering the course of cholera epidemics. Applied orally and usually started after initial rehydration has been completed, antibiotics can reduce patients' diarrhea by 50 percent to an average duration of two days. Antibiotics have also been used as preventatives for family contacts, health workers, and travelers. Antibiotic treatment has been undertaken in severe cases to reduce the duration and severity of both symptoms and the excretion of the vibrio. Nevertheless, evidence of *V. cholerae* o1 El Tor's resistance in Africa and South America to tetracycline, once the drug of choice, together with higher costs that create a false sense of community protection and take resources away from more effective ORT measures, have prompted the WHO to "strongly advise health authorities not to employ this measure."[41]

---

[37] Swerdlow et al, "Cholera in the Americas," 1497.
[38] N.A. Daniels et al., "First do no harm: Making oral rehydration solution safer in a cholera epidemic," *American Journal of Tropical Medicine and Hygiene*, 60 (1999), 1051–5.
[39] Carpenter, "Treatment," 153.
[40] Ruxin, "Magic bullet," 396.
[41] WER, 67 (1992), 260.

Growth of antimicrobial resistance in cholera has been rapid. This has happened first with tetracycline and its replacement, doxycycline; trimethoprimsulfamethoxazole and furazolidone came later but succumbed to the "the relentless progression of antimicrobial resistance."[42] Ciprofloxacin, superbly effective only a decade ago with a single dose, fails 73 percent of time. In 2006, the latest effective antimicrobial agent is a single dose of azithromycin.[43] As Richard Guerrant puts it so well, antibiotics used against cholera are at best "fingers in leaky dikes" that divert the focus from preventive sanitary measures: "However, the most important message is that our reliance on curative antimicrobial agents is misplaced. We must increasingly relearn that no one should lack access to basic clean water and sanitation."[44] Antidiarrheal and antisecretory agents have also been tried for cholera sufferers. These have included kaolin, pectin, activated charcoal, and bismuth subsalicylate, but none of these has proven to be of value.[45]

The fourth approach to clinical management of cholera is the use of oral cholera vaccines. Vaccine therapy for cholera dates back to the bacteriological golden age of Koch and Pasteur, and remains a defining marker of success among older, heroic approaches to infectious disease. Some indication of the quest for a miraculous cholera vaccine can be extrapolated even in current medical writing. For example, as recently as 1998, Michael Oldstone, a prominent American laboratory scientist, paid only cursory attention to socioeconomic foundations of disease, but saw vaccinology as a sure path to medical triumph: "The obliteration of diseases that impinge on our health is a regal yardstick of civilization's success, and those who accomplish that task will be among the true navigators of a brave new world."[46]

Despite the pressure to endorse OCVs, the WHO has been very cautious. The older vaccines were never considered satisfactory for general public health use because of their low protective efficacy, and in 1973 the Twenty-sixth World Health Assembly abolished the requirement in International Health Regulations for a certificate of vaccination against cholera. Three years before that, the U.S. Public Health Service ended the vaccination requirement for persons returning to the United States from

---

[42] Richard L. Guerrant, "Cholera – Still teaching hard lessons," *New England Journal of Medicine*, 354 (2006), 2500.

[43] D. Saha et al., "Single-dose azithromycin for the treatment of cholera in adults," *New England Journal of Medicine*, 354 (2006), 2452–62.

[44] Guerrant, "Cholera – Still teaching," 2501.

[45] Mahalanabis et al., "Clinical Management," 268.

[46] Michael B.A. Oldstone, *Viruses, Plagues, and History* (New York: Oxford University Press, 1998), 192.

cholera-affected areas. Currently, no country officially requires cholera vaccine for visitors.[47]

In the early 1990s, two rival OCVs emerged. The first was an attenuated live oral cholera vaccine developed in Switzerland containing a genetically manipulated *V. cholerae o1* strain, made available in a few countries for travelers, and coded as CVD 103-HgR. Licensed by the Swiss Serum and Vaccine Institute under the name Orochol Berna, this OCV required only a single dose, gave evident protection one week after immunization, and lasted at least three months. Useful against either classical or El Tor cholera biotype and either Inaba or Ogawa serotype, the Swiss product successfully passed trials in a number of countries, including the United States. In 1995, a large-scale trial began in Indonesia to determine its results in a region where cholera had become endemic. Unfortunately, the vaccine did not show convincing protection in a population exposed to cholera a long time after immunization. By 1998, Orochol Berna was licensed in Argentina, Canada, Finland, Peru, the Philippines, and Switzerland, but for several years now, its manufacturer has interrupted production.[48]

The second cholera vaccine, developed first in Sweden under the brand name Cholerix by SBL Vaccine AB, has proved more promising. It is an oral vaccine of killed whole-cell *V. cholerae o1* El Tor in combination with purified recombinant B-subunit of cholera toxin. This killed vaccine (WC/rBS) t has successfully passed trials in Peru, Bangladesh, Colombia, and Sweden, and was also licensed in Norway and Central America. Cholerix, given with a buffer solution and in two doses separated by at least seven days, provided 85 to 90 percent protection for four to six months, with no significant side effects. Its drawbacks were that protection was poorer for children younger than five (disappearing after one year), long-term protection was poorer for O blood-group recipients than others, and it was expensive to purchase. By 1998, its use for travelers was licensed in Argentina, Guatemala, El Salvador, Honduras, Nicaragua, Norway, Peru, and Sweden.

Beginning in 1992, a variant of the killed OCV entered production and testing in Vietnam as an exercise in technology transfer. Its small volume (a single dose was only one and a half milliliters) and lower cost made this OCV easy to deliver and convenient for mass immunization.

---

[47] D.L. Swerdlow and A.A. Ries, "*Vibrio cholerae* non-o1: The eighth pandemic?" *Lancet* 342 (1993), 1498.
[48] WER, 85 (2010), 303.

In 1992 and 1993, a Vietnamese team performed an open-field trial among 22,653 households in the central coastal city of Hue.[49] During a cholera outbreak, they found the number of cases to be 60 percent less among vaccinated families. Protective efficacy for those receiving the two-dose course was 66 percent for all segments of the population sample. The OCV has become licensed for production in Vietnam itself.

In May of 1999, the WHO convened a further meeting of experts on the potential use of OCVs in emergency situations.[50] The panel recommended that the killed Swedish OCV, Cholerix, be maintained in a stock of at least two million doses for use in high-risk populations. The vaccine in this stock needed to be replenished in timely fashion, and potential donors should be approached for financial support to create and maintain the supply. An advisory group within the WHO secretariat would determine case-by-case requests by countries and agencies to use the stock and to interact with manufacturers. The idea was to prevent cholera in populations at risk of an epidemic within six months, but not yet experiencing an epidemic. Often these were refugees and urban slum residents.[51]

As the seventh cholera pandemic spread, OCV trials were extended. In 2001, health authorities in the thinly populated island settings of the Federated States of Micronesia and the Marshall Islands conducted successful mass-vaccination campaigns. Vietnam continued to use its locally manufactured OCV to protect high-risk populations affected by floods in the Mekong Delta. On the Indian Ocean island of Mayotte, the entire population was vaccinated against a potential outbreak that might have spread from the neighboring island of Anjouan.[52] In 2004, another demonstration project for OCVs in an endemic setting took place in Mozambique, where Cholerix was administered in the cholera-endemic city of Beira. Beginning in December 2003, Cholerix was administered to forty-three people diagnosed with cholera during follow-up, and to 172 controls. The results were highly encouraging, with 77 percent protective efficacy. Later that same year, mass-vaccination campaigns with killed OCV took place in Darfur, Sudan, and after the tsunami of early 2005, in Aceh, Indonesia.

The original vaccine transferred to Vietnam was modified to eliminate the recombinant B subunit and thus does not require a buffer. It has

[49] Zosia Kmietowicz, "Oral cholera vaccine raises hopes," *British Medical Journal*, 314 (1997), 323.
[50] *WER*, 75 (2000), 255.
[51] *WER*, 76 (2001), 233–40.
[52] *WER*, 76 (2001), 237–8.

undergone phase II clinical trials successfully and is now licensed as mOr-vac by the National Institute of Hygiene and Epidemiology of Vietnam. A closely related vaccine, called Shanchol, is now produced in India by Shantha Biotechnics.

The WHO, in short, does not see vaccines as "magic bullets." It con-tinues to argue that basic cholera control and relief measures should be maintained. But it does now concede that immunization with either the Vietnamese or Indian vaccine is an important complement wherever chol-era has become endemic as well as in areas at risk for outbreaks.[53]

Researchers who have studied cholera vaccines share the WHO's caution.[54] Thus far, cholera vaccines are expensive, provide only short-term relief while imparting a false sense of security among the public, and are least effective among young children – the very group most at risk from cholera. As Kabir argues, not until the emergence of a single-dose, long-lasting cholera vaccine, effective against all serotypes, will vaccine therapy replace ORT as the treatment of choice.[54]

Fortunately, the medical world has had this effective and inexpen-sive therapy at its disposal since the 1970s. The continuing attraction of ORT, developed by multinational teams in Calcutta and Dhaka, is that it does not even require professionals to administer treatment. Needing only sugar and salt, ingredients available throughout the world, ORT can be administered by immediate family caregivers. In the meantime, a role exists for those tested vaccines that do have short-term value. During terrible cholera emergencies such as those that emerge in refugee camps, these vaccines will save lives.

[53] *WER*, 85 (2010), 303.
[54] Shahjahan Kabir, "Cholera vaccines: The current status and problems," *Reviews in Medical Microbiology*, 16 (2005), 101–16; John Clemens, Dale Spriggs, and David Sack, "Public Health Considerations for the Use of Cholera Vaccines in Cholera Control Programs," in I. Kaye Wachsmuth, Paul A. Blake, and Orjan Olsvik, eds., *Vibrio Cholerae and Cholera: Molecular to Global Perspectives* (Washington: American Society for Microbiology Press, 1994), 425–40.

6

The Seventh Cholera Pandemic in Africa

The seventh cholera pandemic's severe impact on Africa represents a paradox. Why should a disease that had become well understood scientifically, and for which an effective and inexpensive therapy had emerged, have become more widespread and lethal, not less? The answer lies in the increased severity of risk factors, a minority of which stemmed from natural phenomena, and a majority from the deteriorating social, political, and economic conditions most sub-Saharan Africans endured after the mid-1970s.

As indicated in the introduction to this book, the quality and provenance of epidemiological statistics for cholera are colored by political and other considerations. The traditional homeland of cholera, Bangladesh, has as of 2008 not reported annual cholera cases to the WHO.[1] It is impossible to know how many people suffer and die from cholera, given its confusion with other forms of acute diarrhea. Some reporting might overestimate reported cholera by assuming, as is routinely done, that if a wide outbreak occurs, then cholera drives out other diarrheas. But in a diarrhea epidemic in Dhaka following severe floods in 2004, the rate of cholera infection was only 22 percent compared to other acute diarrheas.[2] This would, of course, inflate cholera rates. Yet denial and fear lead to the more likely prospect that, in general, cholera cases are underreported everywhere. One study estimates the annual global burden of cholera runs in the millions rather than one or two hundred thousand. The authors claim that cholera accounts for 0.6 percent of all diarrhea cases, or eleven

---

[1] Hamlin, *Cholera: The Biography*, 283.
[2] Hamlin, *Cholera: The Biography*, 282–3.

million cases annually.[3] Another study agrees, citing WHO unpublished reports that indicate an annual global case and fatality rates at least ten times higher than annual official reports indicate.[4]

A team of researchers at the Fogarty International Center, National Institutes of Health (NIH), Bethesda, MD, has provided a valuable addition to the analysis of global cholera data between 1995 and 2005.[5] The NIH team recognizes that the WHO tabulates annual incidence data, but rarely breaks cases down by regions or provinces. Nor do they find African governments to be the worst reporting offenders. They note that cholera is significantly underreported in Asia, and that outbreaks in Africa are more reliably reported because of "international interest and less commercial consequences."[6]

One obvious finding of the NIH study was that cholera by the turn of the twenty-first century had become essentially a sub-Saharan African disease.[7] Between 1995 and 2005, West Africa accounted for 19.6 percent of all global outbreaks, East Africa, 20.1 percent, Central Africa, 10.6 percent, and Southern Africa, 15.7 percent. The study fails to point out the high outlier of South Africa in 2001 and 2002, which alone accounted for almost 126,000 cases. More valuable is their map indicating that the highest concentration of multiple outbreak reports was in eastern Democratic Republic of the Congo (DRC) and western Uganda, and extending down to southeastern DRC and northern Zambia. It was also noted that all regions of the world saw a spike in cholera in 1998 and 1999, possibly explained by extreme global weather conditions, and all except Europe and the Americas experienced another peak in 2005.[8] The NIH researchers did, however, insist that misdiagnosis was not an issue, because cholera has distinct symptoms that experienced health professionals would not miss. One projection they chose not to make was how the study of concentrated outbreaks might indicate future patterns.

[3] C.F. Lanata, W. Mendoza, and R.E. Black, *Improving Diarrhea Estimates* (Geneva: WHO Child and Adolescent Health Development Monitoring and Evaluation Team, 2002).

[4] Jane Zuckerman, Lars Rombo, and Alain Fisch, "The true burden and risk of cholera: Implications for prevention and control," *Lancet Infectious Disease*, 7 (2007), 522.

[5] David C. Griffeth, Louise Kelly-Hope, and Mark A. Miller, "Review of reported cholera outbreaks worldwide, 1995–2005," *American Journal of Tropical Medicine and Hygiene*, 75 (2006), 973–7.

[6] Griffeth, "Review," 976.

[7] Griffeth, "Review," 974, table 1.

[8] Griffeth, "Review," 977. For the effects of higher temperature, increased rainfall, and flooding brought about by ENSO, see R.S. Kovats et al., "El Nino and health," *Lancet*, 362 (2003), 1481–9.

Neither this nor any other study has been able to predict where in Africa severe cholera outbreaks would strike next, as for example in Angola and Ethiopia in 2006, two countries that had rarely reported cholera in the past.

The NIH team devoted significant attention to those risk factors that played a role in outbreaks, but they must have been disappointed by their results. Many of the qualitative reports of outbreaks did not identify more than one risk factor – or any at all – and they ended their study with a plea for a "clearer definition of risk factor parameters" in the future.[9] Also, the NIH study examined risk factors for contracting cholera, but not risks of dying. A Scandinavian team working in Guinea-Bissau, West Africa reached the logical conclusion that the major risk of death was closely related to delays in reaching rural treatment centers, a finding that surely applied throughout rural Africa.[10]

Even if the NIH exercise was flawed, the discussion and categorization of risk factors is useful. The researchers sought to identify risk factors based upon the primary cause cited by the reporter of an outbreak. The most common choice was heavy rainfall and flooding, cited in 33 percent of the West African outbreaks, and 39 percent of those in Southern Africa. This is hardly surprising given that research in Bangladesh, for instance, has identified rainfall, water temperature and depth, and copepod counts as major factors in the growth of *V. cholerae*.[11] In East Africa, however, heavy rains were only 10 percent of the risk factors, whereas 36 percent cited refugees or internally displaced persons as primary. Water-source contamination was the second highest cited factor in all regions of Africa.[12] In contrast to South America and East Asia, where contaminated food was considered an important risk factor, this factor was rarely indicated for Africa.

Such indications of risk factors are clearly qualitative and perhaps subjective, because the accuracy of the reporter's observations was never assessed. A qualitative assessment is of value, however, especially when more than a single risk factor can be identified. Multiple factors may

[9] Griffeth, "Review," 977, and table 3.
[10] G. Gunnlaugsson et al., "Epidemic cholera in Guinea-Bissau: The challenge of preventing deaths in rural West Africa," *International Journal of Infectious Diseases*, 4 (2000), 8–13.
[11] A. Huq et al., "Critical factors influencing the occurrence of *Vibrio cholerae* in the environment of Bangladesh," *Applied and Environmental Microbiology*, 71 (2005), 4645–54.
[12] Griffeth, "Review," 975–6.

indeed have been at work in specific outbreaks. For example, cholera outbreaks in Senegal, as will be discussed in Chapter 8, can be interpreted as primarily a function of environmental changes, or the failure of the state to address the public health issue of crumbling water and sewage infrastructure, or even the risk posed by huge gatherings of pilgrims at religious shrines, a common nineteenth-century risk factor and one not even listed by any of the reports used in the NIH study.

Unlike the localized if severe experiences with cholera in 1868 and 1893, during the Seventh Pandemic from 1971 to the present day, every sub-Saharan African country, with a handful of exceptions, would report at least some cholera to the WHO. Free-standing cholera developed in the coastal lagoons and large river valleys of West Africa, in Lake Chad, on the coast and in the oases of Somalia, in the Great Lakes of East and Central Africa, throughout Mozambique, on selected Indian Ocean islands, and finally in northern provinces of South Africa. Newly created reservoirs permitted the entrenchment of endemic cholera, which usually attacked affected regions at the start of the rainy season and died away at its end.

The Seventh Pandemic struck Africa in four phases (Table 6.1).[13] The first, from 1971 to 1990, was probably the mildest, though early reporting to the WHO was erratic. From 1991, the same year cholera exploded in Latin America, until 1997, Africa also underwent a significant increase in cholera's intensity. A third phase began in 1998, with another large spike in continental cases, and continued to 2005. The fourth, and ongoing, phase began with a large spike in 2006, when a record 234,000 cases were registered. Following a small decline, Africa's cholera cases in 2009 climbed to 217,333–98 percent of the world total. At the time of writing, 2010 is proving to be another deadly year, featuring large outbreaks in East Africa, and in northern Cameroon and Nigeria near the Lake Chad Basin.

PHASE ONE, 1971–1990

In August 1970, Conakry, the capital of the remote and reclusive West African Republic of Guinea, was one of the least likely corners of Africa to find a cholera pandemic of Southeast Asian origin. Yet it is a measure of growing globalization and of the rapidity of air travel that, possibly for the first time, cholera benefited from air transport to gain a significant new foothold in Africa. Guinea was highly dependent on the Soviet Union

---

[13] Unless otherwise indicated, all statistics for this chapter are from the annual reports on cholera published by the *WER*.

TABLE 6.1. *Cholera in Africa, four phases, 1971–2009*

Phase One, 1971–1990*

Year	Cases	Year	Cases
1971	69,000	1981	18,000
1972	7,000	1982	37,000
1973	9,000	1983	37,000
1974	8,000	1984	17,000
1975	6,000	1985	27,000
1976	3,000	1986	41,000
1977	8,000	1987	31,000
1978	23,000	1988	23,000
1979	19,000	1989	36,000
1980	18,000	1990	38,000
Total	475,000		
Yearly			
Ave.	23,750		

Phase Two, 1991–1997

Year	Cases	Deaths	CFR
1991	153,000	13,998	9.1
1992	91,000	5,291	5.8
1993	77,000	1,843	2.4
1994	162,000	8,128	5.0
1995	71,000	3,024	4.3
1996	109,000	6,216	5.7
1997	118,000	5,853	5.0
Total	781,000	44,353	5.7
Yearly			
Ave.	111,571	6,336	5.7

Phase Three, 1998–2005

Year	Cases	Deaths	CFR
1998	212,000	9,856	4.7
1999	207,000	8,728	4.2
2000	119,000	4,610	3.9
2001	173,000	2,590	1.5
2002	138,000	4,551	3.3
2003	108,000	1,884	1.7
2004	96,000	2,331	2.4
2005	125,000	2,230	1.8
Total	1,178,000	36,780	3.1
Yearly			
Ave.	147,250	4,598	3.1

(continued)

TABLE 6.1 (*continued*)

Phase Four, 2006–2009

Year	Cases	Deaths	CFR
2006	234,000	6,303	2.7
2007	166,000	3,994	2.4
2008	190,000	5,147	2.7
2009	217,000	4,883	2.3
Total	807,000	20,327	2.5
Yearly			
Ave.	201,750	5,082	2.5

Source: WER, annual reports on cholera, 1971–2008.
* No data for deaths or CFRS before 1991.

at that time, and its students often pursued higher studies in Moscow and other Soviet cities. On their way home to Conakry, a group of such students stopped briefly for a holiday on the Black Sea coast at a time when the seventh cholera pandemic was making its initial progress through the Crimea. One of them probably was the index case. Within five years, cholera in Africa became "one of the major natural disasters" of the era.[14]

Cholera's rapid spread from Conakry was astonishing. In only six months, cholera reached everywhere in West Africa except Guinea-Bissau, which may simply not yet have reported its presence to the WHO. Soon after the students' return, on August 18, Guinea reported a significant number of suspected cholera cases to the WHO. When the WHO confirmed these as cholera, Guinea refused to make the announcement official, and when the WHO unilaterally announced cholera's presence in the country on September 4, 1970, Guinea resigned from the WHO in a huff. That first epidemic resulted in at least 2,000 cases and 60 deaths.

Cholera then began to spread throughout West Africa along a major coastal axis, progressing systematically southeast through Sierra Leone, Liberia, Côte d'Ivoire, Ghana, Togo, Benin, Nigeria, and extending as far as Cameroon. Cholera moved along the lagoon system just inside the West African coast, carried along by various fishing communities. Lagoon villages near large cities like Abidjan, Monrovia, Accra, and Lagos, with their swamps and brackish water, provided an especially attractive setting for *Vibrio cholerae*. Free-standing cholera may even have developed in the coastal lagoons of West Africa during this period. Nigerian research

---

[14] Robert F. Stock, *Cholera in Africa* (London: International African Institute, 1976), dust jacket. His work remains the main source for cholera in Africa in the first phase.

indicates that higher counts of *Vibrio cholerae* have been found in the dry season when coastal estuaries are shallow and fishing as well as local trade in fishery products are more intense.[15]

Cholera also progressed into the West African interior in 1970. It reached the major market town of Mopti on the Niger River in Mali, some 1,500 kilometers inland. From there it fanned out south to Burkina Faso and west into the Senegal River valley. Yet Upper Niger regions of the Sahel such as Mali and Burkina Faso proved over time to be more modestly touched by cholera than the Lake Chad Basin to the east. As Chapter 7 indicates, the four countries bordering on this important body of water, Niger, Chad, Cameroon, and Nigeria, all suffered cholera outbreaks in 1970 and 1971, and almost annually thereafter.

In 1971, the Lake Chad Basin became a springboard for cholera heading east to the Horn of Africa. In Ethiopia, which reported cholera in 1971 for the first time in sixty-five years, thousands made their way across the porous border to refugee camps supported by the United Nations High Commission for Refugees (UNHCR) in neighboring Sudan; cholera broke out soon after their arrival.[16] Cholera also touched down in Somalia and Djibouti in 1971, and then spread south to Kenya, Uganda, and Angola. In 1974, Nairobi and its environs became infected, and Kenya reported 2,773 cases and 770 deaths nationally (a catastrophic CFR of almost 28 percent).[17] In Angola, cholera appeared first in the capital of Luanda in late December 1973. From there, it easily made its way to other national ports, and then into the interior along the Luanda-Malenge rail line, where its impact was exacerbated by warfare between the Portuguese colonial army and those fighting for the independence of Angola.

Links between Angola and the other major Portuguese colony of Mozambique helped introduce the Seventh Pandemic to Southern Africa. The seaport of Beira suffered a cholera outbreak imported by air from Angola in late 1973. Cholera then traveled along the Beira-Zambezi rail line, entering the Zambezi River valley and crossing the border into Malawi. Significant interaction among Mozambique liberation troops in Tete Province of Mozambique probably facilitated cholera's crossing into Zimbabwe. Migrant workers from Mozambique were said to have

---

[15] S.J. Utsalo, F.O. Eko, and E.O. Antia-Obong, "Features of cholera and *Vibrio parahae-molyticus* diarrhoea endemicity in Calabar, Nigeria," *European Journal of Epidemiology*, 8 (1992), 856–60.

[16] Kim Mulholland, "Cholera in Sudan: An account of an epidemic in eastern Sudan, May–June, 1985," *Disasters*, 9 (1985), 247–58.

[17] Stock, *Cholera in Africa*, 29.

been responsible for introducing cholera to the Transvaal mines of South Africa in March of 1974.

The Seventh Pandemic also gained purchase in one of its old stomping grounds, a cluster of three small Indian Ocean islands comprising the Comoros. In 1975, an old cholera linkage was believed to have been operative when it was reported that pilgrims returning to the Comoros from Mecca triggered an outbreak of 2,675 cases and 238 deaths (a CFR of slightly less than 9 percent).[18]

For all of Africa, the cholera numbers during the first phase of the Seventh Pandemic were clearly low in comparison with what came later (Table 6.1). The twenty-year average of 23,750 cases yearly was, nevertheless, somewhat deceiving in that annual rates were on the rise in the 1980s. Death rates and, therefore, CFRs, were not published annually by the WHO during this phase, but data show that, in 1971, the continent recorded 73,000 cases and 11,427 deaths. This extremely high CFR of 15.7 percent came before the development of ORT therapy, and was also a function of minimal cholera surveillance in these early days. A decade later, by 1981, the case total had dropped to 19,000; the number of deaths were reported as 1,581, a CFR of 8.3 percent, which suggested that cholera treatment in Africa lagged far behind the rest of the world. Globally in 1981, the CFR was 4.8 percent versus 2.7 percent for Asia.

PHASE TWO, 1991–1997

The tremendous surge of cholera in South America in 1991 marked a large spike in cholera numbers globally (Figure 6.1). The surge did not spare sub-Saharan Africa. After tapering off in the 1980s, the Seventh Pandemic struck twenty-one countries. The toll in 1991 involved fewer cases than the Americas, but the absolute number of deaths, 13,998 (a CFR of 9.1 percent), was three times as large as the global average. This terrible death toll would prove to be the worst recorded in Africa during the Seventh Pandemic to this day. African CFRs in phase two dropped somewhat, running close to 6 percent. Case rates also increased as a portion of global totals, hitting 80 percent by 1997.

For coastal West Africa from Guinea east to Benin, phase two saw cholera outbreaks proliferate. High numbers in 1994, especially for Sierra Leone and Liberia, were no doubt a function of escalating armed conflict. Liberia was gripped by civil war from 1989 to 2003, when its military dictator Charles Taylor was finally forced into exile. Beginning

---

[18] Stock, *Cholera in Africa*, 32.

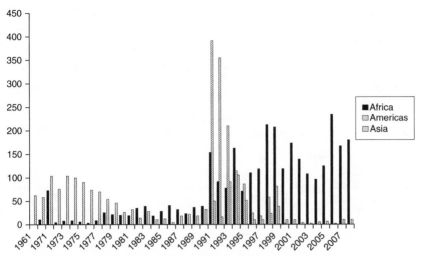

FIGURE 6.1. Seventh cholera pandemic, cases in thousands reported to WHO, 1961–2008 (data from WHO).

in 1991, Liberian warlords destabilized neighboring Sierra Leone, and this country suffered 50,000 dead and hundreds of thousands of refugees until peace was finally restored in 2001. Liberia's eastern neighbor, Côte d'Ivoire, suffered higher case and death rates from 1994 through 1996, coinciding with political unrest; it plunged into full civil war from 2002 to 2007. In Ghana, which experienced cholera every year since 1991, and which was one of the few countries with such a high incidence (see Table 6.2), cholera peaked in 1991, the same year cholera peaked in Togo with around 3,200 cases, and in Benin with 7,400 cases. Another difficult year occurred in 1997 when floods produced high death rates in much of the region.

In Central and Southern Africa, major outbreaks dominated the region, and although not every country was involved every year, the WER always indicated the region as a hotspot, especially through 1993. In just four months, from November 1989 to April 1990, Malawi had the highest case load in all of Africa, 13,457, compared to 37,968 for Africa combined. In 1990, most of Zambia's cases were in Lusaka initially, but by the end of the year, seven of nine provinces had been infected. Other major epidemics occurred in Angola, Mozambique, and Tanzania. In 1993, war-torn Mozambique, together with Zambia, Zimbabwe, and Malawi, accounted for 85 percent of Africa's 77,000 cases. Civil war and genocide in Rwanda during 1994 caused the WHO spotlight to shift to the Great Lakes region, and especially to Goma in the eastern DRC,

TABLE 6.2. *Country incidence for cholera in Africa,* 1991–2007 (17 years)*

West Africa

High (13–17 years)		Medium (7–12 years)		Low (0 – 6 Years)	
Nigeria	17	Guinea	12	Mali	6
Ghana	17	Chad	11	Mauritania	4
Cameroon	16	Guinea-Bissau	10	Gambia	1
Liberia	15	Côte d'Ivoire	10		
Benin	14	Burkina Faso	8		
Togo	14				
Niger	13				

Horn of Africa

		Somalia	12	Ethiopia	2
		Djibouti	7	Sudan	2
				Eritrea	1

Central and East Africa

High (13–17 years)		Medium (7–12 years)		Low (0 – 6 years)	
DRC	17	Angola	7	Congo-Brazzaville.	4
Tanzania	17			Sao Tome	3
Burundi	16			Equatorial	
Uganda	16			Guinea	2
Kenya	14			CAR	1
Rwanda	13			Gabon	1
Southern Africa					
Mozambique	15	Zimbabwe	12	Swaziland	6
Malawi	15	South Africa	8	Namibia	1
Zambia	14			Botswana	0
				Lesotho	0

Indian Ocean

				Comoros	6
				Madagascar	2

Source: WER, annual reports on cholera, 1991–2007.
* Incidence when 50 or more cases occur.

where overcrowded and unsanitary refugee camps were the scene of a cholera catastrophe.

PHASE THREE, 1998–2005

The spike in African cases in 1998 was part of a global rise in cholera triggered by extreme weather, and illustrated by phenomena such as Hurricane

Mitch or the ENSO current. Major cholera outbreaks, among the worst to date, occurred in the DRC, Angola, Mozambique, Tanzania, Kenya, Uganda, and the Comoros. A year later, Madagascar suffered its first cholera attack in twenty years. Indian Ocean cholera again surfaced in 2000, but far and away the worst outbreaks occurred in Southern Africa in 2000 and 2001. South Africa alone reported 54 percent of all African cases in 2001, whereas the continent itself accounted for 94 percent of WHO's global figures. It provided small comfort that the WHO could praise South African health authorities for "dealing with cholera in an open and transparent way."[19]

Parts of the Horn of Africa endured dismal cholera rates in this phase. Somalia suffered especially severe outbreaks in 1999, 2000, 2003, and 2004. To the south, cholera ravaged Kenya, Uganda, and Tanzania in 1998, when the countries reported a combined total of 86,434 cases. In West Africa, Ghana experienced more than 5,000 cases in 2001, then saw falling rates for the rest of this period. Guinea maintained high CFRs and cases from 2004, the same year Sierra Leone's cases spiked. Liberia in 2003 had its worst year ever, reporting 34,740 cases, four times as many as its second-worst year in 1996, but only thirty-eight deaths, for a suspiciously low CFR of 0.1 percent; they maintained these extremely low CFRs thereafter. By then its civil war had ended, and cholera patients undoubtedly benefited from the presence of a large number of NGO emergency teams. Nevertheless, such low CFRs lack credibility and must be what the WHO euphemistically called "limitations in the surveillance and reporting system."[20] Côte d'Ivoire reported virtually no cholera until its rates spiked in 2001 and 2002, a time when the country was falling into civil war; cholera has remained sporadic since, but the country's CFRs were never less than 3.4 percent in phase three. Heavy rains in 2005 caused several West African countries to suffer high cholera rates, as was the case in Senegal, Mauritania, Guinea-Bissau, and Guinea.

PHASE FOUR, 2006 TO THE PRESENT.

By phase four of the Seventh Pandemic, cholera had become an African disease. The worst year to date has been 2006, when Africa registered 234,000 cases, fully 99 percent of the global total of 237,000. What was especially alarming about the 2006 figures was that four countries, the DRC, Angola, Ethiopia, and Sudan, accounted for almost three quarters

---

[19] WER, 77 (2002), 260.
[20] WER, 78 (2003), 270.

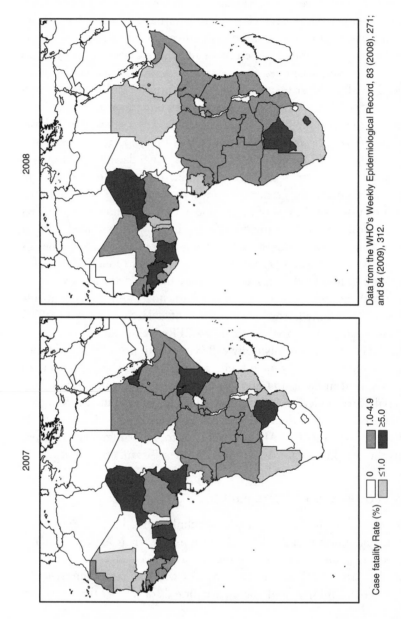

2008

2007

Case fatality Rate (%)

☐ 0

☐ ≤1.0

▨ 1.0-4.9

■ ≥5.0

Data from the WHO's Weekly Epidemiological Record, 83 (2008), 271; and 84 (2009), 312.

MAP 6.1. Distribution of countries in Africa reporting cholera in 2007 and 2008 (adapted from WHO, *Weekly Epidemiological Record*, 83 [2008], 271; and 84 [2009], 312).

TABLE 6.3. *Cholera in selected African countries in 2006*

Country	Cases	Deaths	CFR %	Cases as % of whole
Angola	67,257	2,722	4.1	29
DRC	20,642	426	2.1	9
Ethiopia	54,070	575	1.1	23
Sudan	30,662	1,011	3.3	13
Rest of Africa	61,718	1,569	2.5	26
Total	234,349	6,303	2.7	100

Source: WER, 82 (2007), 274.

of the African total (Table 6.3). It was not a surprise that the DRC was among the four. It had reported cholera annually to the WHO since 1991, and was the African state worst afflicted during the Seventh Pandemic. Such was not the case for the other three countries. Ethiopia and Sudan had rarely if ever reported cholera since 1961, whereas Angola had reported cholera only five times since 1991. Not only were these specific epidemics a surprise, but they also suggest that cholera's annual appearance cannot be predicted, and is now capable of exploding almost anywhere in sub-Saharan Africa in a given year.

The latest bout of cholera in the Horn of Africa began in late January 2006 in the southern Sudan. Cholera then made its way northward to infect fifteen states, eventually crossing over to Gambella, Ethiopia in April. After ravaging Ethiopia, cholera infected vulnerable Somali-speaking populations in the interior of Djibouti, which reported the high CFR of 8.9 percent (11 deaths among 123 cases). According to the WHO, this very high CFR reflects the difficulty of providing timely treatment for vulnerable groups living in remote areas. Overall, the subregion of the Horn reported 36 percent of Africa's cases.[21]

The situation was only slightly improved in 2007. This time Ethiopia registered 24,121 cases and 272 deaths, with a low CFR of 1.1 percent; but Djibouti and Sudan continued to record alarming CFRs of 6.7 and 3.6 percent, based on 372 cases and 25 deaths, and 500 deaths on 13,731 cases, respectively.[22] Worse, Somalia, which reported an absence of cholera the year before, now admitted to the highest number of cases ever – 41,643 cases and 1,182 deaths, for a CFR of 2.8 percent. The lowland state of Eritrea, which achieved its independence from Ethiopia in 1993,

---

[21] WER, 82 (2007), 275, 278.
[22] WER, 83 (2008), 270, 273.

reported cholera for the first time, with 119 cases and 9 deaths (a CFR of 7.6 percent). The Horn's totals of 79,986 cases represented 48 percent of cases notified for Africa in 2007. Cholera in West Africa, which was diminished in 2006, experienced a spike in 2007 with 14,082 cases, 422 deaths, and a CFR of 3 percent.

The latest data, from 2009, show an increase in African cholera cases. Although the worst of the massive outbreak in Zimbabwe (discussed in Chapter 9) is over, Southern Africa, the DRC, and the Horn remain cholera hotspots.[23]

This chapter has detailed how Africa's cholera problem has grown worse despite the availability of inexpensive ORT therapy and the precedent of effective controls being implemented in the rest of the world (Figure 6.1). In the early years of the Seventh Pandemic, cholera experts did not anticipate that Africa would account for a majority of the world's totals.[24] Africa's share of cholera cases clung close to the 20 percent mark, whereas Asia accounted for the majority of cases. Even when world totals spiked alarmingly in 1991 to an all-time high of 595,000 cases, two-thirds of these came from Latin America, which was newly victimized after having been free of cholera for almost a century.

Since 2000, Africa's cholera cases account for 90 percent or more of the world's totals. The latest figures, for 2009, show 217,000 African cases, representing 98 percent of the global total of 221,000.

Not only does Africa have the most cases, it also suffers from the highest case fatality rates (see Figure 6.2). In the early years of the Seventh Pandemic, CFRs were high everywhere, but with the spread of effective oral rehydration therapy the rates declined dramatically, enabling the WHO to establish a benchmark of 1 percent as the maximum a sound public health system should tolerate. Only very recently have some African countries fallen below this benchmark. For example, in 2007, the African CFR stood at 2.4 percent, representing 3,994 cholera deaths among 166,000 cases. By contrast, the Asian CFR was only 0.3 percent, or 37 deaths from 11,000 cases.

Table 6.2 shows incidences of African cholera outbreaks over the past seventeen years. Cholera is endemic in at least twenty-one African countries, those which have reported cases at least ten times since 1991. Outbreaks have varied in size, but Table 6.4 indicates that the attack rates per 100,000 in population in the most severe outbreaks have been devastating in each and every region of Africa. It can also be seen that many countries have

[23] WER 85 (2010), 294.
[24] Barua, "The global epidemiology," 428.

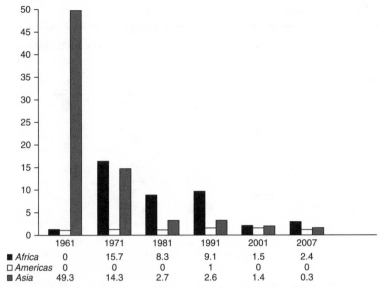

	1961	1971	1981	1991	2001	2007
■ *Africa*	0	15.7	8.3	9.1	1.5	2.4
□ *Americas*	0	0	0	1	0	0
■ *Asia*	49.3	14.3	2.7	2.6	1.4	0.3

FIGURE 6.2. Seventh cholera pandemic, case fatality rate reported to WHO, 1961–2007 (data from WHO).

experienced their worst cholera epidemics very recently. Worst year attack rates in countries with small populations like Djibouti, Guinea-Bissau, Liberia, and the Comoro Islands have been especially alarming, as have those in failing states like Zimbabwe, Angola, Somalia, and Guinea.

Countries with habitually low incidences of cholera do not appear in Table 6.4. The Central African Republic (CAR), Gabon, Congo-Brazzaville, Botswana, Namibia, and Lesotho have never reported more than a handful of imported cases to the WHO. Questions do arise with regard to two countries in the Horn of Africa – Ethiopia and Sudan – because they have usually chosen to describe and report their intestinal infections as "acute watery diarrhea," or AWD (see Introduction).

If it is slightly encouraging that CFRs have been slowly trending downward, the reality is that case loads are increasing. The African case load average for phase four, through 2009, is almost 202,000 the highest ever reported. The high number of people infected is a serious medical issue, an indication that basic cholera surveillance is inadequate, and a confirmation that public health care in Africa is now being seriously eroded.

The next chapters take us away from dry numbers and to case studies that show the human dimensions of the seventh cholera pandemic. As a caveat, this arbitrary grouping of cases will not do justice to the diversity of local experiences with cholera in Africa. Nor is it intended to deny that in each case, multiple risk factors have been at work. Ultimately, sudden

TABLE 6.4. *Attack rates in year of worst outbreak*

Country	Year	Cases	Population in millions	Attack Rate per 100,000
West Africa				
Guinea-Bissau	2005	25,111	1.4	1,894
Liberia	2003	34,740	2.8	1,241
Guinea	1994	31,415	7.2	436
Senegal	2005	31,719	12.0	264
Chad	1991	13,915	6.0	232
Benin	1991	7,474	4.9	153
Ghana	1991	13,172	15.8	83
Togo	1998	3,217	4.6	70
Nigeria	1991	59,478	99.0	60
Cameroon	2004	8,005	16.9	47
Niger	1991	3,238	8.0	40
Horn of Africa				
Djibouti	1995	10,055	0.5	2,011
Somalia	2007	41,643	9.3	448
Sudan	2006	30,662	38.5	80
Ethiopia	2006	54,070	77.4	70
Central and East Africa				
Angola	2006	67,257	12.0	560
Uganda	1998	49,514	22.5	220
Tanzania	1997	40,249	31.0	130
DRC	1994	58,057	44.5	130
Kenya	1998	22,432	29.1	77
Southern Africa				
Zimbabwe	2008–09	98,000	11.4	860
South Africa	2001–02	125,000	45.6	274
Malawi	2002	32,618	12.5	261
Mozambique	1999	44,329	17.7	250
Zambia	1991	13,154	8.2	160
Indian Ocean				
Comoros	2000	3,297	0.6	550
Madagascar	2000	29,083	15.7	185

Source: WER, annual reports on cholera, 1991–2009.

changes in the relationship between water and sanitation facilities, as well as the size of the population requiring these essentials of health, can trigger cholera outbreaks. Both natural disasters like flooding or drought and societal breakdowns produced by civil strife are capable of overwhelming water systems.

7

Risk Factors

Environment and Geography, Armed Conflicts, and the Dispersal of Refugees

This chapter examines two sets of factors making cholera a high risk. First, changing ecological conditions in Lakes Chad, Tanganyika, and Malawi (Nyasa) have enabled cholera to become free-standing and thus endemic to thousands of people living in these large lake basins. The second set involves armed conflict and the ensuing dispersal of refugees, and how these factors have exposed people to cholera in the DRC and in Mozambique.

THE LAKE CHAD BASIN

Lake Chad is a large, shallow lake in the heart of the vast West African Sahel. It is a major source of water and fish for more than twenty million people in the four countries touching its shores: Cameroon, Chad, Niger, and Nigeria. More than 90 percent of its water comes from the Chari River, originating to the south in the tropical forest of the Central African Republic (CAR).

Lake Chad has experienced dramatic environmental cycles of expansion and contraction over the past thirteen millennia. Recently, its diminution has accelerated, from an area of 26,000 square kilometers in 1960 to less than 1,500 square kilometers in 2000, with an exceptionally shallow average depth of only one and a half meters. Experts attribute this shrinkage to a combination of factors: cyclical patterns of reduced rainfall in what is an arid part of Africa; greatly increased amounts of irrigation water drawn from the Chari River system; and population growth, which has dramatically increased water demand in the past half century.[1]

[1] Graham Chapman and Kathleen M. Baker, eds., *The Changing Geography of Africa and the Middle East* (London: Routledge, 1992); Michael T. Coe and Jonathan A. Foley,

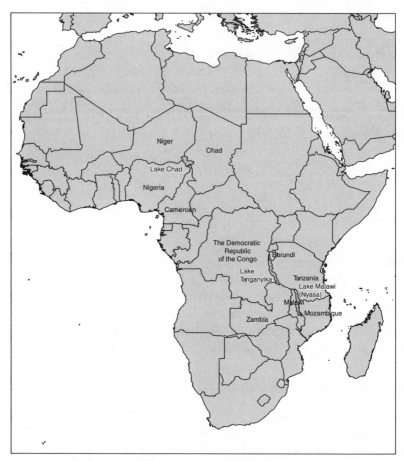

MAP 7.1. Lake basins in Africa.

It is not surprising that water rights in the Lake Chad Basin have produced political and social tensions. Disputes among farmers, herders,
and fishers have been an issue for generations and are exacerbated by
diversion of the water by these groups. Since the 1960s, various plans to
address the water crisis have been broached. One was to divert the Ubangi
River into the lake. These interbasin transfer schemes led to the creation
of the Lake Chad Basin Commission (LCBC) in the early 1990s. At a
March 2008 summit, the heads of state of the LCBC member countries

"Human and natural impacts on the water resources of the Lake Chad basin," *Journal of
Geophysical Research*, 106 (2001), 3349–56; "Africa at a watershed: Ubangi-Lake Chad
inter-basin transfer," *New Scientist*, March 23, 1991; "Vanishing lake Chad – A water crisis in Central Africa," *Circle of Blue*, June 24, 2008, www.circleofblue.org/waternews.

committed to a diversion project and requested a World Bank–funded feasibility study.[2]

The region's first encounter with the seventh cholera pandemic began in May of 1971 when the disease arrived from southern Nigeria. After Lagos was infected late in 1970, cholera spread to urban centers throughout the country. Ibadan – 150 kilometers to the north and then a city of one million – was infected on January 3, 1971, and reached a peak of 1,095 cases in the seventh week; the epidemic continued for more than a year. Next came the Northern Territories, with its large urban centers of Zaria and Kano, where cholera arrived in February 1971.[3] Finally, cholera also touched rural areas, spreading through Maiduguri and entering the Lake Chad Basin.

The May 1971 outbreak centered on the town of Goulfrey in northern Cameroon. There, an estimated 20,000 people from Nigeria, Cameroon, Chad, and Niger gathered for the circumcision ceremony held for the son of an important Muslim *shaykh*.[4] A cholera outbreak struck the day after, and in May alone, Goulfrey recorded 801 cases and 121 deaths (a CFR of 15 percent). Medical authorities rushed in to chlorinate drinking water and disinfect all latrines, but the infection spread throughout the Lake Chad Basin. Some isolated Cameroonian villages endured CFRs of more than 50 percent. Fifty kilometers across the border in Chad, the capital city of N'Djamena experienced 176 cases and 33 deaths (a CFR of 18.8 percent) between May and July, despite a massive vaccination campaign that administered 189,000 inoculations in three days. A French medical observer described the cholera outbreak in the Lake Chad Basin as a "scene of desolation and horror."[5]

Cholera outbreaks in the Lake Chad Basin were mild and sporadic for the next twenty years. But beginning in 1991 and continuing to the present, WHO cholera statistics suggest that the Lake Chad Basin has suffered from a continuing endemic presence; rarely a year passed without significant outbreaks. Persistently high CFRs, among the worst in Africa, suggested that little treatment of patients occurred.

Niger's poverty and the remoteness of Lake Chad from the capital city of Niamey are no doubt factors in that country's inability to control

[2] Voice of America News, March 28, 2008, www.voanews.com/english/2008-03-28-voa33.cfm.
[3] Femi Ogunleye, "Filth: A health hazard in Kano," *Daily Times*, Lagos (September 8, 1973), 7.
[4] H. Félix, "Le Choléra Africain," *Médecine Tropicale*, 31 (1971), 619–28.
[5] Félix, "Le Choléra Africain," 624.

cholera. Poor road transportation networks have made cholera surveillance and treatment a significant challenge for national public health systems throughout the region. In the case of Chad, it has been subject to warlord rule since the early 1990s, and has not taken care of its civic responsibility to provide a minimum of public health care. On the other hand, although Cameroon and Nigeria have the financial resources available to have kept cholera under control, they have failed to do so. Remoteness of the region and its marginal participation in the national economies of the two states only partially explain their poor records in containing cholera.

THE LAKE TANGANYIKA BASIN

A second endemic focus of cholera is the shore area of Lake Tanganyika, implicating populations of the DRC, Burundi, western Tanzania, and Zambia. Lake Tanganyika is the third largest freshwater lake in the world by volume, and the second deepest after Lake Baikal in Siberia.[6] It extends for 673 kilometers north-south and averages fifty kilometers in width. The lake holds at least 400 species of fish, most of which live along the shoreline, as well as numerous invertebrates, especially mollusks. It is estimated that this marine life supplies up to 40 percent of the protein for more than one million people living in the lake basin. Approximately 100,000 people are directly involved in the fisheries at roughly 800 sites in the four countries touching on the lake. Free-standing *Vibrio cholerae* would also find Lake Tanganyika attractive, because its average surface temperature is twenty-five degrees Celsius, and plankton abound.

The Kaputa district in the northern province of Zambia illustrates the problems posed by cholera to fishing communities in the Lake Tanganyika Basin.[7] This remote area incorporates a population of roughly 50,000, many of whom engage in seasonal fishing to supplement subsistence. Each rainy season sees the opening of temporary, unsanitary fishing camps, and the expansion of the port village of Nsumbu on the shore of Lake Tanganyika. Migration of traders from neighboring Tanzania and the DRC also runs the risk of importing cholera from these countries. The result since the 1970s has been a cholera season corresponding to the rains between November and February. The worst year in the Kaputa

---

[6] "Data summary: Lake Tanganyika," www.ilec.or.jp/database/afr.

[7] J.E.A.M. Van Bergen, "Epidemiology and health policy – A world of difference? A case-study of a cholera outbreak in Kaputa District, Zambia," *Social Science and Medicine*, 43 (1996), 94–5.

district was 1991, when 573 cases and 63 deaths brought the CFR to the unprecedented level of 11 percent.

In an effort to address this ongoing risk, Zambian health authorities did attempt control measures. They established eleven cholera treatment centers, but the limited public transport and the remoteness of the region led to shortages of rehydration fluids and staff. Although there was talk for years of improving the water supply by cementing wells and building pit latrines, little progress occurred. In 1991, however, the villagers of Kampinda on Lake Mweru decided to take their own initiative instead of waiting for the Department of Water Affairs to act. They set up their own health committee, and with money raised in part by funds from UNICEF, 80 percent of the 2,453 households dug pit latrines; they also built their own cement-protected well, placing one villager in charge of chlorinating the water.

The local community was as proactive as could be expected, given the constraints they faced in struggling against cholera. Malnutrition was on the rise in Zambia, and in Kaputa health workers have noted scabies levels as high as 40 percent.[8] The price of copper was declining, and because it was Zambia's main export, it sent the country's GNP into sharp decline in the 1980s and early 1990s. The government, therefore, was determined to keep the fishing camps active and open despite poor living conditions and the health risk from cholera. Meanwhile, simple educational admonitions to "boil water, wash hands" foundered because firewood was scarce, charcoal was expensive, and soap was not readily available.

Over the seventeen years since 1991, endemic cholera has been an annual health problem for the peoples of the Lake Tanganyika Basin. Although CFRs have fallen recently, in 2006 for example, the basin experienced approximately 19,000 cases.[9] The Kaputa experience suggests that only as Africa's national economies improve will the risk of cholera be reduced for thousands of vulnerable individuals.

THE LAKE MALAWI BASIN

A third endemic focus for cholera is Lake Malawi, also known as Lake Nyasa, the third-largest lake in Africa.[10] It has much in common with another large Rift Valley body of fresh water to the north, Lake

---

[8] Van Bergen, "Epidemiology," 97.
[9] *WER*, 82, (2007), 274.
[10] *World Lakes Database*, International Lake Environment Committee Foundation, www.ilec.or.jp/database/afr/afr-13.html.

Tanganyika. Its surface temperature ranges from twenty-four to twenty-nine degrees Celsius, and its waters teem with more fish species than any other lake on earth. Like its cousin to the north, Lake Malawi is famous for its cichlids, popular in the aquarium trade. Snails in the southeast portion of the lake carry bilharzia, a threat to bathers. Though unconfirmed, conditions in Lake Malawi would support a hypothesis that freestanding *Vibrio cholerae* are present. Annual cholera data for seventeen years since 1991 show that both Malawi and Mozambique have reported cholera fifteen times (see Table 6.2).

The peoples of the Lake Malawi Basin have been tied to a long history of labor migration in the direction of South Africa. Population movements, both voluntary and involuntary, have triggered cholera outbreaks in the rest of Mozambique, Zimbabwe, and the northern provinces of South Africa.

THE DEMOCRATIC REPUBLIC OF THE CONGO (DRC)

Throughout the seventh cholera pandemic, overcrowded refugee camps globally have exposed vulnerable civilians to cholera. Cholera among refugees was a feature of the Bangladesh war of independence in 1971.[11] The terrible Ethiopian famine of 1985 drove an estimated half million starving civilians from the Ethiopian regions of Tigray, Wollo, and Eritrea into neighboring Sudan, where many contracted cholera.[12]

Four years later, refugees from conflict in Liberia and Sierra Leone brought cholera with them when they took shelter in Guinea. In this instance, the United Nations High Commission for Refugees (UNHCR) acceded to the Guinean government's wish to settle the refugees amidst existing border villages and towns rather than in camps.[13] Elsewhere, challenged health workers have struggled to provide basic services such as latrines, sufficient quantities of safe water, appropriate rehydration fluids, and enough soap and food for distribution.

---

[11] Dhiman Barua and Michael H. Merson, "Prevention and Control of Cholera," in Barua and Greenough III, eds., 345–6.

[12] Mulholland, "Cholera in Sudan," 247–58; Eigil Sorensen and Klaus Dissler, "Practical experience with the management of a cholera outbreak in a refugee camp in Eastern Sudan, 1985," *Disasters*, 12 (1986), 274–81.

[13] The UNHCR paid a fee to the Guinean health service, and foreign donors made supplementary payments. Small epidemics of cholera, measles, and meningitis did occur, but most refugees living in Guinea enjoyed a high degree of autonomy, and avoided the squalor and acute illness typical of camps. William Van Damme, "Do refugees belong in camps? Experiences from Goma and Guinea," *The Lancet*, 345 (1995), 360–4.

The DRC dominates the center of Africa, with a diversified geography that includes much of the African tropical rain forest, the Great Lakes in its northeast, and the southern savanna in the south. Cholera has been a constant threat to the people of this vast country, and from three different directions. First, the eastern DRC shares borders with western Uganda and with Rwanda. Cholera was an enormous problem in and around the town of Goma in 1994, site of displaced persons from Rwanda and Burundi. Second, southeastern DRC touches on Lake Tanganyika, as do Burundi, western Tanzania, and Zambia. This basin has had frequent visitations of cholera, often enough to indicate that free-standing cholera now infests part of Lake Tanganyika. Third, southwestern DRC shares a border with Angola, and imported cholera from Angola spilled over to the DRC in 2006.

The worst cholera disaster of the Seventh Pandemic struck at Goma in July 1994, following quickly after the Rwandan genocide. Medical statistics in the Goma region were estimates, especially in the first few weeks. The toll was terrible, not only from cholera, but from dysentery and meningococcal meningitis as well. In the three weeks following July 20, Oxfam estimated cholera deaths on some days at 3,000, until more emergency help could take hold. By mid-August, the death count reached 13,000, and the WHO reported a decline in the CFR from 22 percent in the first days to 3 percent, following the massive response of the international community.[14] Fatalities were higher still for untreated people in the streets of Goma.

Goma is a border town on the northern shore of Lake Kivu, next to the Rwandan city of Gisenyi, only four kilometers away. It is less than twenty kilometers south of the crater of the active Nyiragongo Volcano. Geography and regional politics have brought great hardship to this city of 250,000. The Rwandan refugees in 1994 completely overwhelmed resources in the already overcrowded city, because it housed many displaced Congolese as well as Rwandans and Burundians, known as Banyamulenge, from earlier displacements. In 2002, Nyiragongo erupted, sending lava into the center of Goma and destroying 40 percent of the city, including more than 4,500 houses and buildings. Warned in time, the population fled to UN refugee camps or to nearby Gisenyi.

The presence of displaced ethnic Hutu militias – at odds with local Banyamulenge and with the Tutsi dominated Rwanda Patriotic Front, in power in Rwanda since 1994 – has generated considerable violence in the

---

[14] WER, 70 (1995), 201–8.

Goma region. The failure of the nominally sovereign Congolese Army to maintain even a semblance of law and order has added to the prevailing anarchy. What has emerged are the First and Second Congo Wars, the latter continuing to the present day. Only NGOs and the various UN organizations are able to deliver food, water, and shelter to more than a million people, and then only when fighting among various factions abates enough to allow these humanitarian efforts to operate.

The Rwandan genocide provides political context for the cholera epidemic of 1994.[15] Between July 14 and 17, large numbers of Hutu civilians, defeated members of the genocidal former Rwandan regime, ex-FAR (Forces Armées Rwandaises) soldiers, and the *Interahamwe* (Hutu militias) fled west in panic, arriving in the Goma area of the DRC. Initial estimates of the refugees were as high as 1.2 million people arriving at a rate of 25,000 a day. The first refugees were installed in Goma itself, but four additional camps were soon opened nearby.

The exodus of so many hundreds of thousands of civilians was orchestrated by the ideologues of the genocide, called *génocidaires*, and their armed supporters. They demanded sexual favors from mothers desperate to care for their children, gave themselves priority in the distribution of food, water, and medicine, and sold the extra rations. Adding insult to injury, the *génocidaires* perpetuated ethnic stereotyping and hatred by encouraging the belief that Tutsis caused the cholera by poisoning the water.[16]

What took place was a death march in search of water and food. Authorities were forced to set up camps on volcanic rock, so that there was no surface or well water, no latrines, and poor burial capacity. People trekked more than twenty kilometers to obtain untreated water from Lake Kivu. As the cholera epidemic waned, leaving an estimated 50,000

---

[15] For medical data, see Goma Epidemiology Group, "Public health impact of Rwanda refugee crisis: what happened in Goma, Zaire, in July 1994," *Lancet*, 345: 1995, 339–44; for the political story, Mahmood Mamdani, *When Victims Become Killers: Colonialism, Nativism, and the Genocide in Rwanda* (Princeton: Princeton University Press, 2001), and Gérard Prunier, *The Rwanda Crisis: History of a Genocide* (New York: Columbia University Press, 1995).

[16] Prunier, *The Rwanda Crisis*, 314; for poisoning rumor, see Liisa Malkki, "Speechless emissaries: Refugees, humanitarianism, and dehistoricization," *Cultural Anthropology*, 11 (1996), 395. For the continuing politicization of the camps, Sarah Kenyon Lischer, *Dangerous Sanctuaries: Refugee Camps, Civil War, and the Dilemmas of Humanitarian Aid* (Ithaca: Cornell University Press, 2005), and Kate Halvorsen, "Protection and Humanitarian Assistance in the Refugee Camps in Zaire: The problem of security," in Howard Adelman and Astri Suhrke, eds., *The Path of Genocide: The Rwanda Crisis from Uganda to Zaire* (New Brunswick, NJ: Transaction Press, 1999), 307–20.

dead, multiresistant dysentery (*Shigella dysenteriae*) took over as a major killer.[17]

Refugee assistance was in the hands of several UN agencies, French military forces, and NGOs like CARE, Oxfam, and Médecins sans Frontières (MSF). The UNHCR coordinated efforts, but was overwhelmed by the enormous number of refugees appearing in such a short time. Hunger, disease, and death stalked the camps from the outset, and news agencies reported the catastrophe globally. Media coverage of Goma's cholera disaster was dramatic; "Hell on Earth" was the headline in *Newsweek* on August 1, and it may not have been hyperbole.[18]

What was absent from news coverage was the moral ambiguity involved in alleviating the suffering of perpetrators of genocide. The French government used humanitarianism as a cover, while protecting the Rwandan *génocidaires*, whom they had supported throughout the crisis. The UN and the NGOs treated these armed camps strictly as refugee settlements and saw their actions as humane and charitable. Yet they turned a blind eye to political coercion exercised in the refugee camps, just as they had failed to help stop the original genocide from unfolding. Mahmood Mamdani makes a persuasive case for judging the international emergency health relief efforts at Goma as a moral failure, whatever were the various claims to have brought cholera under control.[19]

Nor can the medical intervention in its first days be applauded. One of the emergency teams sent by the UN to render assistance in Goma came from the International Centre for Diarrhoeal Disease Research in Bangladesh. Experienced with cholera emergencies, the team later published a report blaming inexperience and incompetence among first responders in Goma for the inordinate number of deaths:

The slow rate of rehydration, inadequate use of oral rehydration therapy, use of inappropriate intravenous fluids, and inadequate experience of health workers in management of severe cholera are thought to be some of the factors associated with the failure to prevent so many deaths during the epidemic.[20]

Political instability and state collapse in Central Africa were features of the postcolonial era, and cholera certainly profited. As we have seen, war

---

[17] Van Damme, "Do refugees," 360–4.
[18] For a graphic account of how French military engineers used bulldozers to bury corpses in mass graves, see Thomas P. Odom, *Journey into Darkness: Genocide in Rwanda* (College Station: Texas A&M University Press, 2005), 106.
[19] Mamdani, *When Victims*, 254–5.
[20] A.K. Siddique, et al., "Why treatment centres failed to prevent cholera deaths among Rwandan refugees in Goma, Zaire," *Lancet*, 345 (February 11, 1995), 359–61.

and genocidal violence in Rwanda in 1994 led to a cholera emergency among refugees. The long-suffering people of the DRC who lived on the turbulent border with Rwanda also paid heavy dues to cholera in 1994 and throughout the Seventh Pandemic. Historically victims of a particularly brutal colonialism under King Leopold of Belgium at the beginning of the twentieth century, and of rampant corruption and flagrant mismanagement since independence in 1961, Congolese citizens have also carried a heavy public health burden from HIV/AIDs, ebola, and other scourges.

Cholera has struck the DRC in each of the eighteen years since 1991, and the country has reported more than 300,000 cases and 16,000 deaths (a CFR of 5.3 percent). No other country in the world has reported such high numbers. The latest tally, in 2009, was almost double the annual average – 22,899 cases and 237 deaths, for a CFR of 1.0 percent, which is lower than in the past.[21] These recent results illustrate the burdens of cholera control faced by hard-pressed public health workers in a country as vast and as badly governed as the DRC. Whereas hotspots in the past have included Goma and the Lake Tanganyika regions, the DRC has recently acquired a new source of cholera: a raging epidemic in Angola (see Chapter 8).

MOZAMBIQUE

Armed conflicts and the dispersal of internal and external refugee populations have also played a central role in the recent history of cholera in Mozambique. The ugly and protracted wars that plagued Mozambique for two decades following its independence in 1975 enabled cholera to thrive on malnutrition, the destruction of treatment centers, and on the untreated water that millions of people were forced to consume. Armed rebels opposed to the Mozambique government deliberately targeted public health personnel and infrastructure.[22]

The Mozambican wars also placed a health burden on the country's neighbors. Between 1987 and 1989, an estimated 750,000 refugees fled

---

[21] *WER*, 85 (2010), 294.

[22] For case studies of cholera, see Andrew E. Collins, *Environment, Health and Population Displacement: Development and change in Mozambique's Diarrhoeal Disease Ecology* (Aldershot: Ashgate, 1998). For politics, see J. Hanlon, *Mozambique: Who Calls the Shots* (London: James Curry, 1991), and John Saul, ed., *A Difficult Road: The Transition to Socialism in Mozambique* (New York: Monthly Review Press, 1985). For public health, see G. Walt, and A. Melamed, eds., *Mozambique: Towards a Peoples' Health Service* (London: Zed Books, 1984).

armed conflict and took refuge in southern Malawi. About 270,000 inhabitants at eleven camps set up by the UNHCR, MSF, and the Malawian Ministry of Health, experienced seven different cholera outbreaks between 1988 and 1989. Attack rates ranged up to 2.6 percent and CFRs as high as 11 percent in the worst outbreaks, though the overall CFR was 2.6 percent as a result of 45 deaths among 1,704 cholera cases.[23] In retrospect, these numbers proved modest, both in comparison to rates among refugees elsewhere in Africa as well as in Mozambique as the Seventh Pandemic intensified in the 1990s.

The seventh cholera pandemic first reached Mozambique in September 1973, as the country was nearing the end of a decade of armed conflict between the Portuguese colonial state and the Liberation Front of Mozambique, better known by its Portuguese abbreviation FRELIMO. The first cholera emergency broke out in the coastal port of Beira, and then spread along the Beira-Zambezi rail line. It then made its way up the so-called Beira corridor into the Zambezi River valley, and then on to Malawi, where it struck hard among fishing communities. Historically persistent colonial labor migration patterns helped bring cholera to the mines of Zimbabwe and South Africa as well (see chapter 8).

Brutal warfare destabilized Mozambique over much of its recent history. Soon after its founding in 1962, FRELIMO gained control over most of the northern region of the country, but it could not oust the Portuguese from urban areas. By 1974, FRELIMO's resistance, together with that of kindred groups in Angola and Portuguese Guinea, prompted the Portuguese colonial army in Africa to begin a revolution in the mother country. In 1975, FRELIMO negotiated Mozambique's independence under the leadership of its first president, Samora Machel.

Before joining FRELIMO in 1962, Machel trained as a nurse in the colonial health care system, and he valued public health investment. Until he died in a suspicious plane crash in 1986, Machel stressed primary health care in every district and devoted more than 10 percent of his government's total expenditure to health, more than any other African country.

Machel was committed to ending colonialism in Southern Africa. He permitted liberation movements fighting white minority regimes in Zimbabwe and South Africa to train and operate within Mozambique. In retaliation, the two white regimes encouraged a rebel group called

[23] A. Moren, et al., "Epidemiological surveillance among Mozambican refugees in Malawi, 1987–89," *Disasters*, 15 (1991), 369–71.

Mozambique National Resistance (MNR) to destabilize the government by destroying schools, hospitals, and clinics.[24] These disruptions were an integral part of a low-intensity war that lasted more than a decade and exacted a heavy toll. Armed conflict displaced more than one million people and damaged preventive programs, raised mortality rates, and exacerbated food shortages. Several infectious disease epidemics followed. Fighting continued through to 1992, when the Rome Peace Accords finally took hold. Both Beira and Quelimane suffered siege conditions at various times in this protracted conflict, although Beira kept up its port functions, enabling people to move in and out more readily than in Quelimane.

The costs of destabilization have been substantial. Between 1982 and 1985, a quarter of the total primary health care network was looted, more than twenty ambulances were destroyed, drug supplies were stolen, many health workers were kidnapped, and twenty-one were murdered. Insecurity drove skilled health care professionals to the coastal cities, leaving rural Mozambicans to suffer most. Health expenditures also shrank because of military priorities. In 1982, health costs were 11.2 percent of the national budget, but by 1985 the percentage dropped to 8.1.[25]

Measles was the most pernicious disease to run amok, but cholera illustrates the plight of the population best. In 1983, a cholera epidemic produced 10,000 cases and 447 deaths in southern Mozambique, a CFR of 4.5 percent. The high CFR for Mozambique arose not only because clinics had been disrupted, but also because life-saving ORT packets could not be supplied because of rebel activity. It is a credit to the Machel government that primary health care did not collapse. In fact, in the cities between 1982 and 1986, the percentage of children vaccinated against childhood diseases rose from 32 to 84 percent, though numbers declined in rural Mozambique.

Mozambique's sanitary inheritance from Portugal also contributed to health issues. At independence in 1975, some resentful departing Portuguese settlers spitefully poured cement into drainpipes. Impoverished urban Africans who occupied abandoned houses and apartments later added to the problem by selling items of value such as copper and lead

---

[24] For the war, P. Johnson and D. Martin, eds., *Destructive Engagement. Southern Africa at War* (Harare: Zimbabwe Publishing House, 1986). For the devastation to public health, Julie Cliff and Abdul Razak Noormahomed, "Health as a target: South Africa's destabilization of Mozambique," *Social Studies of Medicine*, 27 (1988), 717–22.

[25] Cliff and Noormahomed, "Health as a Target," 717–22.

piping. By the 1990s, high-rise buildings had no piped water and people purchased water by the bucket in markets.[26]

Whereas armed conflict has placed a heavy disease burden on Mozambicans, the complex ecology of the region has constituted a second set of risk factors for cholera and other water-borne diseases. To the northwest, *Vibrio cholerae* originating in Lake Malawi has made cholera endemic throughout Mozambique since 1991. To the east, low-lying estuarine environments like Mozambique's Indian Ocean coast are vulnerable to the threat of rising sea levels. Geographer Andrew Collins has contributed significantly to our understanding of Mozambique's vulnerability.[27] Mozambique shares with the Bay of Bengal region in southern Asia a common environment. Both are low in elevation, have large estuarine cities with concentrated populations around aquatic environments, high humidity and temperature, and heavy seasonal rainfall. Mozambique's sedimentary basin occupies 31 percent of the country. Collins sees a cholera hazard in the coastal environment throughout Southern and Eastern Africa. The Indian Ocean coast offers favorable conditions for cholera: an aquatic environment rich in copepods, salinity, amoebae, blue-green algae, and several types of seafood. Although the region suffered significant increases in cholera in the late 1990s, Mozambique, with its 3,000 kilometer coastline, regularly recorded the highest rates of incidence globally. In 1998 and 1999 alone, more than 87,000 recorded cases were reported.[28]

Cholera in Mozambique has benefited from both drought and flooding. A widespread drought throughout Southern Africa in 1992 made Beira's urban ground water source on the Pungwe River too saline to drink. In Quelimane, artificial lagoons alongside the River Licuar, from which the city water was pumped, dried up entirely.[29] By contrast, a devastating flood struck Mozambique in February and March 2000. Five weeks of heavy rains all over the eastern parts of Southern Africa left Mozambique with at least 800 dead, many more homeless, 20,000 head of cattle lost, and 1,400 square kilometers of arable land spoiled. The capital city, Maputo was devastated and the road to Beira was closed.

[26] David A. McDonald and Greg Ruiters, eds., *The Age of Commodity: Water Privatization in Southern Africa* (London: Earthscan, 2005), 46.

[27] See especially Andrew Collins, "Vulnerability to coastal cholera ecology," *Social Science and Medicine*, 57 (2003), 1397–407; Collins, "The Geography of Cholera"; and Collins, *Environment*.

[28] Collins, "Vulnerability," 1397–9.

[29] Collins, *Environment*, 228–9.

As river banks burst in the Limpopo Valley, more than 45,000 people were rescued from trees and rooftops, including Sofia Pedro, the woman who received worldwide notice when she gave birth in a tree to her daughter Rositha. International responses took up to three weeks. The Beira Central Hospital, second largest in the country, and another forty-two health units were ruined. The floods overwhelmed aging colonial water systems and contaminated drinking water.[30]

Popular support for public health initiatives against gastrointestinal disease may have helped treat infection. Local healers in Zambesia province, for example, were reported to have advised mothers not to give their children anything to drink when they had severe diarrhea. But the local health service spread the word that hydration was crucial, and that fresh coconut milk was best because it provided electrolytes and was free of contamination. Traditional healers responded favorably and included coconut milk as a recommended treatment.[31]

Other evidence suggests that Mozambicans' long acquaintance with acute gastrointestinal illness has prepared them culturally to deal with modern cholera.[32] Local culture gave powerful recognition to diarrhea as a persistent problem by assigning no less than eight terms for various kinds of diarrhea, whereas elsewhere in Africa three or four terms would be the norm. Diarrhea, the general term for which was *manyoka*, had a complex etiology. Among infants, contaminated food or water could be responsible, but so too could be improper sexual behavior of the father or mother, even before birth. The local explanation was typical of Bantu-speaking East and Central Africans, and turned around the concept of *nyoka*, which means "snake in the stomach."[33] The guardian of bodily purity, this snake needs to be kept calm. Violations of the body that cause it disturbance, whether attributed to diet, environment, social relations,

---

[30] "Floods take serious economic toll," www.un.org/ecosocdev/geninfo/afrec/subjindx/143moz2.

[31] Collins, *Environment*, 238.

[32] Edward C. Green, Annemarie Jurg, and Armando Djedje, "The Snake in the stomach: Child diarrhea in central Mozambique," *Medical Anthropology Quarterly*, 8 (1994), 4–24; and Julie Cliff, Felicity Cutts, and Ronald Waldman, "Using surveys in Mozambique for evaluation of diarrhoeal disease control," *Health Policy and Planning*, 5 (1990), 219–25.

[33] Green et al., "Snake," 4, 21. For Southern and Central African beliefs see John Janzen, "Health, Religion, and Medicine in Central and Southern African Traditions," in L. Sullivan, ed., *Caring and Curing: Health and Medicine in World Religious Traditions* (New York: Macmillan, 1989), 225–54; and Harriet Ngubane, *Body and Mind in Zulu Medicine* (London: Academic Press, 1977).

taboo violation, death in family, miscarriage, or new pregnancy, require purification through the expulsion of impurities.

Recognized in central Mozambique to be a very serious illness, cholera is held to be brought on by spirits bringing bad luck or perhaps revenge to the community. Treatment is similar to other diarrheas and involves the boiling of roots to produce drinkable liquid. It was not, therefore, a great leap to adapt to modern medicine's rehydration therapy. A few local healers knew about ORT packets, and one urbanized healer claimed to know how to mix his own sugar and salt solution, even if what he described to researchers was incorrect.[34]

Mozambique has long endured endemic cholera in both rural and urban settings. Between the eighteen years from 1991 through 2008, only two – 1995 and 1996 – were cholera-free. It has averaged 16,715 cases and 359 deaths annually, with a relatively low CFR of 2.1 percent. Since the beginning of the twenty-first century, however, Mozambique's local public health officials, with the aid of WHO, have succeeded in driving down the CFR below 1 percent.[35] Given the numerous environmental risk factors that the country has faced, it is not realistic to expect cholera to disappear. But Mozambique's extended peace and stable governance has reduced risks from human mismanagement. The country's success in saving the lives of most of its cholera patients is a commendable achievement, and serves as a model of what can be achieved to high-risk African countries with extended coastal frontage.

---

[34] He is said to have called for a tablespoon of salt and a teaspoon of sugar in a half-liter of water. Green et al., "Snake," 16.

[35] See for example *WER*, 82 (2007), 274, and 83 (2008), 270.

8

Risk Factors

Public Health Policy Choices among Stable and Weak States

Cholera risks are also a function of public health policy choices, especially those involving water and sanitation. The case studies in this chapter include Senegal, South Africa, and Angola.

SENEGAL

On the South Atlantic coast of West Africa, Senegal, together with the region of Senegambia of which it forms a central part, has been vulnerable to extreme weather and thus to high risks from cholera. Several times in the past two decades, extensive flooding following heavy rains has wreaked havoc from Mauritania through to Guinea-Bissau. In Senegal, cholera outbreaks have troubled districts of the capital city of Dakar and the national Muslim pilgrimage site of Touba in the Diourbel region. In Dakar, seasonal flooding exacerbated by climate change has created a cholera danger, and resulted in internally displaced persons who run risks similar to refugees elsewhere in Africa.

Dakar was the capital of the French Colonial Federation of West Africa from 1905 to independence in 1960. Its core urban area, known as the "Plateau," received modern sanitary infrastructure from the colonial government to make it attractive and healthful for French citizens and their families in the public and private sectors. As Assane Seck details, privileged Africans working as colonial intermediaries also benefited from these facilities. Unlike the vast majority of Africans, they could afford housing in the European Plateau, which was also inhabited by Lebanese traders and Portuguese-speaking immigrants from the Cape Verde islands. In short, colonial Dakar was a city where economic, not political, segregation prevailed.[1] After independence especially, urban growth in Dakar accelerated and the infrastructure failed to keep pace. Sanitation and piped water were extended to new and more prosperous districts like Fann Residence, Point E, and SICAP, but for the rest of the rapidly growing Cape Verde peninsula, a shortage of safe drinking water posed a serious problem.

In 1985, when floods struck Dakar, cholera took its heaviest toll in the poor and low-lying neighborhoods of Médina, Gueule-Tapée, and Reubeuss, where the piped water supply was defective and open air sewers were often clogged. Only 36 percent of the district buildings were connected to the sewer network, and more than 60 percent employed poorly built latrines. Senegal itself recorded a total of 2,988 cases and 300 deaths, a CFR of more than 10 percent.[2]

Cholera returned to Senegal ten years later in 1995, when 3,222 cases and 137 deaths (a CFR of 4.3 percent) were reported to the WHO. Senegalese researchers investigating 323 cholera patients at Fann Hospital in Dakar found that only 32 percent used piped water in their homes; most employed either public fountains, well water, or water purchased in plastic bags. Only 49 percent of their homes were connected to the sewage system, and 18 percent did not even have latrines.[3] The researchers blamed the severe Senegalese outbreak on the shortage of clean water; but they also criticized poor local hygiene and recommended tighter surveillance by health workers, more publicity on the need to wash hands and to disinfect latrines, and greater chlorination of drinking water.

In the summer of 2005, major floods contributed to Senegal's alarming national total of 31,719 officially notified cholera cases and 458 deaths (a CFR of 1.4 percent). Once again, several of the same impoverished slums in Dakar became uninhabitable, this time leaving at least 20,000 people homeless.[4] Cholera was much less severe after 2005, but in 2007 Senegal did record 3,984 cases and 24 deaths (CFR of 0.6 percent). The region of Senegambia, however, remained endemic. In 2008, the small republic of Guinea-Bissau reported a staggering 14,323 cholera cases and 225 deaths. Two-thirds of the cases were in the capital city of Bissau,

---

[1] Assane Seck, *Dakar, métropole ouest-africaine* (Dakar: IFAN, 1970), 216–17; and Myron Echenberg, *Black Death, White Medicine: Bubonic Plague and the Politics of Public Health in Colonial Senegal, 1914–1945* (Portsmouth, NH: Heinemann, 2002), 27–31.

[2] P.S. Sow, et al., "L'épidémie de choléra de 1995–1996 à Dakar," *Médicine et Maladies Infectieuses* 29 (1999), 105–9.

[3] Sow et al., "L'épidémie de choléra, 107–9.

[4] *WER*, 81 (2006), 300–2.

but between May and November 2008, cholera made its way into every jurisdiction, racking up CFRs of 9 percent in the more remote and poorly served provinces.[5]

Although its environment has not been cooperative, the government of Senegal has exacerbated risks of cholera through poor policy decisions. A functioning African democracy with a strong civil society and a well-developed public health system, Senegal has become the darling of international health agencies. It has gained a positive public health image as a result of its remarkable success in dealing with Africa's HIV/AIDS crisis.[6]

Unfortunately, the country's record is unsatisfactory when addressing the cholera risks resulting from its exposure to extreme weather and from its aging sanitary infrastructure. In the aftermath of the 2005 cholera crisis, the elected President Abdoulaye Wade announced an ambitious but poorly executed emergency plan costing $104 million to build 4,000 cement homes with electricity and running water for people displaced by the floods. Wade called the plan *Jaxaay*, or "eagle" in Wolof, a symbol of pride.[7] A year later, however, on the site where the houses were to be built, only empty fields stood, and thousands of flood victims still lived in temporary tent camps. Some new housing had been constructed, but the project remained seriously behind schedule. When the rains returned in 2006, the tents sheltering most displaced persons leaked. At one camp called Ganar, 500 people shared six showers and toilets, garbage was never collected, and the infirmary reported numerous cases of malaria and dysentery since 2005.

By 2007, thousands still remained in the tent camps. According to Enda Ecopole, an NGO that assisted the flood victims, conditions in the camps remained so deplorable that only those so impoverished that they have no other choice remained in the tents while waiting for Wade's promises to be realized. Many others moved in with relatives in Dakar or went to surrounding villages and slums in the Cape Verde peninsula. Despair combined with resignation was reflected in the remarks of Coumba Diop as she waited in her tent: "I still keep hoping that one day they will come and bring me to Jaxaay. The president of the republic promised us, but in the meantime I'm getting old."[8]

---

[5] WER, 83 (2008), 270, and 84 (2009), 310, 315–16.
[6] John Iliffe, *The African AIDS Epidemic, A History* (Oxford: James Currey, 2006), 57.
[7] "Utopian Plan Belies Dismal Reality for Flood Victims," December 19, 2006, www.allafrica.com/stories/printable/200612190751
[8] "Utopian," 2.

A second cholera threat to Senegal that combines environmental and political risks is the annual Muslim pilgrimage. Each March, more than a million of the faithful congregate at the holy city of Touba, where the shrine of the venerated founder of the Murid brotherhood, Ahmadu Bamba, is located. This festival, called the *Grand Magal*, is also emulated by other Muslim brotherhoods in the same general region of Diourbel, 150 kilometers to the northeast of Dakar. As was the case in the nineteenth century with Hindu pilgrimages at Hardwar in India and Muslim pilgrimages at Mecca, the congested temporary facilities for millions of people enabled cholera to spread rapidly among pilgrims arriving and leaving such large gatherings.

In Senegal in 2005, health authorities tried to control cholera by installing additional health stations and increasing the amount of chlorinated water for pilgrims, but these measures failed to prevent both an explosion of cholera and the diffusion of the infection by pilgrims returning to their homes throughout the country. Cholera associated with the Touba pilgrimage peaked on April 2, 2005, when 785 new cases were registered in a single day, after which cases declined from more than 3,000 a week to about 500 by June.[9] In an interview, Dr. Pape Salif Sow, Head of Infectious Diseases at the Fann Hospital in Dakar, reported that all the hospitalized cholera cases were Touba pilgrims who drank contaminated water because they had no other choice. He felt it a matter of national importance to recognize the right of people to potable water, and he blamed bad maintenance of septic tanks and canals of stagnant water, which contaminated the water table.[10] President Wade's ambivalence about cholera is not new. None of his predecessors has dared challenge the autonomy of powerful religious authorities by being perceived as interfering with sacred religious practices. Yet no visible effort to reason with the public has been attempted. Instead, Wade's government has continued policies of accommodation toward Muslim, and especially international economic elites. Like most developing nations of the south, Senegal under Wade's mandate has experienced considerable pressure to privatize water services.[11] As we will see in the South African case study, cholera crises and water policies were intimately linked.

9 "Senegal: Lingering cholera epidemic gains new strength," *Integrated Regional Information Networks*, June 23, 2005.
10 Interview, May, 2006, www.sudonline.sn/spip.php? article 1332.
11 For background on water politics in Africa, see Maude Barlow, *Blue Covenant: The Global Water Crisis and the Coming Battle for the Right to Water* (Toronto: McClelland & Stewart, 2007), 35–43; Ann-Christin Sjolander Holland, *The Water Business: Corporations versus*

In the early 1980s, the UN declared an International Drinking Water Supply and Sanitation Decade to set targets for provisioning potable water in the south. They used a public model established in the north as far back as the late nineteenth century. But by 1990, the public model was abandoned in an initiative that European private water companies applauded.

The shift was part of the rise of neoliberalism and its market-based ideology articulated by Margaret Thatcher in Britain and by Ronald Reagan in the United States. Global financial institutions such as the World Bank and the International Monetary Fund were quick to encourage privatization of state services everywhere. In 1989, Thatcher privatized publicly owned regional water authorities in Britain. The private companies raised water rates, laid off thousands of workers, and enjoyed excellent pretax profits as high as 147 percent in the first decade of privatization.[12] Millions, however, had their water cut off when they were unable to pay their water bills.

In the south, indebted countries fell further behind in their debt repayment as interest rates soared in the 1980s. The World Bank only agreed to renegotiate their loans if countries in question accepted Structural Adjustment Programs, or SAPs, which required the sell-off of public enterprises and utilities, and the privatization of education, health care, electricity, and transportation.

Key regional banks such as the African Development Bank and the Inter-American Development Bank encouraged poor countries to permit the large European water corporations to run their water systems for profit. With loans conditional on privatization, it was no surprise that by 2006, the vast majority of African, Asian, and Latin American users were purchasing water from transnational water companies.[13]

Because sources are lacking, the water story in Senegal can only be briefly sketched. Historically, the quantity of water available to Dakar's ever-growing population has long been a problem. The city's water consumption has consistently lagged behind a minimum estimated daily consumption rate of one hundred liters per person. The Senegalese geographer Assane Seck noted in 1970 that over fifty years, Dakar's water consumption had doubled every decade, a rise corresponding roughly to

People (New York: Zed Books, 2005); and Kate Bayliss and Terry McKinley, *Privatizing Basic Utilities in Sub-Saharan Africa: The Millenium Development Goal Impact* (for the UNDP International Poverty Centre (January, 2007).

[12] Holland, *The Water Business*, 9.
[13] Barlow, *Blue Covenant*, 38.

the population increase.[14] By 1970, the city was obliged to draw on a new water source at Pout, some fifty kilometers away, in order to bring the individual daily consumption level to eighty-nine liters. At the time of his writing, Seck indicated that a twenty-year projection based on drawing water from the Senegal River would still leave the per-capita consumption rate below the minimum need. Dakar's failure to come close to the water needs of a population far in excess of what Seck projected is revealed in the rise in endemic cholera that has been documented earlier.

Beginning in the late 1980s, heavily indebted countries of the Third World could not resist the pressure to adopt neoliberalism in exchange for renegotiated loans. Senegal was one of many states to embrace the new ideology of privatization, and by 1995 this shift significantly affected water policy.[15] The national water service provider of Senegal, the Société Nationale d'Exploitation des Eaux du Sénégal (SONEES), was split into the state-owned SONEES and a private operator, La Sénégalaise des Eaux (SDE). Water prices to consumers have risen since, although SDE insisted that the quality of the service did improve.[16] Access to safe and affordable drinking water remained an ongoing nightmare for hundreds of thousands of Senegalese citizens.

If human agency in the form of international economic pressures increased the cholera threat to Senegal, so too did natural forces. Unusually heavy rains not only brought no less than 23,000 cholera cases to Dakar in the first three months of 2005, but they also placed the wider region of Senegambia at risk. The small republics of Gambia, Guinea-Bissau, and Mauritania also saw spikes in cholera outbreaks. In fact, 2005 was the only year when Gambia reported more than a handful of cases. Over seventeen years, Mauritania reported only six times, Senegal seven, and Guinea-Bissau eleven. Their average CFRs over this time have been 2.5 percent, 2.6 percent, and 2.6 percent respectively. Generally, then, the region has been characterized by low incidence and modest CFRs, indicating the ability of health authorities to manage cholera treatment reasonably well. It may, however, be a sign of alarm that Senegal – without any cholera from 1991 to 1994 or from 1998 to 2003 – has not only reported cholera every year since the 2004–2005 outbreaks, but after its number of cases fell 365 in 2006, it spiked to almost 4,000 in 2007.

---

[14] Seck, *Dakar, métropole ouest-africaine*, 216–17.

[15] Meredeth Turshen, *Privatizing Health Service in Africa* (New Brunswick. NJ.: Rutgers University Press, 1999).

[16] "Water for Life," www.un.org/waterforlifedecade/factsheet.html

SOUTH AFRICA

Although it is dwarfed by such terrible chronic diseases as tuberculosis and HIV/AIDS, cholera nevertheless has represented a serious health problem for many South Africans. Not surprisingly, in the apartheid era, old patterns of labor migration and the state's penchant for interfering in the affairs of front-line states north of the Limpopo meant that cholera in Mozambique would soon find its way south. In November of 1973, South African authorities began a large-scale cholera surveillance program in the Transvaal mines out of fear migrant workers would import cholera. Such localized measures could not prevent a small outbreak in a couple of gold mines in the Transvaal during March, 1974.

The South African state preferred to downplay cholera and chose not to report on cholera reliably to the WHO, a practice consistent with apartheid's general approach to health.[17] Although it is therefore difficult to reconstruct an accurate picture of cholera's presence in South Africa before 1990, a few clues emerge from the limited literature available. One study of sources of drinking water during a cholera outbreak in Natal reached the predictable conclusions that treating water with bleach or boiling protected against illness, and those who drank water from a river source were more likely to get cholera than those who imbibed from "safer" sources.[18] Another report on the cholera outbreak in the two Transvaal mines expressed surprise that sixty-three migrant laborers contracted cholera, even though half had received cholera vaccinations before leaving their home countries. Not only did the researchers fail to realize that vaccines only provided protection for a few weeks, they also made the curious claim that cholera may have spread by means of the profuse perspiration of miners, because traces of *Vibrio cholerae* were found on the floor of rooms used for the training and acclimatization of new miners. Typical of the medical mentality prevalent in the mining culture of apartheid South Africa, the research team made no comment on the wider social implications of cholera and its potential to spread in South Africa. Instead, they concluded lamely that the presence of cholera in South Africa showed the importance of "ensuring that sewage disposal plants are in optimal operating condition."[19]

[17] Neil Andersson, and Shula Marks, "Apartheid and health in the 1980s," *Social Science and Medicine*, 27 (1988), 667–81.
[18] G.S. Sinclair, et al., "Determination of the mode of transmission of cholera in Lebowa," *South African Medical Journal*, 62 (1982), 753–5.
[19] Margaretha Isaacson, et al., "The recent cholera outbreak in the South African gold mining industry: a preliminary report," *South African Medical Journal*, 48 (1974), 2560.

Whereas hundreds died from cholera and typhoid fever outbreaks in the so-called tribal Homelands, thousands had been infected by the time apartheid collapsed in 1989.[20] Glimpses of cholera outbreaks appeared occasionally in the pages of the *South African Medical Journal*, where careful readers could learn that the first reported case occurred in the KaNgwane area of Eastern Transvaal in 1980, or that cholera was present in every ward of Eshowe Hospital in Natal in 1983.[21]

During the 1990s, however badly South Africa was hit by the HIV/AIDS pandemic, cholera was rarely seen. A handful of imported cases were reported in some years, as in 1993 and 1998, when the country registered two deaths each year from roughly seventy or eighty cases. Yet cholera was never far from South Africa's borders during these transitional years when power shifted away from whites and to majority rule. Endemic cholera in Malawi and Mozambique represented a serious threat to northern regions of South Africa.

Suddenly, in mid-August of 2000, a cholera epidemic of dramatic proportions struck Madlebe, a semirural community of poor black South Africans living close to the predominantly white town of Empangeni. The region, some 160 kilometers north of Durban, was part of the province of KwaZulu-Natal. Soon the epidemic engulfed most of KwaZulu-Natal and then spread to the Eastern Cape, Mpumalanga, and other provinces of South Africa. Combined official cholera statistics for the 2000–2001 epidemic reveal a total of 125,818 cases, roughly 60 percent of the world total for those years, and far and away the most ever recorded for a modern African epidemic.[22] In the face of this disaster, there was some consolation. Deaths were kept to 264; this remarkable CFR of just one quarter of one percent was the lowest reported anywhere in the world.

The government's rapid mobilization of medical and military personnel led to this great success. Hospitals erected temporary nursing stations to cope with the epidemic. The ministry of health launched a public information campaign using radio, television, and pamphlets to warn against unsafe sources; and it sponsored road shows featuring popular presenters and musicians, as well as demonstrations of how to treat water both by boiling and through the application of freely provided

---

[20] Andersson and Marks, "Apartheid and health," 667–81.
[21] "Notifications of diseases," *South African Medical Journal*, 65 (1982); and J.A. Chapman, and L.P. Collocott, "Cholera in children at Eshowe Hospital," *South African Medical Journal*, 68 (1985), 249.
[22] WER, 76 (2001), 233–40, and 77 (2002), 257–68.

chlorine bleach.[23] They also recruited local women to work (without remuneration) as community health workers all over the Madlebe area. The women went door to door and demonstrated how to use a preparation of the sugar-salt solution for ORT. Finally, the ministry deployed 125 health workers from other provinces to KwaZulu-Natal to boost local capacity.[24]

Equally extraordinary was the intensive mobilization of what were then the formidable resources of the South African Defence Force (SADF). The military bolstered the water tankers provided by municipalities to distribute safe water in rural KwaZulu-Natal. The army medical corps mobilized helicopters and ambulances to evacuate acute cases from some seventy temporary rehydration tents set up in convenient sites such as playing fields and schools. There, medical teams treated more than 1,000 patients a day and roughly 100,000 overall.[25]

Popular responses to the cholera disaster in South Africa have ranged from fear to fatalism, faith-based convictions, and cynicism. Many who felt that water was "a gift from God" and should not be taxed resorted to acts of noncompliance and even vandalism through the smashing of water meters. Fatalism in the face of death and debilitation was also common: "Cholera came and wreaked havoc in this community. Many of our brothers passed away. Our children also passed away. When you had a running stomach you just thought, 'My turn has come to pass on as well.'"[26] Religious beliefs played a role as well. In KwaZulu-Natal, followers of the popular and widespread Shembe faith believed water to have spiritual as well as practical significance, including powers to heal the sick. Prayer served to ensure that water was pure and safe to drink, whatever its source.[27] Although such a position might have made healers and preachers obstacles to beneficial cholera therapy, they in fact cooperated generally with efforts to treat cholera efficaciously.

[23] Hameda Deedat and Eddie Cottle, "Cost Recovery and Prepaid Water Meters and the Cholera Outbreak in KwaZulu-Natal: A Case Study in Madlebe," in David A. McDonald and John Pape, eds., *Cost Recovery and the Crisis of Service Delivery in South Africa* (Cape Town: Human Sciences Research Council Publishers, 2002), 94.

[24] David Hemson, "Still Paying the Price: Revisiting the Cholera Epidemic of 2000–2001 in South Africa," Occasional Papers Series, No.10, *Municipal Services Project*, David A. McDonald and Greg Ruiters, series editors (Grahamstown: Grocott's Publishers, 2006), 17–18.

[25] Ian Crowther, "Saluting the South African medical health service's involvement in cholera prevention and treatment in KwaZulu-Natal," *Milmed*, 17 (2001), 18–19.

[26] Anonymous, interview, Mkhize, July 7, 2003, in Hemson, "Still Paying," 2.

[27] Hemson, "Still Paying," 22.

Stories abounded of how cholera invoked dread. One told of how a terrified young girl died after concealing her symptoms for some time. One informant remembered the fears cholera invoked this way: "The hair still stands on its end and you feel the blood rush through all parts of the body each time when one thinks about the situation."[28] Conspiracy theories involving external agencies were common. One argument held that airplanes were used to contaminate water sources. Another asserted that whites brought down cholera on blacks as part of the pressure to adopt prepaid meters and cost recovery. Some were skeptical and lacked trust in authorities. Many denied public health publicity about the dangers of river water because it had always been used in the past. Some were willing to use bleach, but stopped when its free distribution ended. Some saw cholera as a device to force people to pay monthly water charges.[29] Finally, despair took hold among many who relied on the compassion of water truck drivers to deliver clean water once or twice a week in defiance of official policy.[30]

If some whites had shown compassion for black Africans, others were not so charitable. In 2000, a water board manager in Madlebe expressed his callous disregard for the distress that intermittent breakdowns in water service produced, and the failure of authorities to provide alternative sources: "These people have been without clean water for years. They are used to it. What is a couple of weeks to them?"[31] Although the South African government was accorded virtually universal acclaim internationally for having intervened so successfully during the cholera crisis of 2000–2001, critics within the country took a different view.[32] As members of the Human Sciences Research Council have pointed out, timely provision of safe water and decent sanitation would have left people with decent infrastructure, whereas the use of a vast array of military resources represented hidden costs well in excess of the costs of prevention.[33]

---

[28] Interview, Mr. Madida, July 7, 2003, in Hemson, "Still Paying," 17.

[29] Hemson, "Still Paying," 14.

[30] David A. McDonald, "The Theory and Practice of Cost Recovery in South Africa," in David A. McDonald and John Pape, eds., *Cost Recovery and the Crisis of Service Delivery in South Africa* (Cape Town: Human Sciences Research Council Publishers, 2002), 15.

[31] Deedat and Cottle, "Cost Recovery," 95.

[32] For praise, see *WER*, 77 (2002), 260; for criticism, see McDonald and Ruiters, *The Age of Commodity*.

[33] Hemson, "Still Paying," 37.

TREATMENT OF CHOLERA

1. Does the person have diarrhoea (running tummy) and vomiting?

2. Make this mixture for the person to drink on the way to the clinic.

8 teaspoons of SUGAR + Half a teaspoon of SALT

1l of SAFE WATER

Mix well

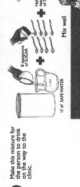

3. Take the person to the clinic IMMEDIATELY.

For more information contact your local clinic or hospital.

Water Affairs and Forestry
Health

Stop
cholera

With clean water
and good hygiene practices

Water Affairs and Forestry
Health

FIGURE 8.1: Stop cholera poster (courtesy of Department of Water Affairs, South African government).

Beginning in 1995, just after majority rule began, Thabo Mbeki's African National Congress (ANC) government adopted a neo-liberal development program. Operation Masakhane ("let's build together") was part of an overall plan called Growth, Employment and Redistribution Strategy, or GEAR. GEAR sought to launch South Africa on a path to sustainable development, and one of its essential features was cost recovery for new water and electrical installations.[34] The World Bank's water expert on Lesotho and South Africa, John Roome, advised Kader Asmal, then South Africa's Minister of the Department of Water Affairs and Forestry (DWAF), to introduce a "credible threat of cutting service" to nonpaying customers.[35]

The close correlation between neo-liberal cost recovery and the cholera explosion is best illustrated by the impact of water policy in Madlebe, where the terrible outbreak began.[36] Madlebe and Empangeni overlook a flat coastal plain and the harbor town of Richards Bay some fifteen kilometers away. The city of uMhlathuze was formed by combining Richards Bay and Empangeni. The population of the whole urban area in 2000 was roughly 50,000.

Empangeni grew rapidly after 1900 with the establishment of a sugar mill, and soon after, the first cotton gin in Zululand. Southern Zululand experienced a cotton crash in the 1920s and its fortunes have been uneven since. Empangeni and its surrounding region boasts South Africa's largest sugar mill in addition to paper factories, aluminum smelters, mines, and upscale game farms. It is today densely populated and very poor. Under apartheid, a tribal homeland separated black Africans from the white areas and provided a cheap labor pool in the Madlebe Tribal Authority.[37]

Most black Africans labor in the nearby sugar plantations, but unemployment is high and has persisted both under apartheid and in the new South Africa. There has been rapid urbanization, together with significant commuting and temporary labor migration, extensive poverty, and low levels of service in rural areas. Politically, most blacks in Zululand

---

34 The most thorough and recent assessment of Mbeki's years in governance of South Africa is William M. Gumede, *Thabo Mbeki and the Battle for the Soul of the ANC* (London: Zed Books, 2007).

35 Jacques Pauw, "Metered to Death: How a Water Experiment Caused Riots and a Cholera Epidemic," *Global Policy Forum* (February 5, 2003), 6.

36 The two sources for the Madlebe case study are Deedat and Cottle, "Cost Recovery" and Hemson, "Still Paying."

37 Shula Marks, *The Ambiguities of Dependence in South Africa: Class, Nationalism and the State in Twentieth-Century Natal* (Johannesburg: Ravan Press, 1986).

supported Inkatha, a cultural nationalist organization turned ethnic party appealing to Zulu loyalties and chiefly patrimony. Led by Chief Mangosuthu Buthelezi, Inkatha challenged the ANC during the apartheid years, but after 1994 Buthelezi became a cooperative cabinet minister in Mbeki's government, and Inkatha no longer threatens ANC hegemony.[38]

During apartheid, public health infrastructure in the Madlebe Tribal Authority was poor. Facilities consisted of mobile clinics and a single hospital at Ngwelezane, but long distances and poor roads made access difficult. As in most of Zululand, the Madlebe region experienced erratic rainfall, and it lacked even a bucket system or latrines; thousands resorted to the bush, or worse, to river banks. Water came from sparsely distributed bore-holes, as well as from these same nearby streams used as toilets, such as the Mfolozi, the Mthlathuze, and the Empangeni rivers.[39] A major drought in 1982 and 1983, which was followed by a cholera outbreak, prompted the state to install nine communal taps, the only purified water available until 1997. Still, the coming of majority rule in 1994 offered hope that a new policy of free primary health care would address the needs of a public that suffered from one of the highest percentages of HIV/AIDS infection in South Africa.

Interviews conducted at the nine communal taps, which dated back to apartheid days, showed that popular hopes for improvements had been dashed. A registration fee for connection to the water supply proved unaffordable for most black Africans, and drove them to use unpurified river water a few months before the cholera outbreak.[40] Even for those who sacrificed to subscribe, the frequent breakdown of the entire system left customers without water for up to three weeks at a time. Clearly, cost recovery represented a terrible threat to health of the poor.

As the KwaZulu-Natal epidemic was unfolding, the Mbeki government responded with a "Free Basic Water policy," to be implemented by DWAF Minister Ronnie Kasrils.[41] All South African households would

---

[38] Gerhard Maré, and Georgina Hamilton, *An Appetite for Power: Buthelezi's Inkatha and South Africa* (Johannesburg: Ravan Press, 1987); and Bill Freund, "Zulu Identity in the International Context," in Benedict Carton, John Laband, and Jabulani Sithole, eds., *Zulu Identities: Being Zulu, Past and Present* (London: Hurst & Company, 2009), 606–12.

[39] Deedat and Cottle, "Cost Recovery," 81.

[40] Deedat and Cottle, "Cost Recovery," 11.

[41] A prominent member of President Thabo Mbeki's cabinet, Ronnie Kasrils had been a senior member of the ANC, a founding member and commander of its armed wing, *Umkhonto we Sizwe*, and a prominent figure in the South African Communist Party during the struggle against apartheid. He was appointed deputy minister of defence from

be guaranteed 6,000 liters of free water per month, based on estimates of eight persons per household and consumption of at least twenty-five liters per person per day.

Kasrils promised "basic supplies" of water and electricity for all South Africans by 2008. As critics pointed out, however, this quantity did not significantly exceed the minimum of four liters a day an individual requires to replenish the body's liquids.[42] It was argued that one hundred liters was the minimum needed for all basic personal and food hygiene, including laundry and washing, but not counting water to grow food. To grow food daily requires between 2,000 and 5,000 liters of water. Clean water consumption in a country well endowed with inexpensive potable water such as Canada exceeded by thirteen times the South African household quota.[43] In the United Kingdom, per-capita domestic water consumption for 1996–1999 was between 145 and 157 liters a day.[44]

Kasrils's fine words offered much more than he or the ANC could deliver. Since 2001, progress in extending access to free water has been slow, especially in semiurban and rural areas, the very places where cholera has been prominent. In addition, inadequate management of water has led to frequent interruptions and cut-offs, burst pipes, slow repairs, and poor general maintenance, so that water delivery in urban as well as rural locales could be interrupted for weeks. As late as 2005, only half of the 170 water service providers met water-quality standards.[45] In rural areas, only 2 percent of blacks had indoor plumbing.[46] In cities, the fundamental unfairness of water policy in a racially divided society persists, which was not supposed to happen in the new South Africa. For example, all-white suburbs of Johannesburg were given discounted bulk rates, and a household could fill its swimming pool and water its garden at less than half the cost per liter faced by a black family in Alexandra township.[47]

Kasrils was not the only minister in the Mbeki cabinet to play an influential role on water and sanitation policy. Dr. Manto Tshabalala-Msimang

---

1994 to 1999, minister of water affairs and forestry from 1999 to 2004, and since then, minister for intelligence services. As head of the DWAF he proved to be an artful dodger of criticism directed toward the ANC government and a loyal supporter of President Mbeki.

[42] "Dead in the water," CBC, The Fifth Estate, broadcast of March 31, 2004, www.cbc.ca/fifth/deadinthewater/africa-printer, 5.

[43] "Dead in the water," 5.

[44] McDonald and Ruiters, *The Age of Commodity*, 72–3.

[45] Hemson, "Still Paying," 37.

[46] Pauw, "Metered," 5.

[47] John Jeter, "South Africa's Driest Season," *Mother Jones* (November/December, 2002), 4.

served as minister of health from 1999 until a reluctant Mbeki finally removed her in 2007, after she was admitted to Johannesburg Hospital suffering from lung disease.[48] Her stance on HIV/AIDS rather than cholera control was a constant embarrassment to the government. Despite angry international and internal opposition to her stubborn reluctance to treat AIDS in the public sector with antiretroviral medicines, she promoted the benefits of beetroot, garlic, lemons, and African potatoes as well as good general nutrition. Dr. Tshabalala-Msimang's emphasis on cholera control was directed toward the building of Ventilated Improved Privies, or VIPs, where no latrines at all were available. She persuaded the European Union to apply part of a $66.6 million grant for the building of toilets, but like Kasrils's Free Water program, the VIPs scheme lagged far behind expectations. In 2003, Dr. Tshabalala-Msimang admitted that although 3.5 million people had received access to sanitation facilities since 1994, the government planned to remove the "backlog" of more than 16 million people by 2010.[49]

The debate over water policy in South Africa requires careful reading. It should not be reduced to the alleged merits of public versus private utilities. Rather, it turns on the issue of commercialization of water rather than ownership of the utility. The question is whether access to water is a basic human right or a commercial commodity that can be sold. The ANC government's position has not been clear. On the one hand, Mbeki and Kasrils have touted their "Free Basic Water policy." On the other, Mike Muller, director-general of the DWAF, remarked disingenuously that the prepaid system benefited consumers because "people don't have to put up with the administration, the paperwork of bills."[50] Muller has shifted his statements frequently. Questioned on national television about the cholera crisis he conceded that "perhaps we were being a little too market-oriented."[51] Meanwhile, his minister, Ronnie Kasrils, rationalized water privatization on the grounds of cost: "The private sector has played and will continue to play an important role in both water resources and water services. The challenges facing us are simply too big to be addressed by government alone."[52] As recently as 2003, Trevor Manuel, South Africa's finance minister and a strong advocate of neo-liberal economic policy,

---

[48] Gumede, *Thabo Mbeki*, 187–215.
[49] Dr. Manto Tshabalala-Msimang, Parliamentary Media Briefing, February 19, 2003, 4.
[50] "Dead in the water."
[51] Mohammed Alie, "South Africa Flounders in its Search for Free Water", *Panos-South Africa*, February 1, 2002, 2.
[52] In "Dead in the water," 2.

remarked that "free water has not benefited the rural poor and is difficult and costly to implement."[53]

The three South African centers of Durban, Johannesburg, and Nelspruit in KwaZulu-Natal reveal how tensions over water have been playing out. Durban was the first city to apply the government's free basic water policy.[54] While maintaining the free six kiloliters per month basic rate, the city doubled the cost for more than six kiloliters. One-third of the city's poorest customers subsequently lowered their consumption from twenty-two to fifteen kiloliters, and their richest customers dropped consumption from thirty-five to thirty-two kiloliters. Durban's water prices have been compared with four other major Third World cities by the UN Human Development Report of 2006. The report found that Durban prices for those consuming from seven to twenty kiloliters per month were the most expensive, a third more costly than those for Dakar and seven times more costly than Bangalore, India. Despite government claims that almost all poor households are connected to the water system, evictions have continued in ever-proliferating shack settlements, where roughly a quarter of all households reside. Particularly vulnerable are women-headed households with AIDS orphans and backyard renters or room tenants.

Johannesburg, South Africa's largest city, with a population of three million, also underwent a transformation in water management through new national legislation in 1999. Its public water utility, lacking management expertise, signed a contract in 2001 with a consortium led by the French water multinational Suez Lyonnaise and British Northumbrian Water. The private companies administered the billing and the quality of the city's water supply. The new utility, called Johannesburg Water Management (JOWAM), installed prepaid water meters in some neighborhoods, obliging customers to pay in advance for what they consumed. Many people had previously drawn water from free communal taps.

JOWAM officials maintained that their private partners would improve revenue collection and quality of service delivery. But it has also been argued that private providers around the world maximize profits and efficiency at the expense of poor peoples' right to water. They focus

---

53 In Patrick Bond and Greg Ruiters, "South Africa: Water for all?" *Pambazuka News*, November 23, 2006, 2, www.pambazuka.org. Patrick Bond is director of the Centre for Civil Society at the University of KwaZulu-Natal; Greg Ruiters directs the Municipal Services Project at Rhodes University's Institute for Social and Economic Research.
54 Bond and Ruiters, "Water for all?" 3–5.

on richer customers and have cut off those who cannot afford to pay.[55] JOWAM clearly behaved like a profit-orientated body when they disconnected the meters of impoverished consumers who could not afford the rates. By contrast, in Britain, the government banned prepaid meters in 1998 on the grounds that disconnections prompted by poverty represented a public health threat. The UN Human Development Report of 2006 has sharply criticized JOWAM's contract with Suez, because transfers of operating authority from local government to utility, and from utility to companies, not only obscures accountability and delivery, but also makes JOWAM both utility shareholder and regulator. Such captive regulators are all too common in South Africa, and the failure of the government to "name and shame," as DWAF Minister Kasrils promised to do in 2003, has left antiprivatization activists as the only watchdogs of JOWAM. Meanwhile, strong dissatisfaction toward prepaid metering persists in black districts such as Soweto and Orange Farm.[56]

Nelspruit lies on the border with Mozambique, a three-hour drive north from Johannesburg.[57] The old town is white and prosperous and serviced by a water network. After apartheid, new boundaries expanded the town in 1999 by an additional 250,000 poor blacks who lacked potable water and basic sanitation. The cost to build additional water and sewage networks was $38 million, so the municipal government hoped that by contracting out water delivery to a private company, the burden of this cost would be alleviated. A consortium called the Greater Nelspruit Utility Company (GNUC) was formed, led by the British water company Biwater, and was granted a thirty-year concession to expand and manage the water and sanitation network. GNUC laid ninety kilometers of new water pipelines, seventeen kilometers of sewage pipes, installed 7,240 new water meters, and made 500 new water connections.

Many of the newly supplied black consumers could not pay the charges, according to Henry Nkuna, a former freedom fighter with the Azanian People's Liberation Army, the armed wing of the Pan-Africanist Congress (PAC). The PAC, a radical nationalist party, favors black empowerment and more aggressive land redistribution. Unemployed in 2002 with six children to support, Nkuna formed the Anti-Privatization Forum to pressure the municipality to cancel the GNUC contract and introduce a flat

[55] Alie, "South Africa flounders" 1–2.
[56] Bond and Ruiters, "Water for all?" 3, 5.
[57] "Dead in the water," 1.

rate of three dollars a month for all municipal services. He also threatened to use violence against the GNUC if necessary:

> If you dare to do cost recovery in the townships, it will spark a fire. It will be
> something you will regret forever ... If they [GNUC] come into the township to
> cut our water supplies or take our goods, we'll vandalize their cars and beat up
> their workers.[58]

Resistance to cost recovery in the provision of basic services is widespread and ongoing throughout South Africa. Protests have ranged from
withholding of payment, to pilfering and sabotage to militant street
demonstrations. Police reported nearly 6,000 protests in a recent twelve-
month period in 2005. Some activities involved not only reconnecting
pipes cut off for nonpayment, but even emptying excrement from the old
apartheid-era "bucket system" at the doors of their elected officials.[59]

In 2002, the South African government sought to make an example of
those who "pilfered" water. In January of that year, one David Shezi, living in a village in KwaZulu-Natal, was caught using a pipe to siphon off
water to override the water meter. He was arrested for theft while claim-
ing that, with an income of only R100 ($8.65) a month, and with eight
children to support, he had no other means of helping his family survive
in conditions of extreme poverty.[60]

Some of this dissent stems from the ANC's own internal resistance to
the earlier apartheid state. Back in the 1980s, it had urged supporters to
make South Africa "ungovernable" by withholding payment to co-opted
and unrepresentative black authorities in the homelands. Millions joined
what became known as the "rates boycott" against electricity and, sometimes, water bills.[61] However effective against an undemocratic state,
aspects of this policy would haunt the ANC once they became the gov-
erning party under majority rule after 1994. The private water and utility
companies, often unable to collect payment for the sale of utilities, have
called this a "culture of non-payment."

Among the most effective opponents of the slow pace of delivery
of promised social and economic benefits has been the South African
Municipal Workers' Union (SAMWU). SAMWU is one of the most militant

---

[58] In Pauw, "Metered," 9–10.
[59] Bond and Ruiters, "Water for all?" 5.
[60] Alie, "South Africa Flounders," 1.
[61] Patrick Bond, *Elite Transition: From Apartheid to Neoliberalism in South Africa*
(Durban: University of Natal Press, 2000); and McDonald, "The Theory and Practice,"
17–37.

affiliates of the Congress of South African Trade Unions (COSATU). As COSATU became increasingly co-opted by Thabo Mbeki's moderate wing of the ANC, SAMWU has spearheaded the rising protests of disadvantaged South Africans.[62] Its members have viewed privatization as a threat to their jobs and to services for the poor. SAMWU argues that South Africa's cholera problem is clearly linked to the delivery system of clean water, and a new policy must "entail recognition of water-cutoffs as unconstitutional, and the principled scrapping of cost-recovery as a determinant of water delivery."[63] Fierce political opposition to privatization also has come from the ultranationalist PAC, which initiated a campaign in 2001 called "Operation Vulamanzi," or Operation Open Water, to reconnect water to all residents cut off for nonpayment. Another group, the Concerned Citizens' Forum (CCF), active in Durban under the leadership of ANC veteran Fatima Meer, has fought utility cut-offs and evictions, using the courts successfully to thwart the Durban Metropolitan Council's plans to relocate rent defaulters.

Strong and increasingly organized civil unrest is manifest among less overtly political groups. Some of the most visible have been the Soweto Electricity Crisis Committee, the Anti-Privatisation Forum, and the Anti-Eviction Campaign.[64] Using old ANC tactics developed against the apartheid state such as marches, pamphleteering, and defiance campaigns, thousands of small civic movements have sprung up since 2005. Many have links to the poor of other countries of the south, such as the Landless Workers' Movement in Brazil and similar groupings in India and the Philippines. Though these social groups have thus far failed to fulfill their initial promises to redress inequalities, they nevertheless represent the only real opposition in a political system where the ANC is so dominant.[65]

Resistance by social activists has had some success, especially against the foreign water companies. Multinational water consortiums throughout Southern Africa have stopped seeking new concessions and are cutting their losses. Saur has withdrawn from Mozambique and Zimbabwe. Suez has not appealed the cancellation of its contract at Nkonkobe (formerly Fort Beaufort) in the Eastern Cape. Biwater says it is committed to Nelspruit but will not seek new concessions. Thames Water has no

---

[62] Gumede, *Thabo Mbeki*, 360–2.
[63] "Joint SAMWU-RDSN (Rural Development Services Network) World Water Day press statement," March 22, 2006, www.worldwaterday.org
[64] McDonald and Pape, *Cost Recovery*, 106.
[65] Gumede, *Thabo Mbeki*, 367.

presence in South Africa, and Vivendi Water is dubious about whether the municipal market is "ready."[66]

In the face of claims and counterclaims, it is helpful to turn elsewhere. Menahem Libhaber, the World Bank's senior water and sanitation engineer for Latin America, offered this insight.[67] A threshold existed beyond which people simply cannot pay. He placed the limit on socially acceptable amounts for utilities at 3 to 4 percent of income, and concluded that South Africa was setting the bar far too high. Supporting this view was a countrywide study by the Department of Local Government in December 2002 showing that many municipalities were gouging the public to such an extent that South Africa's 300 local councils were owed $670 million in outstanding water payments.

Since 1994, the water problem in South Africa has caused untold misery. A national survey by the Municipal Services Project found that as many as 10 million South Africans have had their water cut off for various periods. Two million people have been evicted for failure to pay utility bills, and many poor families spend up to 40 percent of their monthly income for water and electricity. The water cut-offs have driven millions to risk consumption from contaminated sources.[68]

True, some improvements in water and sanitation have occurred since 2001. The VIPs were an asset, and a majority of South Africans did gain access to piped water closer to their residences or through yard connections. Yet only half the 170 water service authorities met water-quality standards. Greater civil-society monitoring was still essential.[69] David McDonald and Greg Ruiters use stronger language.[70] The collective impact of water privatization had devastating effects. Cholera claimed lives of hundreds and exposed thousands, especially the very young, to preventable disease. There was an increase in environmental pollution and degradation from uncontrolled effluent discharges. Morally, making water a restricted privilege was a gross affront to human dignity.

Whether South Africa can avoid another cholera crisis will depend ultimately on access to safe drinking water by most of its citizens. One thing

---

[66] Pauw, "Metered," 11.
[67] Pauw, "Metered," 8.
[68] Pauw, "Metered," 2.
[69] Hemson, "Still Paying," 37.
[70] McDonald and Ruiters, *The Age of Commodity*, 167. David McDonald, a political economist and geographer, is head of Queen's University's Development Studies Program in Kingston, Ontario, and co-director of the Municipal Services Project (MSP) in South Africa.

can be predicted. The SADF, now greatly reduced in personnel and equipment, is no longer a position to save the lives of as many people as were rescued in 2001.

ANGOLA

Angola provides another case study of how public policy can enhance the risk of cholera. Disease and violence have been the sorry lot of the people of Angola for many decades. They suffered greatly through almost thirty years of war, first against Portuguese colonial rule from 1963 to 1975, and then until 2002 as a devastating civil war became a flashpoint for the Cold War. Armed conflict took millions of lives and produced hundreds of thousands of refugees. A country littered with land mines, Angola has needed significant international assistance to accommodate returning refugees since 2002.

On the other hand, Angola's economic fortunes have taken a dramatic turn for the better in recent years. It is now the second-largest petroleum and diamond producer in sub-Saharan Africa. In December of 2006, Angola was admitted as a member of OPEC, and its economy has been enjoying one of the world's biggest booms, averaging about 10 percent growth a year since 2005.[71]

Angola has experienced cholera at various times since 1973, but reported outbreaks were not worrisome until 2006. A massive epidemic began in February 2006 and ended in the spring of 2007.[72] Cholera infected sixteen of eighteen provinces, including urban slums in the two largest cities, the capital of Luanda and Benguela. The two largely urban provinces of the same name recorded more than 50 percent of Angola's cholera total for 2006–2007 of 85,679 cases and 3,235 deaths (a high CFR of 3.8 percent). In nine rural provinces, devastating CFRs ranging from 5 and 15 percent were reported, a measure of poor or nonexistent treatment. In response to the cholera emergency, Médecins sans Frontières (MSF) poured resources into Angola. MSF established six treatment centers in Luanda, one in Benguela, and three others in the smaller provincial towns of Malanje, N'dalatando, and Caxito respectively. It employed 55 international staff, 330 nationals, and treated more than 11,000 patients.[73] Although Angola's civil war was well behind it

---

[71] Angola entry, *The World Factbook*, Washington, D.C.: Central Intelligence Agency, 2008.

[72] WER, 82 (2007), 273–75, and 83 (2008), 270.

[73] *Médecins sans Frontières* report, 2009.

when the outbreak occurred, the government's plea for financial and medical help during the 2006–2007 cholera emergency invoked the argument that nearly 400,000 refugees had returned from neighboring countries since 2002, and the country needed extra assistance. Overcrowding and the scarcity of potable water systems were especially acute in the *Planalto* or central highlands, as well as in Luanda and Mexico province. The country appealed for and received UN funding of more than $2.2 million through the UN's Central Emergency Response Fund, or CERF.[74]

To date, no cholera research beyond the rudimentary and politically correct reports of the WHO are available for the Angola outbreak. But careful reporting by Canadian journalist Stephanie Nolen offers some hints, although she does not mention cholera specifically.[75] She shows how a property and construction boom has been occurring in Luanda over the past few years based on extensive oil and diamond exports. Prime real estate space has become so scarce as to be limited to a little patch of seafront land. Three quarters of the city's four million inhabitants, many of them new urban migrants working in the construction boom, live in appalling conditions. Their shacks have no water services or sanitation, and there are few schools for their children. People pay a dollar a bucket for suspect water provided by tanker trucks. Those who cannot afford such exorbitant prices must scrounge for water from even more dubious sources.

The tanker trucks, some 450 of them, draw 1.3 million gallons of water from the polluted Bengo River just to the north of the city.[76] The trucks supply an estimated 10,000 vendors who fill the jerry cans, buckets, and wash tubs of thousands of slum dwellers. One account of living conditions in the Luanda slums in 2006 provides a picture matching accounts of filth in Zanzibar City 150 years earlier:

Cholera typically spreads through contact with contaminated water or sewage, and in Luanda's slums, both are everywhere. Neighborhoods here are ringed by mountains of garbage, often soaked by rivulets of human waste. Only about half of slum dwellers have even an outdoor latrine. Children stripped to their underwear dance through sewage-clogged creeks and slide down garbage dumps on

---

[74] CERF's money is earmarked for underfunded emergencies in so-called neglected or forgotten crises, and to redress imbalances in global aid distribution. *CERF* Secretariat, United Nations, New York, 2008, www.cerf.un.org.

[75] Stephanie Nolen, "Land of the state, home of the poor," *Toronto Globe and Mail*, September 9, 2008.

[76] Sharon Lafranière, "In oil-rich Angola, cholera preys upon poorest," *New York Times*, June 16, 2006.

sleds made of sheet metal into excrement-fouled puddles. Much of the city has no drainage system; in heavy rains, the filthy water rises hip-high in some of the poorest dwellings.[77]

Cholera in Luanda, which exposes the whole country to risk, is a function of government choices. Enjoying such windfall wealth from its oil revenues, the government might have chosen to provide a modicum of services for its labor force, rather than paying the terrible price in lives and resources needed to control or eliminate cholera. Instead, the Angolan government has opted for a scheme designed to benefit the affluent. Its policy has been to evict people, especially those on prime seafront land, and relocate them some thirty kilometers away from the city. From 2002 to 2006, the government conducted eighteen mass evictions, displaced 20,000 people, and destroyed 3,000 slum dwellings.

Though by no means alone, the Angolan government's cynical policy choices have caused terrible and avoidable suffering for its laboring poor. The tragedy is that the elites have not yet learned the lesson of the late-nineteenth-century European experience with cholera: that is cheaper, as well as in the long-term interest of everyone, to invest in basic sanitation and drinking water than it is to do nothing. Angola's substantial fiscal assets coupled with the availability of international financing and partnerships could turn back cholera in only a few years if its leaders chose to do so.

Sadly, the latest WHO statistics on health are not encouraging. They reveal that Angola remains near the bottom of the Africa region's statistics, with life expectancy and infant mortality rates among the worst in the world.[78] For 2006, Angola spent only 2.6 percent of GDP on health, compared to the regional average of 5.5 percent. On a per-capita basis, the government's expenditure on health was better, averaging $100, compared to $52 for the entire region, yet substantially less than Botswana's $624. For 2007, Angolan health indicators remained poor. Life expectancy at birth stood at fifty-three years, close to regional average, whereas infant mortality and mortality for children under five stood at 116 and 158 per thousand respectively, substantially worse than the Africa region's averages of 88 and 145 per thousand. These deplorable numbers turn up for countries like Guinea-Bissau and Mozambique, where the per-capita annual income in 2008 was only $485 and $465 respectively. However, Angola's per-capita income was $6,331, one of the highest in Africa, although extremely unevenly distributed.

---

[77] Lafranière, "In oil-rich Angola."
[78] "World Health Statistics" (Geneva: WHO, 2009), especially tables 1 and 7.

9

Zimbabwe, Portrait of Cholera in a Failed State

The politics of Zimbabwe have been closely linked – much for the worse – to the fortunes of one man, Robert Gabriel Mugabe.[1] Born in 1924, the wily octogenarian has led his state from prosperity to utter misery, with a ruined economy, a collapsed public health system, and a hungry and sometimes starving population. A massive ten-month cholera outbreak beginning in August 2008 is only the latest in a series of disasters. Details of how such a massive catastrophe occurred require far more space than is available here, but a short overview shows how this failed state has ruined the lives not only of its own population, but of thousands more living in the Southern African region.

Mugabe rose to prominence in the 1960s as the secretary-general of the Zimbabwe African National Union (ZANU). Frequently threatened and sometimes jailed by the dominant white minority in what was then Southern Rhodesia, Mugabe fled the country in 1974 to join the "Second Chimurenga," as the war for liberation was called.[2] Mugabe emerged victorious at the end of the war in 1979 and won a sweeping victory in the general elections the next year. With the help of violent intimidation, Mugabe as prime minister consolidated power over ZANU's rival, the Zimbabwe African Peoples' Union (ZAPU), led by Joshua Nkomo. ZAPU drew most of its support from the Ndebele-speaking region in the south, centered on Bulawayo, the country's second city, whereas ZANU was

---

[1] Stephen Chan, *Robert Mugabe: A Life of Power and Violence* (London: I.B. Tauris, 2003).

[2] David Martin and Phyliss Johnson, *The Struggle for Zimbabwe: The Chimurenga War* (London: Faber & Faber, 1981).

dominated by Shona-speaking peoples in Harare and in rural Zimbabwe outside Matableland. More than an ethnic split, however, the struggle between ZANU and ZAPU also reflected tensions in the Communist world, with Mugabe expressing a pro-Chinese Maoist orientation and Nkomo a Soviet Marxist-Leninist tendency. The often violent conflict with ZAPU ended in 1987 with a merger when Nkomo joined the newly structured ZANU-PF. Mugabe became president of Zimbabwe, a position he has clung to with an iron fist through to the present.

In his first decade of rule after 1980, Mugabe enjoyed widespread national and international support as he presided over a solid economy and a thriving society. His strong endorsement of smallholder agriculture was popular, as was his promise to redistribute more white-held farms once Britain, the former colonial power, delivered on its financial commitments to compensate owners for expropriations. The public health system, which had provided modern care to the white minority, expanded rapidly to deliver services to the black majority. In the first half of the 1980s, social indicators improved for life expectancy, and immunization rose to 80 percent of the population from 25 percent at the beginning of Mugabe's rule.

Like governments throughout Africa, however, ZANU-PF faced two formidable crises not of its making – a medical disaster caused by the spread of HIV/AIDS and a global financial crisis.

The HIV/AIDS epidemic has held Zimbabwe in its thrall for almost two decades.[3] Initially imported stealthily into Southern Africa by migration from the north, HIV/AIDS ravaged Zimbabwe with the aid of an excellent transport system and high levels of internal migration between country and town. By the early 2000s, every village was said to have at least one household headed by a child. The deaths from HIV/AIDS placed tremendous pressure on extended families, and especially on grandparents. By 1995, grandparent caregivers made up 44 percent of households in eastern Zimbabwe. An estimated one in five Zimbabweans are now HIV-positive, and life expectancy has plummeted from sixty-one years in 1998 to thirty-seven in 2007.

John Iliffe has emphasized the importance of recognizing positive trends: HIV/AIDS prevalence in Africa has become stable or is falling.[4] One of the crucial ingredients in this change has been the development of

---

[3] The observations on HIV/AIDS are from Iliffe, *The African AIDS Epidemic*, especially 37–42, and 117–22.

[4] Iliffe, *The African AIDS Epidemic*, 125.

antiretroviral drugs (ARVs) to suppress infection. Some of the Southern African countries facing the same medical crisis, such as Botswana and Namibia, have benefited from ARVs. In South Africa, though ARV treatment was hampered by the resistance of Thabo Mbeki and Manto Tshabalala-Msimang, activism of people with HIV/AIDS has led to more positive developments. Only in Zimbabwe, however, does the situation remain dire. ARV programs have been hampered by Zimbabwe's acute financial crisis, and the refusal of donors like the Global Fund to channel funds "to a government whose probity it distrusted."[5] Little wonder that the disease has lent itself to gallows humor. The local jargon in Zimbabwe has it that some patients suffer from "TB2," derived from "HIV and TB too."[6]

The political will to neutralize HIV/AIDS in Zimbabwe was lacking, and the country's general public health has continued to deteriorate. Mortality rates for children younger than five have climbed from 76 per thousand in 1990 to 105 per thousand in 2006. Maternal mortality has risen from 168 per 100,000 in 1990 to 1,100 in 2005. In 2008 and 2009, all the features of a failed state could be observed in the health sector. Between September and November 2008, as the cholera epidemic raged, most wards in public hospitals gradually closed, and by December there were no functioning critical-care beds in the public sector.[7] Nurses and doctors had been unpaid for months, and medications for HIV/AIDS patients were no longer available. In the main clinic in the capital of Harare, patients were obliged to provide their own food and even latex gloves for their medical attendants.

The global financial crisis of the 1980s affected Zimbabwe, as it did all developing countries. Pressure to adopt "structural adjustment policies" forced Mugabe to bring in austerity programs after 1990. These came down hardest on the poorer black majority, but Mugabe exacerbated the situation politically by targeting white farm owners and castigating Britain for its alleged failure to finance compensation for thousands of confiscated farms. Mugabe's destructive policies have provoked global condemnation since 1998. The international community has watched in disbelief as the ZANU-PF government has triggered the world's worst hyperinflation in memory by printing trillions of Zimbabwe dollars, expropriating

---

[5] Iliffe, *The African AIDS Epidemic*, 153.
[6] Eric Nelson, "Beyond cholera – the Zimbabwe health crisis," *The Lancet Infectious Diseases*, 9 (October 2009), 588.
[7] Geoffrey York, "Crisis in Zimbabwe: a health system nearing total collapse," *Toronto Globe & Mail*, March 14, 2009.

thousands of white-owned farms, and unleashing ZANU-PF thugs – a ragtag group of youths with a smattering of so-called war veterans – on murderous campaigns targeting both white farm families and the black farm workers who supported them. Among the huge errors in judgment, few matched Mugabe's costly military adventure in the DRC, which cost Zimbabwe two million dollars a day.[8]

The chaos unleashed by this failing state has been palpable, as an aging Mugabe clung to power at all costs. By 2004, Zimbabwe, once a breadbasket for the region of Southern Africa, had become dependent on international aid for food and fuel. Internal and external displacement has occurred on a massive scale, driving away talented and well-trained Zimbabweans, especially in the health and education sectors.

By 1999, political opposition to Mugabe's policies had grown significantly. Most notable was the breakaway of the powerful trade union wing of ZANU-PF to form the Movement for Democratic Change (MDC), led by Morgan Tsvangirai. Mugabe responded ruthlessly, unleashing a violent campaign against the MDC, while at the same time accusing them of being puppets of the former colonialists.

Mugabe's ruthlessness would not have succeeded without the "quiet diplomacy" of Thabo Mbeki and the fifteen-member Southern African Development Community (SADC). Indeed, with more than three million Zimbabwean refugees swamping the Republic of South Africa, the Zimbabwean failure has created considerable resonance south of the Limpopo.[9] Trade unionists who formed the core of the MDC had strong support from South African workers in COSATU and among the left wing of the ANC.[10] Nervous about directly toppling Mugabe, Mbeki opted instead for appeasement. Although Mbeki was able to broker a power-sharing coalition government for Zimbabwe, with the protocol signed on September 15, 2008, Mugabe has refused to live up to the agreement, and has defied SADC to do anything about it, choosing to denigrate the MDC as "born-again colonialists" and stalking horses for Western meddling. Mugabe has had at least fifteen MDC members of Parliament arrested on dubious charges since the unity government took office; more white farmers have been murdered and 170 are facing prosecution for refusing to leave their land. The SADC tribunal ruled in

[8] Chan, *Robert Mugabe*, 116.

[9] For an excellent treatment of Mugabe's relations with Mbeki, see chapter 9, "Comrade Bob," of Gumede, *Thabo Mbeki*, 217–41.

[10] Gumede, *Thabo Mbeki*, 223–4.

TABLE 9.1. *Cholera in Southern Africa, 1998–2009*

Year	Cases	Deaths	CFR %	Year	Cases	Deaths	CFR %
1998	45,610	1,472	3.2	2004	38,926	577	1.5
1999	82,440	2,379	2.9	2005	8,487	89	1.0
2000	43,804	645	1.5	2006	83,878	3,050	3.6
2001	126,711	662	0.5	2007	23,870	579	2.4
2002	70,595	1,491	2.1	2008	89,957	3,399	3.8
2003	22,485	258	1.1	2009	109,008	3,128	2.9

Source: WER, annual reports, from 1998 to 2009. The WER defines the region broadly by including the following nine countries: South Africa, Swaziland, Zimbabwe, Mozambique, Malawi, Botswana, Namibia, Zambia, and Angola. Botswana, Swaziland, and Namibia have only had light cholera outbreaks, mostly from imported cases. This was also true of Angola until 2006.

2008 that the seizures were illegal, but Mugabe now refuses to recognize the tribunal's legitimacy. Hopes were raised that the replacement of Thabo Mbeki by Jacob Zuma in South Africa would produce change, because Zuma had been highly critical of Mugabe on public record. As of the summer of 2009, however, it would appear that Mugabe has again out-maneuvered his opponents, because Zuma seems to be continuing Mbeki's non-interventionist policy.[11]

Cholera has been no stranger to Southern Africa. Table 9.1 shows the alarming magnitude of outbreaks over the past decade, whereas Table 9.2 documents Zimbabwe's share of cholera over roughly the same period. Endemic in neighboring Malawi and Mozambique since the 1970s, the disease has been able to attack Zimbabwe frequently, and especially since public health conditions deteriorated after 1999. Zimbabwe's high CFRs would have been a warning, had public health officials been alert, that cholera was a growing endemic threat and treatment particularly deficient. Against this epidemiological background, and in a worsening political and economic climate, an explosive cholera epidemic struck in August of 2008. By the time it had petered out in June 2009 Zimbabwe had endured horrendous numbers, the worst ever seen in Africa. The WHO's recorded figures for Zimbabwe are: roughly 128,000 cases, 5,608 deaths, a CFR of 4 percent, with a punishing attack rate of about 900 per 100,000 population, one of the highest ever recorded globally during the Seventh Pandemic. By contrast, arguably the best possible outcome

---

[11] "Robert Mugabe off the hook as usual," Economist.com, September 10, 2009, Cape Town.

TABLE 9.2. *Cholera in Zimbabwe, 1998–2009*

Year	Cases	Deaths	CFR %
1992	2,039	105	5.1
1993	5,385	332	6.2
1998	995	44	4.4
1999	5,637	385	6.8
2000	1,675	96	5.7
2001	650	14	2.2
2002	3,125	192	6.1
2003	1,009	35	3.5
2004	119	9	7.6
2005	516	26	5.0
2006	789	61	7.7
2007	65	4	6.2
2008	60,055	2,928	4.9
2009	68,153	2,706	4.0*

Source: WER annual reports from 1998 to 2009.
* For the epidemic of 2008 and 2009, the rounded off figures are 128,000 cases, 5,600 deaths, and a CFR of 4.4 percent.

for a modern cholera epidemic was the South African outbreak of 2001, in which 106,000 cases and a remarkably low 232 deaths were recorded. Also impressive had been the South American outcome in Peru during 1991, in which 3,000 deaths occurred among 323,000 cases, a CFR of 0.9 percent.

The index cases seem to have occurred in the Harare dormitory town of Chitungwiza, where two deaths were reported in late August of 2008. Not until December did the Zimbabwe government acknowledge that a full-scale epidemic was underway and request international assistance. As news spread, health workers expressed alarm, and some predicted as many as 60,000 cases, far less than the actual total as it happened.[12] The new year brought no improvement. In retrospect, the epidemic's peak of 8,000 weekly cases was reported for mid-February.[13] By the third week

[12] "UK caused cholera, says Zimbabwe Minister," BBC World News, December 12, 2008, www/news.bbc.co.uk/2hi/7780728.stm

[13] It hardly needs repeating that, as the WER put it, "[d]ata collection and verification remain a challenge throughout the country, affecting the accuracy and completeness of weekly statistics." WER, 84 (April 3, 2009), 109–110. See also "Cholera, Diarrhea, and Dysentery Update, 2009," *ProMed Mail* 17, April 29, 2009, www.promedmail.org, and K. Chambers, "Zimbabwe's battle against cholera," *The Lancet*, 373 (March 21, 2009), 993.

of March, new cases had declined to 2,000, and by the end of May, to roughly 100 cases a week.

Cholera's progress in Zimbabwe after August 2008 was extremely rapid, even before the coming of the rainy season in late October. The entire country became infected, but the worst impact was in the crowded and filthy slums of Harare. Water supplies were especially poor in Harare's townships of Budiriro, Glen Norah, and Glen View, which became cholera epicenters. The country's second city, Bulawayo, also suffered from poor sewage disposal and frequent water shortages, but it was surprisingly not one of the most heavily affected districts.[14] The rural province most affected by cholera was Mashonaland West. In the south, towns like Chinhoyi, Beitbridge, and Chegutu were badly hit before cholera crossed the Limpopo River into South Africa. Similarly, cholera in Manicaland province, bordering on Mozambique, was easily able to cross the border as well.

The Mugabe government chose to ignore the cholera emergency engulfing the country as long as it could. By the time it declared a national disaster on December 3, 2008, opening wider the door for international help, Zimbabwe had experienced 11,735 infections and 484 deaths, a CFR of more than 4 percent.[15] Yet international aid workers did not immediately receive the government's cooperation. It took MSF several weeks to acquire permission to use an empty wing at an infectious diseases hospital in Harare.

The WHO had a large team working with its partners in the Global Outbreak Alert and Response Network and operating out of the national Cholera Command and Control Centre in Harare. It was composed of national teams from five countries: the International Centre for Diarrhoeal Disease Research in Bangladesh; the Burnet Institute of Australia; the London School of Hygiene and Tropical Medicine, Medical Emergency Relief International (MERLIN), and the Health Protection Agency from Britain; the Centers for Disease Control from the United States; and the Swedish National Board of Health and Welfare. International NGOs included MSF and the International Committee of the Red Cross.[16]

---

[14] Bulawayo is located in a semi-arid zone and has suffered several severe droughts since 1980. Issues of water access and management have led to intense political struggles between municipal authorities in Bulawayo and the central government in Harare. See Muchaparara Musemwa, "Disciplining a 'Dissident' City: Hydropolitics in the City of Bulawayo, Matabeleland, Zimbabwe, 1980–94," *Journal of Southern African Studies*, 32 (2006), 239–54.

[15] Chambers, "Zimbabwe's battle," 993–4.

[16] *WER*, 84 (April 3, 2009), 109–10.

The international aid providers did not distinguish themselves in their initial efforts. Poorly conceived public instructions included avoidance of oysters and shellfish, which were unaffordable luxuries for most people in land-locked Zimbabwe. When the ministry of health and UNICEF teamed up to provide text messages, these stressed the boiling of water, avoiding shaking hands, and shunning mass gatherings like funerals. But the cost of boiling water in the poor townships was prohibitive. Donors poured $300,000 to print cholera awareness posters in a country where toilet paper had become an unaffordable luxury. Only as details of the collapse of public health in Zimbabwe became available did the international community begin to appreciate the magnitude of the disaster. Water infrastructure had deteriorated to the point where sewer bursts became common in many parts of Harare. Piped water had been turned off for more than two years, and demoralized workers lacked financial incentive to carry out repairs. People in desperation had been digging shallow, easily contaminated wells, and garbage collection had ceased because of fuel shortages.

Faced with these conditions, NGO interventions were substantial once they were established. MERLIN set up fifty oral rehydration points throughout Zimbabwe.[17] Through March 2009, MSF mobile teams had treated roughly 56,000 people, close to half of the entire infected population, in dozens of cholera treatment centers they established throughout the country. A volunteer gave a moving account of how MSF treated a sick ten-year-old boy in a high-density Harare slum. After his mother had brought the severely dehydrated child in, he was revived with an intravenous drip of Ringer's lactate, and then was able to drink his oral rehydration salts. Each patient in the clinic was given two buckets, one under the bed for diarrhea and one beside the bed for vomit. Gloves and watertight boots were issued to protect workers from contaminated water and soil, and chlorine was applied to disinfect water supplies. Gastric tubes, IV catheters, and syringes completed the list of supplies.[18]

Costly international medical intervention did save some lives even if it did not address preventative issues. As Table 9.2 indicates, the CFR for the period from January 1 to June 30, 2009, fell to 4 percent, as opposed to 4.9 percent from August to the end of December 2008, when international medical intervention was much more limited. The achievement

---

[17] Chambers, "Zimbabwe's battle," 993.
[18] "Dispatch from Zimbabwe," Médecins sans Frontières, *Canada Magazine*, 11 (2009).

FIGURE 9.1. Cholera beds. (Photograph by Luis M. Tello. Used with permission.)

was modest, but far less effective in the long term than efforts to improve Zimbabwe's water infrastructure would have been.

Those members of the Zimbabwean medical community who had not fled the country in despair spoke out against the failing public health system, once the presence of international medical aid organizations made them feel less intimidated. The Zimbabwe Association of Doctors for Human Rights (ZADHR) reported on February 26, 2009, that the human right to safe water and sewage removal had long since disappeared.[19] ZADHR's report itemized the lack of even cheap salt and sugar solutions for rehydration, the violence unleashed on treatment centers, the looting of medical supplies and even telephone lines, and the repeated strikes by doctors and nurses protesting low and often undelivered salaries. The report noted that 61 percent of cholera deaths had occurred outside the inadequate treatment centers.

Facing the consequences of dealing with a failing state, international agencies found themselves appealing to the outside world. To fund a plan to pay health workers and supply treatment centers, they appealed for $51 million in emergency funds. As of the spring of 2009, only 43 percent of the goal had been met, and agencies feared that donors might

---

[19] ZADHR's report was appropriately entitled, "Cholera in a time of Health System Collapse: Violations of Health Rights and the Cholera Outbreak," in Chambers, "Zimbabwe's battle," 993.

be less willing to pay for long-term investment in water, sanitation, and hygiene.[20]

The politics of division continued to hamper efforts to contain cholera. On February 27, 2009, the new minister of health and child welfare in the coalition government, Dr. Henry Madzorewa, attempted to put a bold face on the situation when he reported that international aid had led to "an improvement in our situation," as the CFR fell from 5.7 percent on January 21 to 4.6 percent a month later.[21] Madzorewa hoped that as the rains ended in April, there would be a natural decrease in cholera's intensity. What went unstated was that Madzorewa had long been a member of the opposition MDC, and the finance ministry, controlled by ZANU-PF, chose not to fund health needs when it could rely on international emergency funding instead. Madzorewa provided a more realistic account of the disaster he had inherited in an interview with the *Zimbabwe Times* in August 2009. He noted that his ministry faced critical shortages of all medicines, including antiretroviral drugs for those fighting HIV/AIDS. On the first anniversary of the cholera outbreak, physicians had organized a boycott at major hospitals in Harare and Bulawayo, demanding that their wages of $170 a month be raised to $1,000. Madzorewa could only reply weakly that he was not optimistic about funding because the government was "hamstrung by financial problems at the moment."[22]

When it was forced to acknowledge the presence of a cholera emergency in December 2008, Mugabe's government blamed its familiar scapegoat, the former colonial power. In his press conference on December 11, Information Minister Sikhanyiso Ndlovu called cholera a "serious biological chemical [sic] weapon," unleashed as a "genocidal onslaught on the people of Zimbabwe by the British."[23] A day later, the *Times* reported that after denying the presence of cholera, Mugabe was heralding the success of Zimbabwean doctors in arresting the epidemic. Propaganda about the alleged epidemic was an excuse, according to Mugabe, for "Brown, Bush, and Sarkozy to push for regime change."[24]

Zimbabweans are carrying a terrible health burden. To HIV/AIDS is added cholera and other gastrointestinal ailments resulting from bad water and uncontrolled sewage. Underlying all of this is malnutrition, the result of crop failures and especially of financial mismanagement.

[20] Chambers, "Zimbabwe's battle," 994.
[21] Chambers, "Zimbabwe's battle," 994.
[22] www.thezimbabwetimes.com/?p=14205.
[23] "UK caused cholera," BBC World News, December 12, 2008.
[24] "Mugabe: 'There is no cholera in Zimbabwe,'" *Times*, December 12, 2008.

FIGURE 9.2. Welcome to Zimbabwe cartoon. (Credit: www.CartoonStock.com)

Hunger, especially when children are concerned, makes for a population with weakened constitutions who are highly vulnerable to infection in general.

It is not clear what can be done about the Zimbabwean disaster. In her iconoclastic critique of Western aid for Africa, the Zambian economist Dambisa Moyo maintains that Mugabe has lasted so long in power because he has been "propped up by massive foreign aid receipts," such as the combined aid package of $300 million he received from international aid donors.[25] Without endorsing Moyo's neo-liberal analysis, she has a point. Meanwhile, as she notes ironically, Mugabe's wife Grace makes frequent buying trips to Harrods, London's exclusive department store.[26]

[25] Dambisa Moyo, *Dead Aid: Why Aid Is Not Working and How There is a Better Way for Africa* (New York: Farrar, Straus and Giroux, 2009), 147.
[26] Moyo, *Dead Aid*, 146.

10

Cholera Today

In many respects, the first six cholera pandemics served as prologue to the present. The disease spread rapidly on a path of human destruction that seemed as random as it was terrifying. Medical authorities had flawed understandings of the etiology of the disease, and often developed therapies that did little good and sometimes much harm in an unfortunate reversal of the Hippocratic Oath. Nevertheless, the intensity of cholera diminished, especially in the West, where industrialization eventually brought with it improved treatment of drinking water and the development of better sewage infrastructure. Well before researchers began to determine how the *Vibrio cholerae* pathogen functioned, an empirical understanding emerged of where cholera thrived and how it might be avoided. The gathering of humans, whether voluntary or not, into overcrowded sites where drinking water was suspect and sanitation poor proved deadly for millions. Trade emporia, whether seaports like Hamburg or caravan points like Berbera in Somalia, were dangerous. So too were pilgrimage sites such as Hardwar for Indian Hindus, Mecca for Sunni Muslims, and the Shiite Iraqi towns of Karbala and Najaf. Finally, the displacement of civilians and soldiers alike during military campaigns meant high risks for cholera and other infectious diseases. This held true for besieged towns in the Middle East or in the battlegrounds of the Russian and Austrian empires in the nineteenth century.

Africa's current experience with cholera shows how these risks still apply. The Muslim pilgrimage site of Touba in Senegal is a painful reminder of what happened on numerous occasions at Mecca a century earlier. Cholera epidemics have also been a consequence of the violent displacement of refugees, most strikingly in the terrible aftermath of genocide in the Goma region of the DRC. Weak or failed states have willfully neglected elementary sanitation in the teeming slums of Luanda in Angola and Harare in Zimbabwe, contributing significantly to the misery and suffering of thousands.

Drought and famine have also been closely associated with cholera outbreaks. Nowhere is this more in evidence than in the Horn of Africa. Famine following a serious drought helped propel cholera in Ethiopia in 1835 during the Second Pandemic and in 1893 during the Fifth Pandemic. Almost a century later, during the ongoing Seventh Pandemic, cholera preyed upon thousands of starving migrants searching for food and shelter as a result of devastating famine in Ethiopia and the Horn of Africa in 1971 and 1985.[1] Other correlations between drought, famine, and cholera can be found throughout the continent. In Tunisia, a serious famine in 1865 and 1866 was linked to cholera and typhus. In Southern Africa during the Seventh Pandemic, food shortages made for a vulnerable population, as both Zambia and Mozambique bore witness in 1992. A major drought in 1982 and 1983 preceded a cholera outbreak in the Madlebe region of KwaZulu-Natal. Ranging farther afield to the continent of Asia, malnutrition and deprivation were features of the war for independence in Bangladesh during 1971.

Scientific understanding of the cholera pathogen and its changing environment is much better than it was just a decade ago. Impressive international teams of scientists, no longer confined to the laboratory, have sought out the cholera pathogen in its natural habitats. To assist them, they have exploited new interdisciplinary techniques drawn from oceanography, marine biology, and satellite imagery.[2] One promising new technique uses remote satellite imaging to help predict outbreaks of cholera and other infectious diseases four to six weeks before they happen.[3] In 2000, the mapping of the complete DNA for cholera was accomplished,

---

[1] For discussion of famine, see Amartya Sen, *Poverty and Famines: An Essay on Entitlement and Deprivation* (Oxford: Clarendon Press, 1981); and Alex de Waal, *Famine That Kills: Darfur, Sudan* (New York: Oxford University Press, revised edition, 2005). De Waal argues that Darfurians threatened by famine were more concerned with maintaining an acceptable future livelihood than with hunger. He maintains that famine mortality is a function of health crises that arise, rather than being driven by starvation. Though he does not single out cholera, it has clearly been a threat to drought-stricken Africans.

[2] Colwell, "Global climate," 2031.

[3] The satellite system collects data on the amount of chlorophyll in water, which in turn helps measure the biomass produced by plankton. Patsy Morrow, "Satellites to predict cholera outbreaks," posted October 16, 2008, The Diamondback (www.diamondbackonline.com).

helping advance knowledge of the pathogen.[4] Treatment of those unfortunate enough to contract a serious case of cholera has also advanced. Failures with vaccine therapy and antimicrobial protection should not blind us to the fortunate existence of an inexpensive and readily available lifesaver: a simple solution of sugar, salt, and water in sufficient quantity to accomplish rehydration among patients and prevent serious bodily damage and even death.

Scientists still have unanswered questions centering on how new pandemic strains of cholera develop, and how and when the strains spread around the world.[5] Some, like Andrew Price-Smith, argue that for cholera and other infectious diseases, we have "overestimated our capacities to master the natural world and bend it to our will."[6] Similarly, others invoke climate change as one area where cholera and especially malaria may pose a greater threat in the future.[7] One of the most radical pessimists is James Lovelock, who worries that the low-lying coastal areas of Africa and other continents will be underwater in three decades.[8] Bjorn Lomborg and his Danish associates are a skeptical minority, criticizing what they argue are self-interested agendas of alternative energy advocates.[9] Some of the more extravagant carbon-cutting programs are extremely costly and would take funds away from a world where billions are stuck in poverty and millions die of curable diseases. Significantly for cholera, Lomborg argues that it would only cost about four billion dollars to provide three billion people with access to safe drinking water and sanitation.[10]

Cholera's links to climate change are part of this passionate, and sometimes polemical, debate.[11] The majority of scientific evidence points to serious disruptions to the earth's ecological, climatic, and other natural

---

[4] J.F. Heidelberg, et al., "DNA sequence of both chromosomes of the cholera pathogen *Vibrio cholerae*," *Nature*, 406 (August 3, 2000), 477–83.

[5] B.S. Drasar, "Problems of the Epidemiology of Cholera and the Ecology of *Vibrio Cholerae*," in B.S. Drasar and B.D. Forrest, eds., *Cholera and the Ecology of Vibrio Cholerae* (London: Chapman & Hall, 1996), 333.

[6] Andrew T. Price-Smith, *The Health of Nations: Infectious Disease, Environmental Change, and Their Effects on National Security and Development* (Cambridge: MIT Press, 2002), 184.

[7] J. Patz, et al., "Global climate change," 219.

[8] James E. Lovelock, *The Revenge of Gaia: Earth's Climate in Crisis and the Fate of Humanity* (New York: Basic Books, 2006).

[9] Bjorn Lomborg, *Cool It: The Skeptical Environmentalist's Guide to Global Warming* (New York: Knopf, 2007).

[10] Lomborg, *Cool It*, 111–12.

[11] Lee, et al., "Global change and health," 16–19.

systems through a variety of changes such as the concentration of ozone levels in the stratosphere, the retreat of glaciers, and the depletion of fresh water supplies. A list of changes affecting human health is shorter and not conclusive. It includes the spread of tick-borne encephalitis in Sweden, increased malaria at higher altitudes in Africa, and a rise in dengue fever in several parts of the world.[12] One research finding, using remote sensing, suggests that cholera is profiting from climate change. Sea surface temperature shows an annual cycle similar to the cholera case data. Also, sea surface height could indicate the incursion of plankton-laden water inland (in tidal rivers, for example) and correlates with cholera outbreaks.[13] Throughout this study, the cost of cholera has been an issue. Health authorities from the municipal to the international level have faced the difficult choice between opting for less visible investments in water and sewage infrastructure versus expenditures needed to quell cholera emergencies. For example, South Africa's response to its cholera crisis in 2000 and 2001 was effective but extremely costly. The pivotal role played by army medical units with helicopter teams, equipment, and tented rehydration centers established all over KwaZulu-Natal saved many lives, but the cost was hidden in military budgets. Since 2000, military cutbacks make it unlikely that South Africa could mount such an energetic effort again.

If the human costs of cholera are carefully considered, there should be no doubt about the choice of prevention over cure. Not only does an eminently preventable disease such as cholera now terminate thousands of lives each year, the hidden costs of cholera are exacted upon hundreds of thousands of young children who survive cholera attacks. New research based on case studies from Peru and northeast Brazil suggests that cholera and other diarrheal diseases in early childhood bring staggering costs in the form of cognitive and physical impairment. Diarrheal disease in the first two years of life and the malnutrition often associated with it is rising globally, and so is long-term developmental impairment.[14]

[12] Lee, et al., "Global change and health," 18.

[13] B. Lobitz, et al., "Climate and infectious disease: Use of remote sensing for detection of *Vibrio cholerae* by indirect measurement," *Proceedings of National Academy of Sciences*, 97 (February 15, 2000), 1438–43.

[14] The major studies include Richard L. Guerrant, et al., "Cholera, diarrhea, and oral rehydration therapy: Triumph and indictment," *Clinical Infectious Diseases*, 37 (2003), 398–405; Rebecca Dillingham and Richard L. Guerrant, "Childhood stunting: Measuring and stemming the staggering costs of inadequate water and sanitation," *Lancet*, 363 (2004), 94–5; D.I. Guerrant, et al., "Association of early childhood diarrhea and cryptosporidiosis with impaired physical fitness and cognitive function four-seven years later in a

The main UN body charged with protecting against the depredations of cholera is the WHO. Its approach during the course of the seventh cholera pandemic has reflected the delicate balance between advocacy for public health in the developing world and protection of the developed world. Like its overall performance, the WHO's record on cholera has been mixed. Its approach to cholera reflects the general criticisms leveled at the organization in recent years.[15] The WHO has suffered chronically from financial shortfalls, but entitlements, fancy cars, and lucrative tax-free salaries of its over-centralized bureaucracy at Geneva have been frequent targets for criticism. As for its programs, Richard Smith puts it well: Rather than "doing many of 120 things badly [the WHO] should do a dozen things well."[16]

The WHO's position on cholera in developing societies has often been paternalistic. In ambiguous editorials in its weekly *WER*, the WHO has alternated between blaming Africans and apologizing for them. One example was the allusion to African sanitary and cultural practices, euphemistically expressed as "inattention to food hygiene," or the practice of gathering in large numbers at funerals of cholera victims, "when there is often close contact with the corpse by those involved in the preparation of food."[17] Never was it explained how such practices might have contributed to cholera epidemics. Similarly, when cholera exploded in the Americas in 1991, the WHO, together with several American researchers, blamed careless handling of food and water and unspecified "cultural" practices. Their language sounded clearly like racial and ethnic

poor urban community in Northeast Brazil," *American Journal of Tropical Medicine and Hygiene*, 61 (1999), 707–13; M.A. Mendez and L.S. Adair, "Severity and timing of stunting in the first two years of life affect performance on cognitive tests in late childhood," *Journal of Nutrition*, 129 (1999), 1555–62; and M.D. Niehaus, et al., "Early childhood diarrhea is associated with diminished cognitive function 4–7 years later in children in a Northeast Brazilian shantytown," *American Journal of Tropical Medicine and Hygiene*, 66 (2002), 590–3.

[15] Javed Siddiqi, *World Health and World Politics* (London: Hurst, 1995); Richard Horton, *Health Wars: On the Global Front Lines of Modern Medicine* (New York: New York Review Books, 2003); Fiona Godlee, "The WHO in Africa: Too much Politics, too little accountability," *British Medical Journal*, 309 (1994), 553–4.

[16] Richard Smith, "The WHO: Change or die," *British Medical Journal*, 310 (1995), 543–4.

[17] *WER*, 68 (1993), 154. Some evidence was found that careless handling in the preparation of a rice meal at a funeral in a Guinean village may have been responsible for the spread of a "cholera-like illness." M.E. St. Louis, et al., "Epidemic cholera in West Africa: The role of food handling and high-risk foods," *American Journal of Epidemiology*, 131 (1990), 719–27.

profiling.[18] Blaming food was a common but tiresome accusation that never received scientific support. What the WHO chose to ignore was how the experiences of South America and of Africa during the seventh cholera pandemic reflected global inequalities.[19] In a world featuring movement of people on a grand scale, the poor were at high risk for a disease that spread by means of fecally contaminated drinking water, and which could be prevented by reliable but costly sources of potable water. Maintenance of water infrastructure was surely the responsibility of governments and not the cholera victims. Only later did the WHO regret such vague and unverified attempts to explain the causes of cholera's new energy after 1991. It turned to the general point that war and forced migration often left potential cholera victims with terrible choices. The WHO also remained pessimistic about halting the spread of the Seventh Pandemic until "significant progress is made to improve living conditions in developing countries to allow greater access to clean water, safe food, and a more sanitary environment." [20]

In fairness, the WHO's power to intervene on health matters is circumscribed by its need to obtain consent of national governments. Even when the WHO attempts to assist developing nations deal with the negative economic impact of cholera, it can do little more than scold those countries that penalize victims. In recent years, the WHO has expressed its disapproval of punitive measures imposed by some developed countries, such as the application of antiquated trade, tourism, and travel embargoes. In 1997 and 1998, after ENSO-induced cholera struck hard in East Africa, the European Union banned fish imports from Mozambique, Kenya, Tanzania, and Uganda. Fish exports were the fourth-largest foreign exchange earner for Uganda and worth then an estimated thirty-four to fifty-two million dollars.[21] Although transmission could happen in theory, no research has ever documented a cholera outbreak resulting from

[18] WER, 66 (1991), 257. For racial and ethnic profiling, see Robert V. Tauxe, and Paul A. Blake, "Epidemic cholera in Latin America," *Journal of the American Medical Association*, 267 (1992), 1388. Tauxe was then chief of the Epidemiology section at the Centers for Disease Control headquarters in Atlanta. For a highly insightful and provocative study of racial profiling during the cholera epidemic in Venezuela in 1992, see Charles L. Briggs and Clara Martini-Briggs, *Stories in the Time of Cholera: Racial Profiling during a Medical Nightmare* (Berkeley: University of California Press, 2003).

[19] Lee, "The global dimensions," 16.

[20] WER, 68 (1993), 155.

[21] A. Wachira Kigotho, "European Union bans fish imports from cholera-struck eastern Africa," *Lancet*, 351 (January 17, 1998), 194.

commercially imported food from countries where cholera was endemic. Similarly, travel restrictions against cholera-infected countries are not recommended, because it was impossible to isolate all infected travelers, most of whom presented no signs of illness.[22]

The WHO was slow to deal with the new global threat of cholera in 1991. True, the WHO director-general formed a Global Cholera Control Task Force to coordinate global action. Measures stressed rapid intervention to improve access to safe water and sanitation, as well as education programs and publicity campaigns aimed at the general public. But not until 1995 did the task force provide emergency support in hard-hit African countries.[23]

It is disappointing if not surprising that the WHO continues to treat the current crisis in Africa with excessive discretion. In its annual report on cholera for 2009, it did not direct the slightest hint of criticism to the Mugabe government for having turned a cholera outbreak in Zimbabwe into a regional disaster. Instead, the *WER* weakly proposes "to work with communities to encourage behavioral change to diminish the risks [of cholera]."[24]

Although health is obviously the WHO's mandate, the World Bank has been a major instrument of globalization and has had a profound impact on health in the developing world. Critics have noted that the WHO prefers working in capital cities with health ministries rather than with health workers at the grass roots; and its insistence on structural adjustment policies is said to have helped produce growing food insecurity and malnutrition, as well as declining access to health care for two-thirds or more of the population of Africa.[25] Based on his careful research on cholera and acute diarrhea in Mozambique, Andrew Collins observes that the World Bank's neo-liberal assumption about peoples' willingness to pay for improved services is wrong, and ignores the acute poverty in which many Africans live. Further, globalization policies ignore the views of "affected people who are closest to their own difficulties and appropriate remedies."[26]

On a more general scale, globalization has helped accelerate global migration, making millions more vulnerable to new and reemerging

[22] *WER*, 74 (1999), 263.
[23] *WER*, 71 (1996), 157–64.
[24] *WER*, 85 (2010), 297.
[25] Turshen, Privatizing Health, 8; Rene Loewenson, "Structural adjustment and health policy in Africa," *International Journal of Health Services*, 23 (1993), 717–30.
[26] Collins, *Environment*, 251.

infectious diseases, as well as to stress and psychological disorders in general. Even when this migration is voluntary and economic, individuals in search of a better life must tolerate inferior living conditions. As Kelley Lee and her colleagues argue, our experience and perception of time has certainly changed as globalization accelerates our ability to move about the world and to communicate instantaneously. This brings opportunities but also risks as a result of faster and more frequent human contact.[27]

Former World Bank economist Joseph Stiglitz has documented the failures of the World Bank and the IMF. These bodies, in his view, were insensitive to the health needs of developing countries, refused to let them make their own choices for social and economic development, and instead imposed an unbending free-market ideology.[28]

Yet responsibility for the rising tide of cholera in Africa lies not only with Western institutions. The failures of African leadership have contributed significantly to an environment in which cholera could thrive. Natural phenomena such as ENSO events have also been at work, but it is the decline or collapse of African civil societies that has enabled modern day cholera to profit most from political instability. War refugees from Liberia and Sierra Leone in the 1990s brought increased cholera rates there, as well as in neighboring countries sheltering refugees. Prolonged wars of liberation in Central and Southern Africa smoldered for decades and profoundly harmed the civilian populations of Angola, Mozambique, and Zimbabwe. Failed states such as Liberia, the DRC, and currently Zimbabwe must be added to the list.

Occasionally, cholera's explosion had more to do with misguided government policy than corruption and venality of African leaders. The willingness of otherwise stable and democratic states like Senegal and South Africa to sacrifice public health on the altar of World Bank neo-liberal ideology springs immediately to mind. Commercialization of water policy in both states wreaked havoc among the poor and helped trigger major cholera outbreaks.

Some African leaders have attempted to deflect responsibility for their failures by invoking the poisoned legacy of colonialism. None has done this more cynically than Robert Mugabe. No doubt, many health issues can be traced back to the colonial era. But not only has half a century passed since African independence, African leaders have selfishly allowed

---

[27] Lee, et al., "Global change and health," 18.
[28] Joseph Stiglitz, *Globalization and Its Discontents* (New York: Norton, 2003).

smaller problems to fester until they have grown almost too daunting to address.

Urbanization in Africa is a case in point.[29] Colonial cities universally distinguished between European and African inhabitants. Town planning, health, and sanitation were provided for white residents, while Africans, sometimes original inhabitants but more often labor migrants, were obliged to fend for themselves. After independence, the pace of urbanization accelerated, and by 1990 the distinguished Nigerian urbanist Akin Mabogunje estimated that urban infrastructure was in a state of total collapse for 40 to 70 percent of urban Africans who lived amid the squalor of overcrowded and underserviced shanty towns.[30] He added that neo-liberal ideology contributed to an emerging counterculture among the urban poor. Facing major breakdowns in water, electricity, and sanitation systems, urban dwellers have sought to secure as many services as they can by often illegal means, including sabotage.[31] Twenty years later, the deplorable conditions faced by millions of urban Africans have further deteriorated.

Cholera in Africa is no longer a biomedical riddle. Although climate change and meteorological events can account for cholera surges, they are permissive factors. Active factors are clearly social and economic, and they range from failures of leadership in Africa to those in the wider global community. Implicit in the health tragedy is the glaring structural inequality of the global economy. Western nations may be prepared to intervene in African medical emergencies, but are reluctant, for example, to allow fair trade in African export products.[32] Yet only improvements in their economies will enable enough African states to invest in the affordable public health measures required to end the lethality of cholera, as have developing countries in Asia and Latin America.

---

[29] Akin L. Mabogunje, "Urban planning and the post-colonial state: A research overview," *African Studies Review*, 33 (1990), 121–203; Andreas Eckert, "Urbanization in Colonial and Post-Colonial West Africa," in Emmanuel Akyeampong, ed., *Themes in West African History*, (Oxford: James Currey, 2005), 208–23; and Garth Andrew Myers, *Disposable Cities: Garbage, Governance and Sustainable Development in Urban Africa* (Burlington, VT: Ashgate, 2005).

[30] Mabogunje, "Urban planning," 141.

[31] Mabogunje, "Urban planning," 146.

[32] In his history of malaria, Randall Packard has made a similar argument about bringing malaria under control. Whereas malaria's grip on humans is more tenacious and destructive, cholera can also be tamed when major changes in its disease ecology occur. See Randall M. Packard, *The Making of a Tropical Disease: A Short History of Malaria* (Baltimore: The Johns Hopkins University Press, 2007).

Cholera control rather than eradication is the only realistic goal. Although *Vibrio cholerae* are fragile organisms and require a high dose of infection to bring about person-to-person transmission, the bacteria persist in many aquatic environments for months –perhaps indefinitely. Worse, the density of humans around the world has increased five-fold since 1850, and even more in Latin America and Africa. Urban and peri-urban environments favor the bacteria. The sheer number of extant environmental reservoirs means that cholera is likely to be around indefinitely.[33]

Nevertheless, effective control of cholera in Africa can be achieved. The disease is well understood, and oral rehydration therapy is inexpensive and effective. But the lessons of the past seem difficult to learn. In the West by the end of the nineteenth century, municipal rate-payers realized that improved water systems were in the wider public interest. Yet although preventive public health expenditures for clean water and decent sanitation are cost effective, such measures are not attractive to African politicians or international donors. Instead, millions are spent on emergency relief each time a cholera outbreak careens out of control. As we have so recently witnessed in Zimbabwe, such policies enable a rogue leader like Robert Mugabe to rely on outsiders to pay for what is a state's existential responsibility. What is required is for governments in Africa and in the West to act out of enlightened self-interest, as did their counterparts a century ago. Although emergency cholera fires need to be extinguished, the world must also address prevention of this old scourge.

[33] Robert Tauxe, Paul Blake, Orjan Olsvik, and I. Kaye Wachsmuth, "The Future of Cholera: Persistence, Change, and an Expanding Research Agenda," in Wachsmuth, I. Kaye, Paul A. Blake, and Orjan Olsvik, eds., *Vibrio Cholerae and Cholera: Molecular to Global Perspectives* (Washington: American Society for Microbiology Press, 1994), 443–53.

Bibliography

I. Statistical References

Program for Monitoring Emerging Diseases (ProMed), posted by the International Society for Infectious Diseases as *Pro-Medline*, www.promedmail.org.
World Health Organization, "Cholera," *Weekly Epidemiological Record*, yearly.
World Health Statistics, Geneva: WHO, 2009, Tables 1 and 7.

II. Unpublished Material

Ngalamulume, Kalala J., "City Growth, Health Problems, and Colonial Government Response: Saint-Louis (Senegal) from Mid-Nineteenth Century to the First World War," Ph.D. dissertation, Michigan State University, East Lansing, 1996.
Pam, Adama Aly, "Fièvre jaune et Choléra au Sénégal: Histoire des idées, pratiques médicales et politiques officielles entre 1816 et 1960," thèse de troisième cycle, Université Cheikh Anta Diop de Dakar, December, 2005.
Robertson, Edna, "Christie of Zanzibar, Medical Pathfinder," unpublished mss., cited with permission.

III. Articles and Monographs

Alpers, Edward A., *Ivory and Slaves in East Central Africa: Changing Patterns of International Trade to the Late Nineteenth Century*, Berkeley: University of California Press, 1975.
Andersson, Neil and Shula Marks, "Apartheid and health in the 1980s," *Social Science and Medicine*, 27 (1988), 667–81.
Arnold, David, "Cholera Mortality in British India, 1817–1947," in Tim Dyson, ed., *India's Historical Demography: Studies in Famine, Disease and Society*, London: Curzon Press, 1989, 263–346.
  Colonizing the Body: State Medicine and Epidemic Disease in Nineteenth-Century India, Berkeley: University of California Press, 1993.

Baldwin, Peter, *Contagion and the State in Europe, 1830–1930*, Cambridge: Cambridge University Press, 1999.

Barlow, Maude, *Blue Covenant: The Global Water Crisis and the Coming Battle for the Right to Water*, Toronto: McClelland & Stewart, 2007.

Barua, Dhiman, "The global epidemiology of cholera in recent years," *Proceedings of the Royal Society of Medicine*, 65 (1972), 423–8.

Barua, Dhiman, and William Burrows, eds., *Cholera*, Philadelphia: W.B. Saunders, 1974.

Barua, Dhiman, and William B. Greenough III, eds., *Cholera*, New York: Plenum, 1992.

Barua, Dhiman and Michael H. Merson, "Prevention and Control of Cholera," in D. Barua and W.B. Greenough III, eds., *Cholera*, New York: Plenum, 1992, 329–49.

Bayliss, Kate, and Terry McKinley, *Privatizing Basic Utilities in Sub-Saharan Africa: The Millenium Development Goal Impact* (for the UNDP International Poverty Centre) (January, 2007).

Beachey, R.W., *The Slave Trade of Eastern Africa*, London: Rex Collings, 1976.

Bentivoglio, M. and P. Pacini, "Filippo Pacini: A determined observer," *Brain Research Bulletin*, 38 (1995), 161–5.

Blake, Paul, "Endemic Cholera in Australia and the United States," in I. Kaye Wachsmuth, Paul A. Blake, and Orjan Olsvik, eds., *Vibrio Cholerae and Cholera: Molecular to Global Perspectives*, Washington: American Society for Microbiology Press, 1994, 309–19.

Bond, Patrick, *Elite Transition: From Apartheid to Neoliberalism in South Africa*, Durban: University of Natal Press, 2000.

Bourdelais, Patrice, *Epidemics Laid Low: A History of What Happened in Rich Countries*, translated by Bart K. Holland, Baltimore: The Johns Hopkins Press, 2006.

Bourdelais, Patrice, and André Dodin, *Visages du choléra*, Paris: Belin, 1987.

Briese, Olaf, *Angst in den Zeiten der Cholera*, 4 vols., Berlin: Akademie Verlag 2003.

Briggs, Charles L., and Clara Martini-Briggs, *Stories in the Time of Cholera: Racial Profiling during a Medical Nightmare*, Berkeley: University of California Press, 2003.

Brock, Thomas D., *Robert Koch: A Life in Medicine and Bacteriology*, Madison: Science Tech Publishers, 1988.

Brown, Michael, "From foetid air to filth: The cultural transformation of British epidemiological thought, ca. 1780–1848," *Bulletin of the History of Medicine*, 82 (2008), 515–44.

Brown, P.E., "John Snow – The Autumn loiterer," *Bulletin of the History of Medicine*, 35 (1961), 519–28.

Burton, Richard, *The Lake Regions of Central Africa, A Picture of Exploration*, Vol.2, New York: Horizon Press, 1961 reprint of original edition, London: Longman, 1860.

Zanzibar, City, Island, and Coast, vol.2, London: Tinsley Brothers, 1872.

Carpenter, Charles C.J., "Treatment of cholera – Tradition and authority versus science, reason and humanity," *The Johns Hopkins Medical Journal*, 139 (1976), 153–62.

Chambers, K., "Zimbabwe's battle against cholera," *Lancet*, 373 (21 March 2009), 993–94.

Chan, Stephen, *Robert Mugabe: A Life of Power and Violence*, London: I.B. Tauris, 2003.

Chapman, Graham, and Kathleen M. Baker, eds., *The Changing Geography of Africa and the Middle East*, London: Routledge, 1992.

Chapman, J.A., and L.P. Collocott, "Cholera in children at Eshowe Hospital," *South African Medical Journal*, 68 (1985), 249.

Chase, Allan, *Magic Shots: A Human and Scientific Account of the Long and Continuous Struggle to Eradicate Infectious Disease by Vaccination*, New York: William Morrow and Company, 1982.

Chatterjee, H.N., "Control of vomiting in cholera and oral replacement of fluid," *Lancet* (1953), 1063.

Christie, Dr. James, "Notes on the cholera epidemics in East Africa," *Lancet* (1871), 113–15; 186–8; and "Additional notes on the cholera epidemics on the east coast of Africa," *Lancet*, (1872), 573–4.

Christie, James, *Cholera Epidemics in East Africa*, London: Macmillan, 1876, reprinted, USA: Kessinger Publishing, 2008.

"Cholera in Gambia," *Lancet*, (May 22, 1869), 727, and (June 5, 1869), 727.

"Epidemics of dengue fever: Their diffusion and aetiology," *Glasgow Medical Journal*, 1881.

Clemens, John, Dale Spriggs, and David Sack, "Public Health Considerations for the Use of Cholera Vaccines in Cholera Control Programs," in I. Kaye Wachsmuth, Paul A. Blake, and Orjan Olsvik, eds., *Vibrio Cholerae and Cholera: Molecular to Global Perspectives*, Washington: American Society for Microbiology Press, 1994, 425–40.

Cliff, Julie, and Abdul Razak Noormahomed, "Health as a target: South Africa's destabilization of Mozambique," *Social Studies of Medicine*, 27 (1988), 717–22.

Cliff, Julie, Felicity Cutts and Ronald Waldman, "Using surveys in Mozambique for evaluation of diarrhoeal disease control," *Health Policy and Planning*, 5 (1990), 219–25.

Clot Bey, A.B., *Relation des épidémies de choléra-morbus qui ont regné à l'Heggiaz, à Suez et en Egypte*, Marseilles: Feissat ainé et Demonchy, 1832.

Coe, Michael T., and Jonathan A. Foley, "Human and natural impacts on the water resources of the Lake Chad basin," *Journal of Geophysical Research*, 106 (2001), 3349–56.

Collins, Andrew E., *Environment, Health and Population Displacement: Development and Change in Mozambique's Diarroeal Disease Ecology*, Aldershot: Ashgate, 1998.

Collins, Andrew, "The Geography of Cholera," in B. S. Drasar, and B.D. Forrest, eds., *Cholera and the Ecology of Vibrio Cholerae*, London: Chapman & Hall, 1996, 255–94.

"Vulnerability to coastal cholera ecology," *Social Science and Medicine*, 57 (2003), 1397–407.

Colwell, Rita R., "Global climate and infectious disease: The cholera paradigm," *Science*, 274 (1996), 2025–31.

Colwell, Rita R., and W.M. Spira, "The ecology of vibrio cholera," in Dhiman Barua, and William B. Greenough III, eds., *Cholera*, New York: Plenum, 1992.

Cooper, Donald, "The new 'Black Death': Cholera in Brazil, 1855–56," *Social Science History*, 10 (1986), 467–88.

Cooper, Frederick, *Plantation Slavery on the East Coast of Africa*, New Haven: Yale University Press, 1977.

Crowther, I., "Saluting the South African medical health service's involvement in cholera prevention and treatment in KwaZulu-Natal," *Milmed*, 17 (2001), 18–19.

Curtin, Philip D., *Disease and Empire: The Health of European Troops in the Conquest of Africa*, Cambridge: Cambridge University Press, 1998.

Dalsgaard, A., P. Reichert, H.F. Mortensen, Anita Sandstorm, Paul-Erik Kofoed, Jens Laurits "Application of lime (Citrus aurantifolia) juice to drinking water and food as a cholera-preventive measure, *Journal of Food Protection*, 60 (1997), 1329–33.

Daniels, N.A., S.L. Simons, A. Rodrigues,G.Gunnlagsson, T.S. Forster, J.G. Wells, L. et al, "First do no harm: Making oral rehydration solution safer in a cholera epidemic," *American Journal of Tropical Medicine and Hygiene*, 60 (1999), 1051–55.

Davies, J.P.N., "James Christie and the cholera epidemics of East Africa," *East African Medical Journal*, 36 (1959), 1–6.

Daws, Gavin, *Prisoners of the Japanese: POWS of World War II in the Pacific*, New York: Morrow, 1994.

Deedat, Hameda, and Eddie Cottle, "Cost Recovery and Prepaid Water Meters and the Cholera Outbreak in KwaZulu-Natal: A Case Study in Madlebe," in David A. McDonald and John Pape, eds., *Cost Recovery and the Crisis of Service Delivery in South Africa*, Cape Town: Human Sciences Research Council Publishers, 2002, 81–97.

Delaporte, Francois, *Disease and Civilization: The Cholera in Paris, 1832*, Tr. by Arthur Goldhammer. Cambridge: MIT Press, 1986.

Desai, Ashwin, "Neoliberalism and Resistance in South Africa," *Monthly Review*, 54 (2003), 1–15.

Dillingham, Rebecca, and Richard L. Guerrant, "Childhood stunting: Measuring and stemming the staggering costs of inadequate water and sanitation," *Lancet*, 363 (2004), 94–5.

Dorolle, Pierre, "International Surveillance of Cholera," in Dhiman Barua and William Burrows, eds., *Cholera*, Philadelphia: W.B. Saunders, 1974, 427–33.

Drasar, B.S., "Problems of the Epidemiology of Cholera and the Ecology of *Vibrio Cholerae*," in B.S. Drasar and B.D. Forrest, eds., *Cholera and the Ecology of Vibrio cholerae*, London: Chapman & Hall, 1996, 333.

Drasar, B.S., and B.D. Forrest, eds., *Cholera and the Ecology of Vibrio Cholerae*, London: Chapman & Hall, 1996.

Echenberg, Myron, "'Scientific Gold': Robert Koch and Africa, 1883–1906," in Chris Youe and Tim Stapleton, eds., *Agency and Action in Colonial Africa: Essays for John Flint*, London: Palgrave, 2001, 34–49.

Black Death, White Medicine: Bubonic Plague and the Politics of Public Health in Colonial Senegal, 1914–1945, Portsmouth, NH: Heinemann, 2002.

Eckert, Andreas, "Urbanization in Colonial and Post-Colonial West Africa," in Emmanuel Akyeampong, ed., *Themes in West African History*, Oxford: James Currey, 2005, 208–23.

Epstein, Paul, "Cholera and the environment," *Lancet*, 339 (1992), 1167–8.

"Climate, Ecology, and Human Health," in Andrew T. Price-Smith ed., *Plagues and Politics: Infectious Disease and International Policy*, New York: Palgrave, 2001, 27–58.

Evans, Richard J., *Death in Hamburg: Society and Politics in the Cholera Years*, New York and London: Penguin, 2005, second edition.

Farley, John, *Bilharzia: A History of Imperial Tropical Medicine*, Cambridge: Cambridge University Press, 1991.

Feith, Herbert, and Daniel S. Lev, "The end of the Indonesian rebellion," *Pacific Affairs*, 36 (1963), 32–46.

Félix, H., "Le choléra africain," *Médecine Tropicale*, 31: 1971, 619–28.

Freund, Bill, "Zulu Identity in the International Context," in Benedict Carton, John Laband, and Jabulani Sithole, eds., *Zulu Identities: Being Zulu, Past and Present*, London: Hurst & Company, 2009, 606–12.

Frieden, Nancy M., "The Russian cholera epidemic of 1892–93 and medical professionalization," *Journal of Social History*, 10 (1977), 538–59.

Fukuda, Mahito H., "Public Health in Modern Japan: From Regimen to Hygiene," in Dorothy Porter, ed., *The History of Public Health and the Modern State*, Atlanta: Rodopi, 1994, 385–402.

Gallagher, Nancy, *Medicine and Power in Tunisia, 1780–1900*, Cambridge: Cambridge University Press, 1983.

Egypt's Other Wars: Epidemics and the Politics of Public Health, Syracuse: Syracuse University Press, 1990.

Garrett, Laurie, *Betrayal of Trust: The Collapse of Global Public Health*, New York: Hyperion, 2000.

Gilbert, Pamela K., *Cholera and Nation: Doctoring the Social Body in Victorian England*, Albany: State University of New York Press, 2008.

Glass, Roger, and Robert Black, "The Epidemiology of Cholera," in Dhiman Barua, and William B. Greenough III, eds., *Cholera*, New York: Plenum, 1992, 129–50.

Godlee, Fiona, "The WHO in Africa: Too much politics, too little accountability," *British Medical Journal*, 309 (1994), 553–4.

Goma Epidemiology Group, "Public health impact of Rwanda refugee crisis: What happened in Goma, Zaire, in July 1994," *Lancet*, 345 (1995), 339–44.

Gradmann, Christoph, *Laboratory Disease: Robert Koch's Medical Bacteriology*, translated by Elborg Forster, Baltimore: Johns Hopkins University Press, 2009.

Green, Edward C., Annemarie Jurg, and Armando Djedje, "The snake in the stomach: Child diarrhea in central Mozambique," *Medical Anthropology Quarterly*, 8 (1994), 4–24.

Griffeth, David C., Louise Kelly-Hope, and Mark A. Miller, "Review of reported cholera outbreaks worldwide, 1995–2005," *American Journal of Tropical Medicine and Hygiene*, 75 (2006), 973–7.

Guerrant, D.I., S.R. Moore, A.A.M. Lima, P.D. Patrick, J.B. Schorling, and R.L. Guerrant, "Association of early childhood diarrhea and cryptosporidiosis with impaired physical fitness and cognitive function four–seven years later in a poor urban community in Northeast Brazil," *American Journal of Tropical Medicine and Hygiene*, 61 (1999), 707–13.

Guerrant, Richard L., "Cholera – Still teaching hard lessons," *New England Journal of Medicine*, 354 (2006), 2500.

Gumede, William M., *Thabo Mbeki and the Battle for the Soul of the ANC*, London: Zed Books, 2007.

Gunnlaugsson, G., F.J. Angulo, J. Einarsdottir, A.Passa, R.V. Tauxe, "Epidemic cholera in Guinea-Bissau: The challenge of preventing deaths in rural West Africa," *International Journal of Infectious Diseases*, 4 (2000), 8–13.

Halvorsen, Kate, "Protection and Humanitarian Assistance in the Refugee Camps in Zaire: The Problem of Security," in Howard Adelman and Astri Suhrke, eds., *The Path of Genocide: The Rwanda Crisis from Uganda to Zaire*, New Brunswick, NJ: Transaction Press, 1999, 307–20.

Hamlin, Christopher, *Cholera: The Biography*, Oxford: Oxford University Press, 2009.

A Science of Impurity: Water Analysis in Nineteenth Century Britain, Berkeley: University of California Press, 1990.

Hanlon, J., *Mozambique: Who Calls the Shots*, London: James Curry, 1991.

Harris, Sheldon H., *Factories of Death*, New York: Routledge, 1994.

Harrison, Mark, "Quarantine, pilgrimage, and colonial trade: India 1866–1900," *The Indian Economic and Social History Review*, 29 (1992), 117–44.

Public Health in British India: Anglo-Indian Preventive Medicine, 1859–1914, Cambridge: Cambridge University Press, 1994.

"A Question of Locality: The Identity of Cholera in British India, 1860–1890," in David Arnold, ed., *Warm Climates and Western Medicine: The Emergence of Tropical Medicine, 1500–1900*, Atlanta: Rodopi, 1996, 133–59.

Hays, J.N., *The Burdens of Disease: Epidemics and Human Response in Western History*, New Brunswick: Rutgers University Press, 1998.

Epidemics and Pandemics: Their Impacts on Human History, Santa Barbara, CA: ABC-CLIO, 2005.

Heidelberg, J.F., Eisen J.A., Nelson, W.C.,Clayton, R.A., Gwinn, M.L., Dodson, R.J. et al., "DNA sequence of both chromosomes of the cholera pathogen Vibrio cholerae," *Nature*, 406 (August 3, 2000), 477–83.

Hemson, David, "Still Paying the Price: Revisiting the Cholera Epidemic of 2000–2001 in South Africa," Occasional Papers Series, No.10, *Municipal Services Project*, series editors, David A. McDonald and Greg Ruiters, Grahamstown: Grocott's Publishers, 2006.

Holland, Ann-Christin Sjolander, *The Water Business: Corporations versus People*, New York: Zed Books, 2005.

Horton, Richard, *Health Wars: On the Global Front Lines of Modern Medicine*, New York: New York Review Books, 2003.

Howard-Jones, Norman, "Cholera therapy in the nineteenth century," *Journal of the History of Medicine and Allied Sciences*, 27 (1972), 373–95.

"Choleranomalies: The unhistory of medicine as illustrated by cholera," in *Perspectives on Biology and Medicine*, 15 (1972), 422–33.

The Scientific Background of the International Scientific Conferences, 1851–1938, Geneva: WHO, 1974.

Huber, Valeska, "The unification of the globe by disease? The international sanitary conferences on cholera, 1851–94," *The Historical Journal*, 49, 2 (2006), 453–76.

Huq, A., R.R. Colwell, R. Rahma, A. Ali, M.A. Ali, S. Praveen, et al., "Detection of Vibrio cholerae o1 in the aquatic environment by fluorescent monoclonal antibody and culture method," *Applied and Environmental Microbiology*, 56 (1990), 2370–3.

Huq, A., et al., "Simple water filtration for cholera prevention," Proceedings of the U.S.-Japan Cholera Meeting. U.S.-Japan Cooperative Medical Science Program, Tokyo, 2001, 15.

Huq, A., R.B. Sack, A. Nizam, I.M. Longini, G.B. Nair, A.Ali, et al., "Critical factors influencing the occurrence of Vibrio cholerae in the environment of Bangladesh," *Applied and Environmental Microbiology*, 71 (2005), 4645–54.

Iliffe, John, *The African Poor, A History*, Cambridge: Cambridge University Press, 1987.

The African AIDs Epidemic, A History, Oxford: James Currey, 2006.

Isaacson, Margaretha, K.R. Clarke, G.H. Ellacombe, W.A. Smit, P. Smit, H.J. Koomhof, et al., "The recent cholera outbreak in the South African gold mining industry: A preliminary report," *South African Medical Journal*, 48 (1974), 2557–60.

Jannetta, Ann Bowman, *Epidemics and Mortality in Early Modern Japan*, Princeton: Princeton University Press, 1987.

Janzen, John, "Health, Religion, and Medicine in Central and Southern African Traditions," in L. Sullivan, ed., *Caring and Curing: Health and Medicine in World Religious Traditions*, New York: Macmillan, 1989, 225–54.

Johnson, P., and D. Martin, eds., *Destructive Engagement: Southern Africa at War*, Harare: Zimbabwe Publishing House, 1986.

Johnson, Steven, *The Ghost Map: The Story of London's Most Terrifying Epidemic, and How It Changed Cities and the Modern World*, London: Allen Lane, 2006.

Kabir, Shahjahan, "Cholera vaccines: The current status and problems," *Reviews in Medical Microbiology*, 16 (2005), 101–16.

Kalapeni, Ezekiel, and Joseph Oppong, "The refugee crisis in Africa and its implications for health and disease: A political ecology approach," *Social Science and Medicine*, 46 (1998), 1637–53.

Kamal, A. M., "The Seventh Pandemic of Cholera," in Dhiman Barua and William Burrows, eds., *Cholera*, Philadelphia: W.B. Saunders, 1974, 1–14.

"Cholera in Egypt," *Journal of the Egyptian Public Health Association*, 3 (1948), 184–90.

Kiple, Kenneth, "Cholera and race in the Caribbean," *Journal of Latin American Studies*, 17 (1985), 157–77.

Klein, Ira, "Cholera: Theory and treatment in nineteenth century India," *Journal of Indian History*, 58 (1980), 35–51.

Kmietowicz, Zosia, "Oral cholera vaccine raises hopes," *British Medical Journal*, 314 (1997), 323.

Koponen, Juhani, *People and Production in Late Precolonial Tanzania: History and Structures*, Helsinki: Finnish Society for Development Studies, 1988.

Kovats, R.S., M.J. Bouma, S. Hajat, E. Worrall, and A. Haines, "El Nino and health," *Lancet*, 362 (2003), 1481–89.

Kuhnke, Laverne, *Lives at Risk: Public Health in Nineteenth-Century Egypt*, Cairo: The American University in Cairo Press, 1992.

Lanata, C.F., W. Mendoza, and R.E. Black, *Improving Diarrhea Estimates*, Geneva: WHO Child and Adolescent Health Development Monitoring and Evaluation Team, 2002.

Landes, David S., *Bankers and Pashas: International Finance and Economic Imperialism in Egypt*, London: Heinemann, 1958.

Lee, Kelley, "The global dimensions of cholera," *Global Change & Human Health*, 2 (2001), 6–17.

Lee, Kelley, Tony McMichael, Colin Butler, Mike Ahern, and David Bradley, "Global change and health: the good, the bad and the evidence," *Global Change & Human Health*, 3 (2002), 16–19.

Lischer, Sarah Kenyon, *Dangerous Sanctuaries: Refugee Camps, Civil War, and the Dilemmas of Humanitarian Aid*, Ithaca: Cornell University Press, 2005.

Livingstone, David, *Last Journals*, Vol.1, London: [s.n.], 1874.

Lobitz, B., L. Beck, A. Huq, B. Wood, G. Fuchs, A.S. Faruque, et al., "Climate and infectious disease: Use of remote sensing for detection of Vibrio cholerae by indirect measurement," *Proceedings of National Academy of Sciences*, 97 (February 15, 2000), 1438–43.

Loewenson, Rene, "Structural adjustment and health policy in Africa," *International Journal of Health Services*, 23 (1993), 717–30.

Lomborg, Bjorn, "Cool It": The Skeptical Environmentalist's Guide to Global Warming, New York: Knopf, 2007.

Lovejoy, Paul, *Transformations in Slavery: A History of Slavery in Africa*, second edition, New York: Cambridge University Press, 2000.

Lowy, Ilana, "From guinea pigs to man: The development of Haffkine's anticholera vaccine," *Journal of the History of Medicine*, 37 (1992), 270–309.

Lovelock, James E., *The Revenge of Gaia: Earth's Climate in Crisis and the Fate of Humanity*, New York: Basic Books, 2006.

Mabogunje, Akin, L., "Urban Planning and the Post-Colonial State: A Research Overview," *African Studies Review*, 33 (1990), 121–203.

Madoff, L.C., and J.P. Woodall, "The Internet and the global monitoring of emerging diseases: Lessons from the first 10 years of ProMED mail," *Archives of Medical Research*, 36 (2005), 724–30.

MacPherson, Kerrie L., *A Wilderness of Marshes: The Origins of Public Health in Shanghai, 1843–1893*, New York: Oxford University Press, 1987.

Mahalanabis, Dilip, A.B. Choudhuri, N.G. Bagchi, A.K. Bhattacharya, and T.W. Simpson, "Oral fluid therapy of cholera among Bangladesh refugees," *Johns Hopkins Medical Journal*, 132 (1973), 197–205.

Mahalanabis, Dilip, A.M. Molla, and David A. Sack, "Clinical Management of Cholera," in D. Barua and W.B. Greenough III, eds, *Cholera*, New York: Plenum, 1992, 253–83.

Malkki, Liisa, "Speechless emissaries: Refugees, humanitarianism, and dehistoricization," *Cultural Anthropology*, 11 (1996), 377–404.

Mamdani, Mahmood, *When Victims Become Killers: Colonialism, Nativism, and the Genocide in Rwanda*, Princeton: Princeton University Press, 2001.

Maré, Gerhard, and Georgina Hamilton, *An Appetite for Power: Buthelezi's Inkatha and South Africa*, Johannesburg: Ravan Press, 1987.

Marks, Shula, *The Ambiguities of Dependence in South Africa: Class, Nationalism and the State in Twentieth-Century Natal*, Johannesburg: Ravan Press, 1986.

Martin, David, and Phyliss Johnson, *The Struggle for Zimbabwe: The Chimurenga War*, London: Faber & Faber, 1981.

McDonald, David A., "The Theory and Practice of Cost Recovery in South Africa," in David A. McDonald and John Pape, eds., *Cost Recovery and the Crisis of Service Delivery in South Africa*, Cape Town: Human Sciences Research Council Publishers, 2002, 17–37.

McDonald, David A., and Greg Ruiters, eds., *The Age of Commodity: Water Privatization in Southern Africa*, London: Earthscan, 2005.

McGrew, Roderick E., *Russia and the Cholera, 1823–1832*, Madison: University of Wisconsin Press, 1965.

McKeown, Adam, "Global Migration, 1846–1940," *Journal of World History*, 15 (2004), 155–89.

McNeill, William H., *Plagues and Peoples*, New York: Anchor Books, 1976.

Mendez, M.A., and L.S. Adair, "Severity and timing of stunting in the first two years of life affect performance on cognitive tests in late childhood," *Journal of Nutrition*, 129 (1999), 1555–62.

Mitchell, Timothy, *Rule of Experts: Egypt, Techno-politics, Modernity*, Berkeley: University of California Press, 2002.

Moren, A., D. Bitar, I. Navarre, M. G. Etchegorry, A. Bordel, G. Lungu, et al., "Epidemiological surveillance among Mozambican refugees in Malawi, 1987–89," *Disasters*, 15 (1991), 363–72.

Moulin, Anne-Marie, "Révolutions Médicales et Révolutions Politiques en Egypte (1865–1917)," *Revue du monde musulman et de la méditerranée*, 52/53 (1989), 115–23.

Mouriño-Pérez, Rosa R., "Oceanography and the seventh cholera pandemic," *Epidemiology*, 9 (1998), 355–57.

Moyo, Dambisa, *Dead Aid: Why Aid Is Not Working and How There Is a Better Way for Africa*, New York: Farrar, Straus and Giroux, 2009.

Mulholland, Kim, "Cholera in Sudan: An account of an epidemic in eastern Sudan, May–June, 1985," *Disasters*, 9 (1985), 247–58.

Musemwa, Muchaparara, "Disciplining a 'dissident' city: Hydropolitics in the city of Bulawayo, Matabeleland, Zimbabwe, 1980–94," *Journal of Southern African Studies*, 32 (2006), 239–54.

Myers, Garth Andrew, *Disposable Cities: Garbage, Governance and Sustainable Development in Urban Africa*, Burlington, VT: Ashgate, 2005.

Nations, Marilyn K. and Cristina M.G. Monte, "'I'm not dog, no!': Cries of resistance against cholera control campaigns," *Social Science and Medicine*, 43 (1996), 1007–24.

Nelson, Eric, "Beyond cholera – The Zimbabwe health crisis," *The Lancet Infectious Diseases*, 9 (October 2009), 587–8.

Nesse, Randolph M., and George C. Williams, "Evolution and the origins of disease," *Scientific American* (November, 1998), 86–93.

Ngubane, Harriet, *Body and Mind in Zulu Medicine*, London: Academic Press, 1977.

Niehaus, M.D., S.R. Moore, P.D. Patrick, L.L. Derr, B. Lorntz, A.A. Lima et al., "Notifications of diseases," *South African Medical Journal*, 65 (1982), 54.

"Early childhood diarrhea is associated with diminished cognitive function 4–7 years later in children in a Northeast Brazilian shantytown," *American Journal of Tropical Medicine and Hygiene*, 66 (2002), 590–3.

Odom, Thomas P., *Journey into Darkness: Genocide in Rwanda*, College Station: Texas A&M University Press, 2005.

Oldstone, Michael B.A., *Viruses, Plagues, and History*, New York: Oxford University Press, 1998.

Packard, Randall M., *The Making of a Tropical Disease: A Short History of Malaria*, Baltimore: The Johns Hopkins University Press, 2007.

Pankhurst, Richard, "The history of cholera in Ethiopia," *Medical History*, 12 (1968), 262–9.

Panzac, Daniel, *Quarantine et Lazarets: L'Europe et la Peste d'Orient (XVII – XXe siecles*, Aix-en-Provence: Edisud, 1986).

Population et santé dans l'Empire Ottoman (XVIIe – XXe siècles), Istanbul: Editions Isis, 1996.

Pascual, M., X. Rodo, S.P. Ellner, R.R. Colwell, and M.J. Bouma, "Cholera dynamics and El Niño – southern oscillation," *Science*, 289 (2000), 1766–9.

Patz, Jonathan A., M.A. McGeehin, S.M. Bernard, K.L. Ebi, P.R. Epstein, A. Grambsch, et al., "The potential health impacts of climate cariability and change for the United States: Executive summary of the Report on the Health Sector of the U.S. National Assessment," *Environmental Health Perspectives*, 108 (2000), 367–76.

Patz, J., P. Epstein, T. Burke, and J. Balbus-Kornfeld, "Global climate change and emerging infectious diseases," *Journal of the American Medical Association*, 275 (1996), 219–20.

Pelis, Kim, *Charles Nicolle: Pasteur's Imperial Missionary: Typhus and Tunisia*, Rochester: University of Rochester Press, 2006.

Pelling, Margaret, *Cholera, Fever and English Medicine, 1825–1865*, Oxford: Oxford University Press, 1978.

Pollitzer, Robert, *Cholera*, Geneva: WHO, 1959.

Price-Smith, Andrew T., *The Health of Nations: Infectious Disease, Environmental Change, and their Effects on National Security and Development*, Cambridge: MIT Press, 2002.

Prunier, Gérard, *The Rwanda Crisis: History of a Genocide*, New York: Columbia University Press, 1995.

Rockel, Stephen J., *Carriers of Culture: Labor on the Road in Nineteenth-Century East Africa*, Portsmouth, NH: Heinemann, 2006.

Rodrigues, Amabélla, Anita Sandstrom, Tomé Cá, H.Steinsland, H. Jensen, P Aaby, "Protection from cholera by adding lime juice to food-results from community and laboratory studies in Guinea-Bissau, West Africa," *Tropical Medicine and International Health*, 5 (2000), 418–22.

Rosenberg, Charles E., *The Cholera Years: The United States in 1832, 1849, and 1866*, Chicago: University of Chicago Press, 1962; reprint, with an an afterword, 1987.

Ruxin, Joshua N., "Magic bullet: The history of oral rehydration therapy," *Medical History*, 38 (1991), 363–97.

Saha, D., M.M. Karim, W.A. Khan, S. Ahmed, M.A. Salam, and M.L. Bennish, "Single-dose azithromycin for the treatment of cholera in adults," *New England Journal of Medicine*, 354 (2006), 2452–62.

Saul, John, ed., *A Difficult Road: The Transition to Socialism in Mozambique*, New York: Monthly Review Press, 1985.

Schram, Ralph, *A History of the Nigerian Health Services*, Ibadan: Ibadan University Press, 1971.

Seck, Assane, *Dakar, métropole ouest-africaine*, Dakar: IFAN, 1970.

Sellassie, Guebre, *Chronique du règne de Ménélik II, roi des rois d'Ethiopie*, translated from the Amharic by Tesfa Sellassie and annotated by Maurice de Coppet, Paris: Maisonneuve Frères, 1930.

Sen, Amartya, *Poverty and Famines: An Essay on Entitlement and Deprivation*, Oxford: Clarendon Press, 1981.

Shears, Paul, "Recent developments in cholera," *Current Opinion in Infectious Diseases*, 14 (2001), 553–8.

Siddiqi, Javed, *World Health and World Politics*, London: Hurst, 1995.

Siddique, A.K., A. Salam, M.S. Islam, K. Akram, R.N. Majumdar, K.Zaman, et al., "Why treatment centres failed to prevent cholera deaths among Rwandan refugees in Goma, Zaire," *Lancet*, 345 (1995), 359–61.

Sinclair, G.S., M. Mphahlele, H. Duvenhage, R. Nichol, A. Whitehorn, and H.G. Kustner, "Determination of the mode of transmission of cholera in Lebowa," *South African Medical Journal*, 62 (1982), 753–5.

Smith, Richard, "The WHO: Change or die," *British Medical Journal*, 310 (1995), 543–4.

Snow, John, *On the Mode of Communication of Cholera*, London: J. Churchill, 1849.

On the Mode of Communication of Cholera, 2nd edition, *Much Enlarged*, London: J. Churchill, 1855.

"Cholera and the water supply in the south districts of London," *British Medical Journal*, (1857), 864–5.

Snowden, Frank M., *Naples in the Time of Cholera, 1884–1911*, Cambridge: Cambridge University Press, 1995.

Sorensen, Eigil, and Klaus Dissler, "Practical experience with the management of a cholera outbreak in a refugee camp in eastern Sudan, 1985," *Disasters*, 12 (1986), 274–81.

Sow, P.S., B.M. Diop, M. Maynart-Badiane, A. Sow, C.T. Ndour, N.M. Dia, et al., "L'épidémie de choléra de 1995–1996 à Dakar", *Médicine et Maladies Infectieuses* 29 (1999), 105–9.

Speck, Reinhard S. 1993. "Cholera," in Kenneth Kiple, ed. *The Cambridge World History of Human Disease*, New York: Cambridge University Press, 642–9.

Stiglitz, Joseph, *Globalization and its Discontents*, NY: Norton, 2003.

St. Louis, M.E., J.D. Porter, A. Helal, K. Drame, N. Hargrett-Bean, J.G. Wells, et al., "Epidemic cholera in West Africa: the role of food handling and high-risk foods," *American Journal of Epidemiology*, 131 (1990), 719–27.

Stock, Robert F., *Cholera in Africa*, London: International African Institute, 1976.

Swerdlow, D.L., E.D. Mintz, M.Rodriguez, E. Tejada, C.Ocampo, L. Espejo, et al., "Severe life-threatening cholera associated with blood group O in Peru: Implications for the Latin American epidemic," *Journal of Infectious Disease*, 170 (1994), 468–72.

Swerdlow, D.L, and A.A. Ries, "Vibrio cholerae non-o1: The eighth pandemic?" *Lancet*, 342 (1993), 392–3.

Swerdlow, David L., M.D. Allen, and A. Ries, "Cholera in the Americas: Guidelines for the clinician," *Journal of the American Medical Association*, 267 (1992), 1495–9.

Tamplin, N.L. and C.C. Parodi, "Environmental spread of Vibrio cholerae in Peru," *Lancet*, 338 (1991), 1216–17.

Tauxe, Robert, Paul Blake, Orjan Olsvik, and I. Kaye Wachsmuth, "The Future of Cholera: Persistence, Change, and an Expanding Research Agenda," in I. Kaye Wachsmuth, Paul A. Blake, and Orjan Olsvik, eds., *Vibrio Cholerae and Cholera: Molecular to Global Perspectives*, Washington: American Society for Microbiology Press, 1994., 443–53.

Turshen, Meredeth, *Privatizing Health Service in Africa*, New Brunswick. NJ.: Rutgers University Press, 1999.

Utsalo, S.J., F.O. Eko, and E.O. Antia-Obong, "Features of cholera and Vibrio parahaemolyticus diarrhoea endemicity in Calabar, Nigeria," *European Journal of Epidemiology*, 8 (1992), 856–60.

Van Bergen, J., "Epidemiology and health policy – A world of difference? A case-study of a cholera outbreak in Kaputa District, Zambia," *Social Science and Medicine*, 43 (1996), 93–9.

Van Damme, William, "Do refugees belong in camps? Experiences from Goma and Guinea," *Lancet*, 345 (1995), 360–4.

Van Heyningen, W.E., and John R. Seal, *Cholera: The American Scientific Experience*, Boulder: Westview Press, 1983.

Waal, Alex de, *Famine That Kills: Darfur, Sudan*, New York: Oxford University Press, revised edition, 2005.

Wachira Kigotho, A., "European Union bans fish imports from cholera-struck eastern Africa," *Lancet*, 351 (1998), 194.

Wachsmuth, I. Kaye, Paul A. Blake, and Orjan Olsvik, eds., *Vibrio Cholerae and Cholera: Molecular to Global Perspectives*, Washington: American Society for Microbiology Press, 1994.

Wall, Don, *The Heroes of 'F' Force*. Mona Vale, NSW: by the author, 1993.

Walt, G. and A. Melamed, eds., *Mozambique: Towards a Peoples' Health Service*, London: Zed Books, 1984,

Watts, Sheldon, "From rapid change to stasis: Official responses to cholera in British-ruled India and Egypt, 1860–c.1921," *Journal of World History*, 12 (2001), 321–74.

Whitehead, Henry, "The Broad Street Pump: An episode in the cholera epidemic of 1854," *MacMillan's Magazine* (1865), 113–22.

Experience of a London Curate, Clapham: [s.n.], 1871.

Wills, Christopher, *Plagues: Their Origin, History and Future*, New York: Harper Collins, 1996.

Zuckerman, Jane, Lars Rombo, and Alain Fisch, "The true burden and risk of cholera: Implications for prevention and control," *Lancet Infectious Disease*, 7 (2007), 521–30.

IV. Newspapers and Internet

"Africa at a watershed: Ubangi – Lake Chad inter-basin transfer," *New Scientist*, March 23, 1991.

Alie, Mohammed, "South Africa flounders in its search for free water," *Panos-South Africa*, February 1, 2002, 2.

Angola entry, *The World Factbook*, Washington, D.C.: Central Intelligence Agency, 2008.

Bond, Patrick, and Greg Ruiters, "South Africa: Water for all?" *Pambazuka News*, November 23, 2006, www.pambazuka.org

Carlton, James. "Environmental impacts of marine exotics: An action bioscience. org. Original interview," American Institute of Biological Sciences, May, 2004 www.actionbioscience.org/biodiversity/carlton.html.

CERF Secretariat, United Nations, New York, 2008, www.cerf.un.org.

Colwell, Rita, "A global thirst for safe water: The case of cholera," Abel Wolman Distinguished Lecture, National Academy of Sciences, January 25, 2002, www.sofiausgs.gov/publications/lectures/safwater.

Daily Trust, Abuja, Nigeria, November 27, 2001.

"Data summary: Lake Tanganyika," www.ilec.or.jp/database/afr

"Dead in the water," CBC, The Fifth Estate, broadcast of March 31, 2004, www.cbc.ca/fifth/deadinthewater/africa-printer.

"Dispatch from Zimbabwe," Médecins sans Frontières, *Canada Magazine*, 11 (2009).

"Floods take serious economic toll," www.un.org/ecosocdev/geninfo/afrec/subjindx/143moz2.

Harvey, M., "Cholera epidemic may be spreading to rest of South Africa," WOZA Internet October 31, 2000. Interview, May, 2006, www.sudonline.sn/spip. php? article 1332.

Jeter, John, "South Africa's driest season," *Mother Jones*, November/December, 2002, 1–6.

"Joint SAMWU-RDSN (Rural Development Services Network) World Water Day press statement," March 22, 2006, www.worldwaterday.org

Lafranière, Sharon, "In Oil-rich Angola, cholera preys upon poorest," *New York Times*, June 16, 2006.

"Mugabe: 'There is no cholera in Zimbabwe,'" *Times*, December 12, 2008.

Médecins sans Frontières report, 2009.

Nolen, Stephanie, "Land of the State, home of the poor," *Toronto Globe and Mail*, September 9, 2008.

Ogunleye, Femi, "Filth: A health hazard in Kano," *Daily Times*, Lagos, September 8, 1973, 7.

Pauw, Jacques, *P.M. News*, Lagos, November 20, 2001.

"Metered to death: How a water experiment caused riots and a cholera epidemic," *Global Policy Forum*, February 5, 2003, 1–12.

"Senegal: Lingering cholera epidemic gains new strength," *Integrated Regional Information Networks*, June 23, 2005.

"Robert Mugabe off the hook as usual," Economist.com, September 10, 2009, Cape Town.

Tshabalala-Msimang, Dr. Manto, "Parliamentary media briefing," February 19, 2003, 4.

"Unit 731 and war crimes," last updated January 21, 2001, www.ww2pacific.com/unit731.html.

"UK caused cholera, says Zimbabwe minister," BBC World News, December 12, 2008, www/news.bbc.co.uk/2hi/7780728.stm.

"Utopian plan belies dismal reality for flood victims," December 19, 2006, www/allafrica.com/stories/printable/200612190751.

"Vanishing Lake Chad – A water crisis in Central Africa," *Circle of Blue*, June 24, 2008, www.circleofblue.org/waternews/world/vanishing-lake-chad.

"Voice of America news," March 28, 2008, www.voanews.com/english/2008-03-28-voa33.cfm.

"Water for life," www.un.org/waterforlifedecade/factsheet.html.

World Lakes Database, International Lake Environment Committee Foundation, www.ilec.or.jp/database/afr/afr-13.html.

York, Geoffrey, "Crisis in Zimbabwe: A health system nearing total collapse," *Toronto Globe and Mail*, March 14, 2009.

Zimbabwe Times, www.thezimbabwetimes.com/?p=14205.

Index

BOOKS IN THIS SERIES